MW01196603

In this careful study of a valuable and much-ne of the teaching of Scrip his discussion of the theology of the major Reformers, the Puritans and their successors will give them a welcome bonus. And in addition to this he wrestles with the three great B-Titans of twentieth century theology, Barth, Brunner and Bultmann. Ministers, students and all serious-minded Christians should find a work worth turning to again and again.

Sinclair B. Ferguson
St George's Tron Parish Church,
Glasgow

As the theology of Karl Barth, and the neo-orthodoxy in general, becomes more and more marginal (having been relegated to the proverbial museum of out-dated theology by mainstream liberal academia on the charges of being 'too conservative'), a danger remains and is perhaps increasing for evangelicalism. That danger is the evangelical adoption and incorporation of significant elements of a theology whose time has past, and which is manifestly unbiblical at important points in its teaching (why do we always hop on the bandwagon after it's run off the road?!).

In a day in which there is increasing evidence of the syncretism of evangelical theology and neo-orthodoxy, even in the Reformed community, Iain D. Campbell has provided a timely antidote in his excellent study of *The Doctrine of Sin*. Campbell capably summarizes the main lines of biblical and Reformed thinking on the doctrine of the Fall and sin, and contrasts that teaching with the opinions of leading proponents of the so-called new orthodoxy. The result is a sturdy survey of the sound teaching bequeathed to us by our Reformed forebears, and a crucial caveat against our witting or unwitting concession to the subjectivising tendencies of the neo-orthodox view of sin.

Campbell wants to stimulate us to think long and hard about a subject critical to our evangelism. How so? It is crucial because without a proper understanding of sin, grace is unintelligible. Hence, our Gospel witness must begin with a biblical understanding of creation and sin, before it can explain grace meaningfully. May Iain D. Campbell's labors inspire us to a fresh commitment to this task.

J. Ligon Duncan,
Minister, First Presbyterian Church
Adjunct Professor, Reformed Theological Seminary,
Jackson, Mississippi, USA

THE DOCTRINE OF SIN

IN
REFORMED AND
NEO-ORTHODOX THOUGHT

Iain D. Campbell

Mentor

Christian Focus Publications publishes biblically-accurate books for adults and children. The books in the adult range are published in three imprints.

Christian Heritage contains classic writings from the past.

Christian Focus contains popular works including biographies, commentaries, doctrine, and Christian living.

Mentor focuses on books written at a level suitable for Bible College and seminary students, pastors, and others; the imprint includes commentaries, doctrinal studies, examination of current issues, and church history.

For a free catalogue of all our titles, please write to
Christian Focus Publications,
Geanies House, Fearn,
Ross-shire, IV20 1TW, Great Britain

For details of our titles visit us on our web site
http://www.christianfocus.com

Published in 1999
in the Mentor Imprint
by
Christian Focus Publications,
Geanies House, Fearn, Ross-shire,
IV20 1TW, Great Britain.

Contents

Section 3: The Neo-orthodox View of Sin

Section 4: The Relationship Between Neo-Orthodoxy and Reformed Thought

Dedicated to

my wife

ANNE

with thanks to God for the gift of an
encourager, home-maker and friend

Preface

This book is by no means a definitive word on the subject of sin. It has grown out of a study of the differences in approach to this doctrine on the part of Reformed theologians on the one hand, and the theologians in whose work modern theology is rooted on the other. I should like to thank those who supervised the study in its earlier stages: Dr Mark N. Gretason, London, and Dr Noel W. Wallis, Queensland, Australia. The work leans heavily on a trilogy of writings by the late Dr. Harold Whitney, of the Presbyterian Church of Australia, who served as evangelist in that denomination, as well as being President of Illawarra Bible College and Principal of Queensland Presbyterian Theological Hall. His evangelical critique of Barth, Bultmann and Brunner opened avenues of thought along which I have trundled in this volume. My aim is to introduce the leading themes of Neo-orthodoxy to a wider Christian readership, and to encourage the study of Reformed and Puritan thought by demonstrating its faithfulness to the Biblical position. Others, I acknowledge, have done this more ably and more skilfully than I; but if I can deepen commitment to our Reformed heritage at a popular level through this work, it will not have been in vain. I am grateful to Mr Malcolm Maclean for his editorial help in the production of this volume. My thanks are due especially to my wife and children for their patience, love and affection at all times, not least when work on the manuscript interrupted our routine. The constancy of their devotion is one of the great joys of my life.

Free Church Manse
Vatisker, Back
Isle of Lewis
June 1998

Introduction

Religion and theology have always taken the problem of deviant behaviour, and related matters of conscience and ethics, seriously. Religious groups and practices differ to the degree in which various solutions are proposed to deal with the problem of sin. On the surface of it, there is little significant difference between Ludwig Feurbach's assertion that

'Our world – not only our political and social world, but our learned, intellectual world as well – is a world upside down. The great achievement of our education, of our culture, our science, our erudition has been, above all, to stray as far as possible from nature, from the simple palpable truth'[1]

and the Lord's own assertion, in John 3:19, that 'this is the condemnation, that the light has come into the world, and men loved darkness rather than light, because their deeds were evil'. However, religious experience and doctrine vary in terms of understanding and defining the precise nature of the darkness from which salvation is possible.

The Christian faith proclaims one Saviour, the Lord Jesus Christ, who alone is able to define sin for us, and to save us from sin. Yet many people have what Dr. Harold Whitney called 'a vitiated sense of sin'.[2] The context of Dr. Whitney's assertion was an address as Assembly Evangelist for the Presbyterian Church of Australia, and he went on to show that a weakened sense of sin is evidenced in personal life, in home life, in social circles, in business, in politics and in the church. 'We must,' he urged, 'press for Christian standards.'[3]

The problem can be defined at this point in the following way: what are the standards of Christian ethics and morality which set it off against other standards? In the midst of a world of confused ethical signals, the Christian voice carries a distinctive tone and presses for a distinctive ethic. Yet Christian theologians vary in their interpretation of the nature and meaning of Christ's ministry of salvation. What is the darkness out of which He claims to deliver men and women? What is the 'sin' from which He claims – and for which He came – to save? Unless the preaching of the Christian church is directed to this question, then the occupant of the Christian pulpit can only deal with apparent needs – or even felt needs – while the *real* need of man will go unchallenged.

The question itself is part of a much larger question – the question of theological mode and method. Modern theology can trace is roots to Neo-orthodox theologians like Karl Barth and Emil Brunner; yet the claim that such theology 'represents a retreat from both Scripture and Reason into subjectivism and irrationalism and a reliance upon secular philosophical presuppositions instead of upon Scriptural principles'[4] is one which must be taken seriously. If truth is subjectivised, then propositional doctrine is meaningless. And it is at this level that tensions arise between the recorded, propositional claims of Christ, and the so-called 'insights' of modern theology.

Ninian Smart, in his popular work, *The Religious Experience of Mankind*, sheds light for us on the practical implications of such subjectivising tendencies. He says that 'in the whole field of human knowledge, whether in the liberal arts or the sciences, there is always a margin of disagreement between expert scholars. But very often knowledge advances precisely because of this. It is out of the dialogue and argument that new insights are won.' Smart continues: 'The foregoing may be summed up by saying that here revelation will be treated as "non-propositional"...it is possible to approach revelation from the human standpoint, by considering what it means to the recipients and how they interpret it.'[5]

Interpretation of sacred texts, therefore, in Smart's view, depends as much upon the condition of the reader as upon the content of the texts themselves. Any biblical doctrine is valid only insofar as the reader is able to make sense of it in terms of his or her own subjective condition. Therefore, in connection with the doctrines of sin and grace, much depends not on the statements of the Bible and the recorded utterances of the Lord, but on the experiential reception of relevation.

This is precisely the characteristic of much modern theology, whose twentieth-century roots are to be found in Neo-orthodoxy (a definition of these terms is given elsewhere in this volume). This dialectical, crisis theology is examined by Dr. Harold Whitney in his trilogy, *The New Mythology*, *The New Infallibility* and *The New Heresy,* published in the 1960s and 1970s, when the Barthian influence was at its height following the death of Barth in 1968. *The New Infallibility* begins with a discussion of the existentialist philosophy of Jean-Paul Sartre

(1905-1980), in whose thinking human experience becomes the infallible test of all things. Dr. Whitney concludes that

'Sartre is an apostle of absurdity. He is an expositor of the meaningless. He is a prophet preaching self-salvation. His philosophy urges self-love, self-creation, self-rule, self-annihilation, all in one....His philosophy fitly belongs in the theatre of the absurd...'[6]

The most devastating consequence of this, he argues, is that

'Sartre's existentialism – the product of an atheistic mind – becomes the ground plan of the thinking about God of the dialectical-existential theologians of our day. For them revelation becomes, with Kant, experience.'[7]

Over against this, Dr Whitney asserts that

'Not human experience, but Divine declaration is the ground of our certainty. Only this, preserved as a written, objective, rational, personal record of what God hath both wrought and taught, deserves to be regarded as the infallible Word of God – the only rule of faith and practice.'[8]

For Sartre's existentialism cannot co-exist happily with the objective and propositional revelation of the Scriptures. The consequence of adopting some kind of experientialism as the ground of truth is that it makes the Gospel meaningless. Delivery and salvation from sin is reduced to absurdity if there is no clear revelation concerning sin and its consequences.

Neo-orthodoxy, building on the foundation laid by Barth, Bultmann and Brunner, each of whom took different approaches to the study of theology, sought to return to the Bible. The nature of Neo-orthodoxy will become clear on the following pages, as will the fact that the three men whose works are studied here under the general rubric of 'Neo-orthodoxy' were very diverse in their approaches. On the whole, however, it is true that as a reaction to the liberalism that dominated theology at the beginning of the century, Neo-orthodoxy represented a movement of thought in which theology is 'not a response to the human situation or to human questions; it is a response to the Word of God, which demands a response because of its intrinsic nature'.[9] Karl Barth, for example, says:

'That man who refuses to listen and to obey the Word acts not as a free man but as a slave, for there is no freedom except through God's Word.... Theology responds to the Word which God has spoken, still speaks, and will speak again in the history of Jesus Christ which fulfills the history of Israel.'[10]

Liberal Protestantism dominated theological reflection at the end of the nineteenth century; it had undermined the authority of Scripture by postulating various theories of source and compilation which led to a purely historical and contextual treatment of the Scriptures. On these terms the teaching of Scripture was evacuated of all supernaturalism, and reduced to ethical exemplarism. The Ritschlian school (named after Albrecht B. Ritschl, 1822-1889) in particular, turned religious doctrine into subjective value-judgment; it has been said of Ritschl that he was 'the most influential continental theologian between Schleiermacher and Barth...[he] followed Kant in rejecting metaphysical knowledge of God and stressing the ethical elements of religion. God was not to be known in himself, but in his effects on mankind...'[11]

This was classic liberal theology, the kind of theology that takes

'A view of the Bible as a fallible human record of religious thought and experience rather than a divine revelation of truth and reality'[12];

part of whose legacy is

'A denial that the Fall of a primitive pair brought guilt, pollution and spiritual impotence upon our race, in favour of a vision of mankind moving spiritually upward.'[13]

An example of this in practice may be seen in the interesting dialogue between David Edwards and John Stott, entitled *Essentials*, in which the liberal Edwards writes on various doctrines, and the evangelical Stott responds. There is one point at which Stott says that Edwards' guide

'...seems to be the "world which we have entered through education and through daily experience ('culture')", which teaches us that certain ideas are "either ridiculous or else actually blasphemous". Perhaps the crucial question between us, then, is whether culture is to judge Scripture, or Scripture culture.'[14]

Edwards is a modern disciple of classic liberalism. Neo-orthodoxy was an attempt to return to something more objective than culture or personal experience; to emphasise the objectivity of divine revelation. It assumed the fallibility of Scripture, but postulated the 'otherness' and absolute transcendence of God. Scripture can be relied upon, in Neo-orthodox thinking, not as final revelation, but as one means of revelation.

The following chapters are an attempt to introduce and assess the claims and methods of Neo-orthodox theology. The doctrine of sin is examined, first of all, in terms of the Bible's own teaching, and then in terms of Reformed thought. In the third section of the book, the thought of the leading exponents of Neo-orthodoxy, Karl Barth, Emil Brunner and Rudolf Bultmann, is assessed. It is all too evident that while claiming on the one hand to protest against theological liberalism, the Neo-orthodox theologians themselves build on theological presuppositions and foundations which are every bit as subjective as those of classic liberalism. As such, such theology as emerges is confusing at best and highly dangerous at worst. This study confirms the truth of Dr. Whitney's assessment that in Neo-orthodoxy,

'faith is being moved over into an area where it cannot be subjected to rational scrutiny, and is therefore a completely personal thing beyond the reach and the need of verification.'[15]

On the other hand, it is because Reformed theology has posited an objective, propositional revelation that evangelism is possible. For Christ came into the world to save sinners, whose sin God, and not man, defines.

NOTES

1. Feurbach, L., 'The Essence of Religion', quoted in *The World Treasury of Modern Religious Thought*, (J. Pelikan, ed.),(1990), p.57
2. Whitney, H.J. *Evangelism the Heartbeat of the Church*, (1987), p.114.
3. Ibid., p.117.
4. Whitney, H.J., *The New Heresy*, p.1.
5. Smart, N., *The Religious Experience of Mankind*, (1989), pp.26-27.
6. Whitney, H. *The New Infallibility*, p.32.
7. Ibid., p.33.
8. Idem.
9. McGrath, A.E. *Christian Theology: An Introduction* (1994), p.99.
10. Barth, K. *Evangelical Theology: An Introduction*, (1979), pp.19-20.

11. Article on 'Albrecht Ritschl' in *New Dictionary of Theology*, p.595.

12. Article on 'Liberalism and Conservatism in Theology', Ibid., p.385.

13. Idem. James Packer, author of the article, summarises thus: 'Liberalism dominated European Protestantism for half a century till the First World War shattered its optimism and the lead passed to the existentialist biblicism of the neo-orthodox genius Karl Barth' (Ibid.).

14. John Stott writing in *Essentials: A Liberal-Evangelical Dialogue*, (1988), p168.

15. Whitney, H. *The New Infallibility*, p.280.

Section 1

The Biblical Doctrine of Sin

Introduction

Dr. Harold Whitney concludes his introduction to the impact of Neo-Orthodoxy on modern theological reflection, as set forth in his *The New 'Myth'-ology* with a clarion call to evangelical scholars. In their attempt to meet the massive groundswell of Barthian thinking, Whitney proposes that only one course of action remains for them. His exhortation is as follows:

'... Evangelicals should study the acknowledged teaching of the Church. They should master the core of Reformed doctrine. They should commit themselves wholeheartedly to the plain teaching of Scripture on the essentials of the faith....They should accept the straightforward meaning of the Bible and not seek subtle or far-out interpretations.'[1]

In the conviction that this is the only sure method of advancing towards an examination of the Neo-Orthodox treatment of the doctrine of sin, the attempt will be made in the first section of this book to set forth both 'the plain teaching of Scripture' (in section 1) and 'the core of Reformed doctrine' (in section 2).

It must be admitted at the outset that there is a wealth of biblical material relevant to our purpose in this connection. The complexity of the subject under investigation revolves around both the multi-faceted biblical vocabulary employed by the writers of Scripture, and the differing emphases of each progressive epoch of revelation. Any discussion of the Bible's teaching about sin must do justice both to the linguistic evidence and to the gradual development of revelation.

These aims will be best served by taking a *biblical* rather than a *systematic* approach to the doctrine of sin as it appears on the pages of the Word of God. That is to say, rather than attempting to systematise the teaching of Scripture on such themes as the nature and character of sin and its entrance into the world, its effects, solution and final dissolution, this section will pay respect rather to the differing emphases of each progressive epoch of scriptural revelation, following largely the schema set forth by Geerhardus Vos in his *Biblical Theology*.[2] In this great work, Vos identifies three such epochs, and he distinguishes between what he calls 'The Mosaic Epoch of

Revelation', 'The Prophetic Epoch of Revelation' and revelation of the New Testament. The discussion of the following chapters will pay regard to the differing emphases of these three great movements in the history of God's unfolding disclosure of His will for mankind in sin. First, however, it will be necessary to comment on the complexity of the semantical issue involved.

The Biblical Vocabulary

The Bible uses a wide-ranging vocabulary when addressing the problem of sin. Neither the Hebrew nor the Greek confine their concept of sin to any one word in isolation. It is necessary, therefore, to summarise the lexical evidence.

In studying the Old Testament vocabulary for sin, R.B. Girdlestone makes the following remark:

'The pictorial power of the Hebrew language is seldom exhibited more clearly than in connection with the various aspects of evil. Every word is a piece of philosophy; nay, it is a revelation.'[3]

Girdlestone goes on to list eleven distinct Hebrew roots, each one laden with its own etymology and contribution to the study of the doctrine. R.C. Trench, in the companion New Testament volume, lists nine different Greek nouns bearing on the whole question of sin and transgression.[4]

The language of the Old Testament is, as Girdlestone correctly identifies, more pictorial than etymological; that is, the Hebrew language builds up *word-pictures*, more than relying on root meanings. For example, the most frequently used Hebrew root for sin is *ḥāṭā'* (used over 580 times), a word borrowed from archery. The Book of Judges talks of the left-handed slingers of Benjamin (20:16), whose praise was that they never missed their target. It is the concept, the picture, of missing the target, that thus forms the basic concept of sin in the Old Testament. This also becomes foundational in the New Testament, where again the most frequently used word for sin (*hamartia*) bears a similar meaning.

In summarising the content of the Old Testament vocabulary for sin, William Dyrness suggests three major categories.[5] First, he suggests that words usually translated 'sin', 'iniquity', and 'perversion' belong to a word-group in which sin is represented as a *deviation from a right way*. This is echoed, for example, by Isaiah in his universally-applicable confession: 'We all, like sheep, have gone astray, each of us has turned to his own way' (Isa. 53:6). The essence of sin can be understood in the sense of deviating from a pre-set standard.

Second, there is a category which represents sin as *guilt before God*; words like 'guilt', 'ungodly', 'wicked' belong to this group. Here, as Dyrness correctly observes, 'the objective nature of sin comes to the fore'.[6] Whereas concepts like deviation and straying are primarily concerned with sin in its subjective aspect, the idea of guilt brings in the element of responsibility and culpability. Sin is no longer simply abstract but intensely personal. It is transacted on a plane where those who deviate are both answerable and accountable.

Dyrness identifies as a third category that of *rebellion*, often translated 'trespass'. Again, this language is used in a secular sense, as of rebellion against the House of David (cf. 1 Kings 12:19). Especially, however, it is employed on the lips of the prophets as a frequent charge aginst the covenant people who have rebelled against their King and God.

The *Theological Dictionary of the New Testament* (ed. Kittell) evaluates these findings for us in the following statement:

'It is obvious that among the many words to be considered [for sin in the Old Testament], none was exclusively devoted to religious and theological use and therefore none constitutes an exact equivalent to the English 'sin'. All the Hebrew words in question had a secular as well as a religious sense.... They are theologoumena rather than original terms of spontaneous experience, and the meaning falls into different groups.'[7]

The Dictionary makes two points in consequence. First it asserts that, 'Only with the strongest reservations, if at all, can we count on a uniform and self-contained concept of sin in the authors of the Old Testament';[8] and that the variety of words employed in the original language of the Old Testament means that 'justice is hardly done to this variety either in the LXX.... nor by our modern translations'.[9]

These conclusions do not mean that our doctrine cannot be definitive, but they do make for a composite definition, and they alert us to the fact that the doctrine is a complex and not a simple one.

These points must be borne in mind when interpreting the Old Testament. The words used for sin and its related concepts are very often borrowed from secular, rather than religious usage, and in consequence display a great variety of metaphor and accommodate a great variety of thought. This highlights the humanness of the Scriptures and opens to us a rich and multi-faceted doctrine of sin contained within its pages.

The prominent words for sin in the New Testament are related to the root which yields *hamartano* as the verbal form. It is employed both in the classical Greek (literally, in the sense of missing a target, and metaphorically, to denote wrong or erroneous action) and in the Greek version of the Old Testament, the Septuagint (commonly denoted as 'LXX', representing the 70 scholars who allegedly produced it). In the LXX, the root is most often used to translate the noun *ḥāṭā'*, the most prominent Hebrew noun for sin. The New Testament also employs other nouns which will be mentioned in the following chapters.

NOTES
1. Whitney, H.J. *The New 'Myth'-ology* (hereinafter T.N.M.), (1969), p.175
2. There Vos makes the worthwhile statement that 'All truly Christian theology must be biblical theology', but also that 'Biblical theology deals with the material from the historical standpoint, seeking to exhibit the organic growth or development of the truths of Special revelation from .... Eden to the close of the New Testament canon' (preface). In summarising Vos's contribution in this area of work and study, Gaffin says that he is 'the first in the Reformed tradition, perhaps even the first orthodox theologian, to give pointed, systematic attention to the *doctrinal* or *positive* theological significance of the fact that redemptive revelation comes as an organically unfolding historical process, and to begin working out the methodological consequences of this insight' (Gaffin, R.B., Jr. (ed.), *Redemptive History and Biblical Interpretation: The Shorter Writings of Geerhardus Vos*, (1980), p. xv.
3. Girdlestone, R.B., *Synonyms of the Old Testament: Their Bearing on Christian doctrine*, (1978 reprint of 2nd edition of 1897), p. 76.
4. Trench, R.C., *Synonyms of the New Testament*, (1976 reprint of 9th edition of 1880), pp. 239ff.
5. Dyrness, W., *Themes in Old Testament Theology*, (1979), pp. 105-7.
6. Ibid., p. 106.
7. Kittell, G. (ed.), *Theological Dictionary of the New Testament*, (1964), p. 269.
8. Ibid., p. 270.
9. Ibid., p. 267.

Chapter 1

The Old Testament

Sin in the Mosaic Epoch of Revelation

By 'Mosaic Epoch' we mean the period of revelation recorded for us in the Books of Moses, Genesis through Deuteronomy, covering approximately the period from the beginning of the world to the establishing of Israel as a theocratic nation in its own land, in Canaan, and constituted under God by means of His supernaturally revealed law. It needs hardly to be said that this period is radical and pivotal for any true understanding of the biblical doctrine of sin. Without a correct interpretation of these passages, passages which assert the entrance of sin into the world by the disobedience of the first man, and which also give an account of God's law, the standard of perfection against which sin in all its multifarious forms is to be measured, our hamartology is seriously impaired. Unless in our approach to these passages we see in them the revelation of God concerning sin, its entrance into man's experience and the consequences of it, then, to quote Dr. Whitney again:

'Instead of interpreting our present-day sin in the light of a divinely revealed standard, we reduce this standard to a pale reflection of our own man-made standard.'[1]

The kind of approach Dr. Whitney is warning against yields only an impoverished understanding of sin.

The Genesis narratives

The primary aspect of this period of biblical revelation is the fact of sin's entrance into the world, as recorded in Genesis 3. It is clear that this passage is of supreme importance in any correct biblical theology, and the main emphases must be brought out.

It is clear that Genesis 3 presupposes certain things. First, the primitive perfection of man is assumed. This perfection enabled man to fulfil the purpose for which God had made him. So Professor John Murray of Westminster reminds us that:

'...man was created good, good in respect of that which he specifically is. He was made upright and holy and therefore constituted for the demand, endowed with the character enabling him to fulfill all the demands devolving upon him by reason of God's propriety in him and sovereignty over him.'[2]

Man was not originally sinful. The biblical account does not leave open the possibility for us that sinfulness is a necessary predicate of creatureliness or humanness. A good God cannot create a bad man. The teaching of Scripture is that the world was a good place, with good people in it. Sin was alien, intrusive and foreign. It became domesticated, although it had no right to enter at all.

Secondly, Genesis 3 presupposes the fall of Satan into sin. The story of man's Fall is precipitated by sin already existing in the devil, who comes personally to Eve and addresses her. It is clear that the interpreter has to decide at this point on the genre of the narrative – are we here in the realm of historical fact, or in the realm of myth? G.Ch. Aalders summarises the principal difficulty thus:

'Rationalistic unbelief has insisted that animals simply do not speak, and consequently what is recorded here cannot be accepted as literally true.'[3]

But he goes on to say that

'Whoever accepts the Scripture as the Word of God ... will not be swayed by any objections. When God's Word says that the serpent spoke we accept this as a fact without further argument.'[4]

This being our position, therefore, we accept the historical factualness of the Genesis account, averring both that the serpent spoke, and that the speaking recorded demonstrates that sin did not originate with man, although it originated in humankind through a man.

Thirdly, Genesis 3 presupposes a specific probationary command given by God to man. Man was placed in the garden of Eden with a specific prohibition addressed to him by God, namely the command forbidding him to eat of the tree of the knowledge of good and evil (Gen. 2:17). Evangelical scholarship has debated much over whether this form of prohibition was covenantal; it was Robert Rollock, the first Principal of Edinburgh University (1555-99) who first gave expression in English to the term 'covenant of works', a term which is used in conservative theology to describe the probationary arrangement made with man in the garden. Subsequently the term was used in the Westminster documents to describe this arrangement. John Murray has argued against use of the term, however. He presents two arguments against using the phrase 'covenant of works':

'(1) The term is not felicitous, for the reason that the elements of grace entering into the administration are not properly provided for by the term 'works'. (2) It is not designated a covenant in Scripture.... Covenant in Scripture denotes the oath-bound confirmation of promise and involves a security which the Adamic economy did not bestow.'[5]

However, inasmuch as the terms of God's prohibition did offer security, conditional upon Adam's obedience, it seems that the arrangement by which God tested Adam was indeed covenantal. Not only was the blessing of life covenanted to him in promise on condition of his obedience, but the consequences of his actions, as the covenant representative of the human race, were to affect the whole of mankind.

It is clear that in this probationary period, Adam's choice was between good and evil, sin and holiness, right and wrong. Those who favour a mythical interpretation of the passage would agree with this evaluation. There is, however, much more at stake than a personal choice on the part of Adam. It is clear from the terms of the curse meted out (Gen. 3:17-19) that the choice he made had profound consequences for himself and all men after him. Similarly, the curse on Eve in Genesis 3:16 had respect to every child-bearing woman after her. Adam's action had both private and public, personal and covenantal consequences.

What was the nature of the probation? Murray answers:

'The Adamic administration is...an administration in which God, by a special act of Providence, established for man the provision whereby he might pass from the status of contingency to one of confirmed and indefectible holiness and blessedness, that is, from *posse peccare* and *posse non peccare* to *non posse peccare*.'[6]

The choice before him was either to continue in the perfection of goodness as his status before God, or to lose it, in the knowledge that to lose it meant death. J. Gresham Machen's summary of the meaning of Adam's probation is worth noting:

'If the probation had been successfully passed through, then man would have been received at once into eternal life. He possessed life before, but then life would have been assured. The 'if' would all have been removed from the promise of life; the victory would have been won; nothing further could ever by any possibility have separated God from his child.'[7]

As to the Fall itself, it is clear that temptation's arrow struck a chord in the heart of Eve, through whom then Adam was tempted to sin. The account of man's first sin emphasises several points which Calvin, in his summary of the passage, highlights. First, he says that 'the woman is led away from the word of God by the wiles of Satan through unbelief.'[8] Unbelief, says Calvin, 'was the root of defection.... Hence flowed ambition and pride, so that the woman first, and then her husband, desired to exalt themselves against God.'[9]

But, says Calvin, there is not simply apostasy from God in their first sin; there is also the fact that by it, Adam and Eve 'enslave themselves to the devil'[10] – '...unbelief has opened the door to ambition, but ambition has proved the parent of rebellion.'[11] Thus, by questioning the sanctions and promises of God, the way is opened only for man to yoke himself to the devil and become his slave, at enmity with God.

The divine response to Adam's sin is multi-layered, corresponding to the seriousness of the crime of each of the characters at the heart of the great drama. All of Adam's relationships are affected – with himself, with Eve and with God. God places enmity between Himself and His creatures – He declares a state of war between them both. The consequences of this are many – the woman will have pain in child-bearing, and Adam in his work. And at last, with all the authority of a great judge whose word is final and beyond appeal, the primitive couple are driven by God away from the garden, and are subject to laws of death and corruption.

Paradoxically, however, the word of God's curse also bears good news, in the 'protevangelium' of Genesis 3:15, a 'pivotal interpretation on the first human crisis'.[12] The promise of a future victor who would crush the serpent is heralded within the word of the curse pronounced on the devil. Walter Kaiser summarises:

A divinely instigated hostility... climaxes with the triumphant appearance of a 'he' – no doubt a representative person of the woman's seed. He would deliver a lethal blow to the head of Satan while the best the serpent would be able or even permitted to do would be to nip the heel of this male descendant.[13]

This, says Kaiser, would see 'a complete reversal of the serpent's temporary coup....'[14] Or, as Aalders expresses it:

> 'we see that in the sentence that is pronounced upon the serpent the ultimate annihilation of the wicked instigator of evil is clearly announced.'[15]

It is clear, therefore, in the protevangelium, that sin, in biblical terms, is temporal – in the realm of human experience it has an actual point of entry and an anticipated and promised point of defeat. Adam and Eve probably had little awareness of the meaning of the proto-evangelium. Some have suggested that Eve expected in Cain (whose name is explained in her exclamation in Genesis 4:1: 'I have *gotten* a man from the LORD) the fulfilment of the divine promise, and named her second son Abel (meaning 'vapour', 'smoke' or 'vanity') to indicate that these hopes were dashed.

More important for us to enumerate at this juncture are the consequences of man's sin, as these are spelt out for us in the Genesis narrative. Murray's summary (*Collected Writings*, Vol. 2, pp. 71ff.) is useful, and may be taken as the basis of discussion at this point. First, says Murray, man experiences 'internal revolution'. This is the subjective condition of man consequent upon his Fall. Man and Woman both see themselves as naked, their bodies having now become objects of self-loathing and embarrassment. Instead of enjoying the beauty of God's creation in self-harmony and wholesomeness, 'A new complex of disposition, feeling, and emotion took possession of [man's] heart and mind', in Murray's words. Sin affects man's self-awareness, and his deepest psychological impulses. 'Who told you that you were naked?' (Gen. 3:11) is God's question to Adam, and highlights the complete reversal of the satisfaction and contentment he had once enjoyed.

Second, Murray highlights the consequent 'revolution in God's relation to man'. Both on God's part as well as on man's, the mutual fellowship is disturbed and distorted as peace gives way to war, friendship to hostility. Murray calls God's verbal responses to Adam's sin 'the echoes of displeasure and condemnation'. It is this fact that necessitates what the New Testament calls *reconciliation*. A severed relationship requires to be healed in a way that satisfies the offended party, thus bringing both parties together once again in a re-constituted relational unity. Reconciliation is necessary for the repairing of the breach between God and man.

Third, Murray draws attention to the 'cosmic revolution' which is consequent upon man's sin. Although sin is personal, a 'movement in the realm of spirit,'[16] its implications are as large as the universe. The ground is cursed for the sake of man (Gen. 3:17). Adam's sin has consequences which stretch out far beyond and around him, outwith himself and into his very environment. Paul offers the best commentary upon this when he states that the whole creation groans, having been subjected to vanity by man's first sin (Rom. 8:20). The salvation which will effect the final destruction of sin and demonic activity will also require to be cosmic in its consequences and implications.

Murray fourthly emphasises the revolution which takes place in the human family because of man's sin. He draws attention here to various details underlined by the writer of Genesis, for example, the cry of Lamech in 4:23: 'I have slain a young man....' The subsequent history of the human family is written in bloody language – violence and wickedness follow the sin of Adam.

Finally, Murray underlines the 'disintegration in man's own constitution' consequent upon his sin, in the fact of death. Man will return to his constituent element, the dust from which he was created (3:19). Especially telling in this context is the frequently used formula in the genealogies, for example, in Genesis 5, where the names of the patriarchs are followed by the terse summary: 'and he died.'

Here, then, is the dismal record of the entrance of sin into the world, the Bible's testimony to the fact of man's sin as it came to be and now is. Man, originally created good, fails God's test. By doing so, through an act of wilful disobedience for which man alone is responsible, he opens the way for personal, familial and cosmic disintegration, the only hope of remedy lying in the (as yet) obscure promise of a future Saviour coming from the progeny of Eve herself.

At this point the narrative of Genesis leads up to the universal judgment of God expressed in the sending of a flood (Genesis 6-9). Much has been made of the supposed similarities between the Genesis account of the flood and the story of Ziusudra's ark in the Sumerian *Epic of Gilgamesh*. Indeed, S.H. Hooke, in his *Middle Eastern Mythology*, argued that comparisons had to be made between a Sumerian, a Babylonian, a Yahwist and a Priestly account of the flood story,[17] the former two being Mesopotamian, the latter two evolving from the biblical record, and all, allegedly, with a common mythical source. It is indisputable that 'A number of versions of a deluge story have been discovered among the cuneiform documents excavated at various near Eastern sites,'[18] and that 'These cuneiform accounts exhibit points of contact with the biblical narrative.'[19]

Many scholars have, consequently, dismissed the historicity of the flood narrative[20] on the grounds of its being not unique, even though geologists have long established the plausibility of significant changes in the earth's axis due both to erupting volcanoes and melting polar ice-caps.[21] In fact, the one striking difference between the Mesopotamian and biblical accounts of the flood is that the former *are* purely mythological, and purport to be nothing more; the Bible, on the other hand, claims to record actual history, and brings us face-to-face with credible historical reality, even if Harrison is right in saying that 'any attempt to relegate the events described in Genesis to a flood in an actual historical period must be regarded, for the present at least, as tentative'.[22]

For a full and satisfactory defence of the scientifico-historical view of the flood, the research material in Whitcomb and Morris' *The Genesis Flood* (1969) remains pivotal and fundamental. Drs. Whitcomb and Morris are under no doubt that the universal flood is scientifically defensible, and that it evidences further the cosmic results and implications of man's sin in Eden.

The point to be stressed in our evaluation of the biblical hamartology is that universal sin is expressly stated in the Genesis narrative (6:5-7) as the precipitate of the flood as an expression of divine judgment and displeasure. The prodigy of Cain (Gen. 4:16ff.) demonstrated the unremitting nature of sin, and its irreversible consequences in the human family. Now, in the intermarriage of 'the sons of God and the daughters of men' (Gen. 6:2), sin's expression knows no bounds. Aalders is probably correct to accept the traditional orthodox interpretation of this difficult phrase and to say that 'the 'seed of the woman' and the 'seed of the serpent' became mixed by way of intermarriage... these two lines did not maintain their distinctiveness'.[23]

The lines of demarcation have become blurred. Sin, at this point of biblical revelation, reaches its omega-point in the expression of the judgment of God, as the Genesis writer stretches the Hebrew language as well as Old Testament theology to its outer limits by declaring that 'it repented the LORD that he had made man upon the earth' (Gen. 6:6). Whitcomb and Morris are worth quoting at length on this point:

'The constant, almost monotonous repitition of phrases depicting the utter depravity of antediluvian humanity has filled the minds of believers with a sense of awe and astonishment. Every statement seems calculated to impress upon its readers the idea of *universal sin*; not just the exceptional sins of this group or that region, nor even of specific times or occasions, but rather the sin of an entire age and an entire race that had utterly corrupted its way upon the earth, and was now ripe for the judgment of a holy God.'[24]

The other aspect to the flood narrative in Genesis is the fact that the God whose awesome judgment demonstrates the terribleness of sin also provides the only salvation there is from the catastrophe by providing an ark for Noah and his family. Genesis 6 states explicitly that Noah 'found grace in the eyes of God', and O. Palmer Robertson, in his important volume *The Christ of the Covenants* (1984), takes this as an affirmation of 'the particularity of God's program of redemption'.[25]

It is to be noted that the act of salvation proffered by God is expressly covenantal; and, moreover, that the terms of the salvific covenant embrace not only Noah but also his family (Gen. 6:18). All this is reiterated in the post-deluvian revelation by God that He will never so visit the sin of man again. The promise of the world's preservation in Genesis 8 recognises that man innately tends to rebellion against God, but there is an express divine intention to set limits to man's self-destruction. Coupled with this is the law regarding the murderer (Gen. 9:6), demonstrating that responsibility for a correct response to sin and sinful actions is placed on man's shoulders. So Robertson continues:

'If the degenerating character of man is to be stopped short of total self-destruction, adequate curbs to the advancement of wickedness must be erected. In the wisdom of God, the execution of the manslayer provides a major curb to overflowing wickedness.'[26]

In summary, the first nine chapters of Genesis introduce us to the fact of sin in man's life and experience. They tell us of sin's entrance into the world originally created good by a benevolent God, and of the consequences of its entrance. The goodness of God reaches the limits of tolerance in the days of Noah, when patience is exhausted and gives way to judgment. All the while the narrative is reminding us that all hope of deliverance from the results and dominion of sin centres upon the sovereign, saving act of God.

It is God's saving activity in the world that occupies the attention of the writer in subsequent chapters. God's call to Abram to leave Ur and to follow Him (Gen. 12ff.), with the attendant promise that God would make him a great nation, is all to be seen in the light of covenant mercy extended now to a lost humanity. Vos is correct to emphasise the absolute monergism – the sole action on the part of God – of such salvation.[27] The writer's emphasis is on the unconditional sovereignty of the God who thus acts in saving grace to a lost world, and who does so by particular election and involvement. Of Abram's children, Isaac is chosen; of Isaac's, Jacob; of Jacob's, Judah. In this way the writer never lets us lose sight of the promise which was given in the wake of the primal sin, that the death-blow to sin would come through the seed of the woman. In each subsequent generation of world history, the divine rescue plan is being set in motion.

The Revelation of Law

With the giving of the law to Moses we enter a new phase of revelation, in which the nature and reality of sin are given external codification. The basic concept for sin in the Bible, as we have seen, is that of 'action contrary to the norm,'[28] action which 'misses the target'. This raises the question – what precisely *is* the target? The answer given to the people of God in this era of biblical revelation is indelibly written on the two tables of stone given to Moses by a divine hand on Mount Sinai (Exod. 20ff.).

Two points need to be stressed in this connection. First, the law is given within the covenantal relationship sustained by God's people to Him. The remarks of Exodus 19:5, introductory to the giving of the law, set the decalogue firmly within a federal context. Also, the divine directive in Exodus 33:1-3 to the children of Israel to remove from Sinai reiterates the terms of the Abrahamic covenant. Dr Fensham of Stellenbosch University, writing in the *New Bible Dictionary*, puts it exactly right when he says of the legal material in Exodus that

> 'In Exodus this code is placed in a definite historical framework, viz., the forming of the covenant at Sinai. These laws are, thus, intended as the stipulations of the covenant.'[29]

In the thought, therefore, of the Old Testament, the keeping of God's law is expressive of a covenant relationship with Him, and is not to be regarded as itself constitutive of such a relationship. The law is given not in order to establish the bond between God and His people, but in the wake of such a bond having been established. It is to His covenant family that God gives the commandments; law-keeping is the mark of this family, not the entrance into it. Obedience to His commandments is the badge of adoption, not the basis of adoption.

Secondly, there is a legitimate sense in which the Sinaitic law was anticipatory of settlement in the land of Canaan. Of the civil legislation of Exodus 21 ff., Professor Edward J.Young of Westminster wrote:

'It is obvious that they were never intended for observance in the desert, but are anticipatory, pointing forward to the time when Israel should dwell in the land.'[30]

Nevertheless, one must qualify such a statement by saying that the law was binding from the moment of its being given, even if it was not operative within a civic context until a later date. It is this fact that enables us to see in the law of God a full revelation of the nature of sin.

Much has been made of the similarities between the Sinaitic law and other extant lawcodes of the Ancient Near East. Both Anderson[31] and Keller[32] refer to this, but both stress that the similarity is essentially as to form rather than content. American evangelical scholarship – such as the work of Walter Kaiser – has done a great deal of research in this field; Robertson is brought to the conclusion that 'the discovery of the classical Hittite form should continue to be one of the significant factors in contemporary biblical studies'.[33]

Although this naked statement may have the effect of leading people to think of the Israelites' law as one example of a wider genre, Robertson goes on to underline the distinctiveness of the Sinaitic lawcode by defining it as 'an externalised summation of the will of God.'[34] Thus a proper definition of the law of God requires us to view it primarily as self-revelation on the part of God, and, because this is so, to see in it a precise and divine definition of sin. This latter fact requires a great deal of study, more than theological works tend to give it; the following comments are only pointers in this direction.

First, the Sinaitic law reveals something of the multiformity of sin. There is not one commandment but ten. Sin dresses itself in various garbs. Dr. J.E. Hartley, in the *Theological Dictionary of the Old Testament*, summarises it thus: 'Through the law God shows his interest in all aspects of man's life which is to be lived under his direction and care.'[35] In other words, the comprehensiveness of the two tables of the law corresponds to the biblical presentation of sin as complex and involved, and not as simple. Every area of life is open to the scrutiny of God, and has been affected by the Fall of the first man.

Second, the law shows that sin is objective, a noun, not an adjective. It is not merely an inward state. It can be defined according to a moral code. This requires us to guard jealously the doctrine of the personalness of God; Dr. Whitney is correct to maintain that the depersonalisation of God is the foundation for the rejection of absolute ethical standards and the first movement towards the secularisation of morality.[36] Ethical values then become situational, to be maintained or discarded at will. The law of God, as transcribed by the finger of God on the stone tables of Sinai, forbids this line of reasoning. By maintaining the personal nature of the God who legislates, the norms become absolute, uncompromising and non-negotiable. Sin is not a subjective category; the inscription of these commands and prohibitions brings it fully into the category of the objective and absolute.

This is not to suggest that there is no subjective element in sin. It is fundamental to a fully biblical anthropology to emphasise the complete bondage of the fallen human will. But in the context of revealed law, it is clear that no concept of sin can be defined from a totally subjective aspect. Indeed, Eichrodt quotes passages where 'the decisive factor is the objective offence, with no reference to the element of volition'.[37]

Third, the law emphasises the accountable character of the lawbreaker. There is now a written code, the breaking of which requires explanation and presses to a verdict. Culpability attaches now to the shortcoming. Sin is blameworthy. In this area, objective and subjective aspects of the sin question merge. Eichrodt has a thorough discussion of this in Volume 2 of his *Old Testament Theology*. In examining the evolution of the understanding of sin in Israel, he points out that there was a tendency 'to objectivise sin by weakening the element of personal responsibility'[38], which developed into 'a surprisingly sure grasp of the development of sin in man, indicating a high level of understanding of the volitional element in the sinner's conduct'.[39]

The result of this is to objectivise guilt also, by seeing it, according to Eichrodt, 'in the perspective of what God is doing to establish his holy people'.[40] The objectivity of guilt is also brought to our attention in the fact that the casuistic corpus of the Sinaitic law (Exod. 21ff.) itself includes the punishment as an integral part of the inscribed code.[41]

Fourthly, the law demonstrates the seriousness of sin by including within its corpus the stipulated methods of dealing with it. This fact alone underlines for us the fact that the giving of the law, far from implicating man further in his departure from God, was actually given with a salvific purpose in mind. Robertson describes this accurately when he says that

> 'The integral role of a substitutionary sacrificial system within the legal provisions of the Mosaic covenant clearly indicates a sober awareness of the distinction between God's dealings with man in innocence and with man in sin.'[42]

In other words, the very law which demonstrates so clearly and adequately the condition of fallen man, itself prescribes the necessary channels by which such sin may be dealt with. And in this context Robertson is correct to state that

> '...at the very time of its institution, the Mosaic covenant was represented as being progressively related to the totality of God's purposes. While containing a clearer manifestation of redemptive truth than that which preceded, it also contained much less truth than the consummation of the covenant which was to follow.'[43]

The law which reveals sin is integral to the saving purposes which reveal grace. Or, as Dr. Whitney expresses it, 'The whispers of Calvary must not preclude the thunders of Sinai.'[44]

The Histories and the Prophets

The foregoing has given a summary of the teaching of the early chapters of the Bible concerning the nature of sin. These chapters of Genesis and Exodus bear upon the most fundamental aspects of the doctrine of sin, namely its entrance into the world and the divine response to it. Much evangelical scholarship has concerned itself with defending the integrity of these early chapters of the Pentateuch, and much Neo-orthodox thinking has concerned itself, as we shall see, with a new approach to these very chapters. This, as Dr. Whitney has demonstrated, is the 'new hermeneutic' governing much that passes for theology and biblical scholarship; he goes on to suggest that 'nowhere does [it] receive more spectacular illustration than in the treatment accorded by liberal scholars to the first eleven chapters of Genesis'.[45]

Yet, as has been shown in the discussion above, these are the very chapters which give a biblical doctrine of sin its firm theological and historical basis.

The testimony of the remainder of the Old Testament is built upon the foundation of its early opening chapters. The teaching is uniform, yet the revelation progresses with each epoch. Our study at this point will outline the salient features of the biblical teaching on sin in the historical, prophetic and poetic passages of the Old Testament. These distinctions are purely a matter of genre; none of these categories can be separated from each other. At the same time, the demonstration of the Old Testament doctrine will be served only by commenting on them individually. Vos subsumes all of these categories under the heading 'The Prophetic Epoch of Revelation'.

Vos is worth summarising here. He begins by pointing out that the law, which God gave to His people through Moses, established the Israelites as a theocracy. Even a liberal Old Testament scholar like John Bright concedes this when he says that the Decalogue 'brought Israel into being as a people'.[46] The theocracy is consolidated, says Vos, with the accession of David to the throne; all other events centre upon this great moment, and, moreover, the concept of the theocratic kingdom 'remains central in the hopes of Israel'.[47]

Vos' position is that the period of revelation during which God's message was mediated to the people through the prophets attaches itself to this movement of the establishing of the kingdom. Vos is worth quoting at length:

> 'Prophecy is a factor of continuity in the history of revelation both through its retrospective and through its prospective attitude. Its preaching of repentance, and of the sin of apostasy from the norms of the past, links it to the preceding work of Jehovah for Israel in the patriarchal and Mosaic periods. Through its predictive elements it anticipated continuity with the future.'[48]

Patrick Fairbairn, a much neglected nineteenth-century theologian, writing in similar vein, says that

> '...as regards the great stream of prophecy, the past never properly dies; it is perpetually resumed and carried forward in the future. Earlier developments become only the historical basis out of which spring the announcement of more matured and diversified results.'[49]

In other words, it is only against the background of the opening pages of the Old Testament that the meaning of sin in the rest of the Old Testament can be understood. And realising that the prophetic voice from God is the authentic vehicle of revelation, we must turn to examine the revelation of sin found there.

The Historical Narratives (1 Samuel–Esther)

By the designation 'historical narratives' we understand the portions of the Old Testament which together tell the story of Israel as a people from the point of settlement in Canaan up until the point of final return from the Babylonian exile. This history is complex and, in the style of the biblical narratives, usually revolves around various personalities, like the kings, or the charismatic leaders of the covenant community. At the very outset, it has to be borne in mind that the whole question of Old Testament hagiography lies at the centre of current theological debate. Gerhard von Rad has precipitated much of the current controversy by his insistence on distinguishing between Israel's history in 'modern critical research, and that which Israel's faith has built up.'[50] This dichotomy, he has alleged, has been largely ignored by Old Testament scholars, who have forgotten that the Old Testament gives 'only' the theological angle; in von Rad's view, highly interpretative and subjective.

Von Rad's thesis has been attacked by, among others, Walther Eichrodt. His main objection to the severing of faith and history in this way is that it becomes impossible 'to restore any inner coherence between these two aspects of Israel's history'.[51] Eichrodt goes on to suggest that von Rad's approach is 'strongly reminiscent of the trends in New Testament studies inspired by Bultmann'.[52]

A proper approach to the Old Testament requires us to recognise the presence and validity of both avenues of thought, to see both history and kerygma, fact and faith, interwoven. The Old Testament history is true theologically and the Old Testament theology is verifiable historically. Hasel identifies this approach exactly when he says that

> 'In view of the biblical testimony the historical-critical method working
> without a God-given hypothesis of which Scripture testifies brings with
> is a crisis of objectivity and facticity.'[53]

In our surrender to the Old Testament as the inspired revelation of
God, we distance ourselves exactly from such a crisis.

In summarising the salient features of the presentation of the
doctrine of sin in the historical portions of the Word of God, therefore,
we note simply and very generally the main emphases. First, it is to
be noted that sin is generally regarded as a contravention of the
commandments of God. Early in 1 Samuel (2:22-25), Eli registers
the seriousness of sinning against God by contrasting it with a man
sinning against his brother. In the latter case, he suggests, satisfaction
can be obtained before a judge; but if a man sins against the Lord,
'who shall intreat for him?' This seriousness is echoed in 1 Samuel
14:33, where the people recognise that the eating of blood is a 'sin
against the Lord'.

Early, therefore, in the minds of some in Israel, there is a recognition
of sin as a transgression of divine decree. Its seriousness is heightened
by the object of its attack, God Himself. Sin is personal and culpable.
It is the certain violation of absolute standards, the discarding of
absolute ethics and morals. In the mind of Israel, at this stage, there
are still to be heard some echoes of the thunderings of Sinai.

Within the history of this period, the attention of the reader is
drawn to the particular seriousness which attaches to the sin of wilful
disregard for the stated command of God. Thus Samuel, in confronting
Saul with his sin following the battle with the Amalekites in 1 Samuel
15, points out to the king that 'rebellion is as the sin of witchcraft, and
stubbornness is as iniquity and idolatry' (verse 23), adding that because
Saul has rejected the word of God, God has rejected him as Israel's
king. Quite apart from the incidental reference to the regard with which
the particular sin of witchcraft is held,[54] this particular verse reveals
to us the prophetic understanding of the essence of sin as volitional
and self-determined rebellion against the law of God. Saul is culpable
in this connection, and this guilt precipitates his fall from Israel's
throne.

It is interesting to note also that within the framework of these
historical developments, the general designation 'sinner' is used on

occasions as a generic type of the enemies of Israel. In this same passage, 1 Samuel 15, the name 'sinners' is used to describe the Amalekites. The lines of demarcation for Israel are clearly drawn by the law of God. Adherence to its claims and standards are to be the distinguishing characteristics of the redeemed people; whereas the enemies of Israel are known generically as 'sinners'.

Again, it is to be noted that the historical narratives recognise a developing sense of the universalism of sin. In Solomon's dedicatory prayer at the completion of the building of the Temple, the statement is made, parenthetically and incidentally (but made nonetheless): 'there is no-one who does not sin' (1 Kings 8:46, repeated in 2 Chronicles 6:36). 'Here', says Eichrodt, 'all pride is silenced by the realization that there is no man who has not sinned.'[55] However, the bald statement of the universalism of sin is not to be taken as a fully developed doctrine of original sin; Eichrodt is probably correct to make the point, as he does in a footnote, that a statement such as that of 1 Kings 8:46, 'which sounds like an absolute principle... in fact, merely represents the experience of the effort involved in keeping the Law.'[56] In other words, Solomon is registering the recognition of how unyielding the law's demands are; but in doing so he is drawing attention to the fact of universal sinfulness.

Much of the historical narrative is taken up with the fact of Jeroboam's sin in commanding the people to worship two golden calves, one in Bethel and one in Dan (1 Kings 12:25ff.). This was a flagrant breach of the law of God, particularly of the second commandment. It is interesting to note the writer's comment on these two idols and shrines, that 'this thing *became* a sin' (verse 30). The making of idols and the command to worship them was clearly a sin on the part of Jeroboam, and this in turn became a sin for the people. It is important to underline this note of the possibility of an object *becoming* a sin for the covenant community.

It is important to note that this particular sin committed by Jeroboam itself becomes pivotal for the re-telling of Israel's story in subsequent years of her history. God's curse on Jeroboam and his house is recounted in the most violent forms (1 Kings 14:7ff.), and subsequent kings of Israel are judged in terms of whether or not they walked in the ways of Jeroboam,[57] and ultimately the sin of Jeroboam in this regard is stated as the underlying reason for which Israel was exiled (2 Kings 17:21-23).[58]

Indeed, the whole spiritual temperature of Israel and Judah is judged in these writings by the extent to which the king adhered to, or rebelled against, the claims of God's law. Much of the people's fortunes hinge upon whether or not the king 'did right in the sight of God'.[59] Here, the concept of sin is set in a national and political context.

Coupled with the testimony to what sin is and has done, the historical narratives of the Old Testament also demonstrate a deep awareness of the power of God to remove sin. There is clearly an awareness of the forgiving nature of God when Solomon prays at the dedication of the Temple,[60] and the prophet Nathan is able to give David the assurance that 'The LORD has taken away your sin' (2 Sam. 12:13).

Eichrodt points out that there are two elements in the Old Testament presentation of God as able to effect the removal of sin. The first of these concerns the prescriptions for ritual and cultic removal of both personal and national sins. The full significance of this is seen at the return from exile where the immediate concern of Ezra, for example, is that an altar be built and sacrifice offered (cf. Ezra 3:2; 6:16-22). Eichrodt is correct to maintain that the cultic atonement current at the time had its roots in the priestly laws and codes of Leviticus,[61] and makes the important point that

> 'the whole priestly institution of atonement is to be regarded as the gracious creation of the covenant God, who bestows upon his congregation the possibility of expiating all those things that call for expiation, and of assuring themselves, through these visible signs, of his forgiving grace and enduring clemency.'[62]

Secondly, Eichrodt emphasises that guilt may be removed by a special act of intercession, such as Samuel's prayer 'on Israel's behalf' in 1 Samuel 7:9. In common with other intercessory prayers of the Old Testament, Eichrodt suggests that the description given of them

> 'unambiguously subordinates their petition to God's saving dealings with his people, so that both in the acceptance and the refusal of the request the divine plan which dominates history comes to fulfillment.'[63]

Eichrodt also makes the important point that even where God refuses to grant the request specified, such as when Samuel interecedes on behalf of Saul (1 Samuel 15), even the denial achieves 'the realization of God's plan of salvation despite human sin'.[64]

By far the most important contribution of the historical narratives to the question of sin and its meaning is to be found in 2 Samuel 7, where God makes a covenant with David. The passage is skilfully written, and centres upon the concept of 'building a house'. The establishing of the covenant bond between God and David is precipitated by David's desire to build a house for the ark of God. Here David clearly has the temple in view. However, the essence of the covenant is that God will build a house (that is, a dynasty, a kingdom) for David. David's son will sit on David's throne for ever.

Just as Jeroboam's sin is pivotal in describing the subsequent sin and rebellion of the house of Israel, so the covenant established with David becomes pivotal in the historical narratives as the foundation for God's care of Judah. Abijam, for example, sits on the throne 'for David's sake' (1 Kings 15:3-5). In a thorough discussion of this, Robertson highlights how often the formula 'according to the word of the Lord' is used in the description of the kings of Judah, and concludes that 'the unfolding of the history of the kings of Israel may be appreciated from a proper covenantal perspective. God's covenantal word to David will now be verified through the concreteness of historical events.'[65]

In a penetrating and original study of a notoriously difficult phrase in 2 Samuel 7, Walter Kaiser has adequately shown the universal soteriological significance of the Davidic covenant. Like Robertson, Kaiser emphasises the elements of continuity with the past which appear in the covenant with David.[66] The element of discontinuity, which, insists Kaiser, is fully realised by David, is that

'the ancient promise of blessing to all mankind would continue; only now it would involve David's dynasty, throne and kingdom. Indeed, it was a veritable "charter" granted as God's gift for the future of all mankind.'[67]

This is the significant point. The sin of mankind is to be dealt with covenantally, and the covenant finds its focus now in David, whose son will sit on his everlasting throne. It is in the salvific terms of this covenant that the fallen race of Adam will find hope.

The Prophetic Literature (Isaiah–Malachi)

It may appear misleading to deal with the prophetic portions of the Bible separately, as if the ministry of the prophets was divorced from the historical events which shaped them. There is, undoubtedly, an intimate connection between the historical writings and the prophetic literature – witness, for example, the story of Hezekiah, which is recounted both in the narrative of Kings (2 Kings 18ff.) and in the literature of Isaiah (chapters 36-38). In general, liberal approaches to the prophetic literature have emphasised this fact to the exclusion of the significant theological role of the prophets; in some cases the role of the prophets has been reduced to little more than social commentary. For example, Bright says that from the books of Amos and Hosea we are given 'an inside view of contemporary Israelite society... which [makes] it clear that the northern state at least, in spite of its healthy appearance, was in an advanced state of decay, socially, morally and religiously'.[68]

And even although Bright concedes that the prophets 'were certainly of far greater historical significance than any of Judah's kings',[69] it remains that the general picture of the prophets in liberal scholarship is of functionaries who took their society's political, social and religious conditions as the foundation for their address, rather than as spokesmen sent by the living God to bring His word to His people. To be sure, the prophets cannot be divorced from the historical circumstances which gave them birth, but neither can a view of them which ignores the sovereign commission of God do justice to the Old Testament evidence.

In a much neglected study of the church in the Old Testament, the late Rev. W.B. Nicolson sets the role of the prophets correctly within the framework of the historical narratives of the Bible. He says:

'There is no evidence that the prophets were interested in politics as such; their purpose in the kingdom period was to represent the righteous claims of Jehovah, under whose dictation and law the king was to exercise his exalted office. These prophets lived in critical times, and their warnings of judgment against evil doers and their calls to repentance envisaged the weal or woe of Israel and the surrounding nations.'[70]

Similarly, in a booklet which deals with much more than its title immediately suggests,[71] the late Prof. O.T. Allis makes the point that while the Bible 'does attach importance to the authorship, date and situation of the prophetic utterance which it records',[72] the reason it does so is because in many cases the prophecies are predictive and proleptic. Indeed, says Allis,

'It is the predictive element which often makes the biblical situation so important. For according to their biblical situation these predictions reveal an insight into the future which clearly transcends anything that is possible to the dim and short-sighted vision of mortal man.'[73]

Or, to put it otherwise:

'God thus permitted the prophets to hear words and see visions regarding matters that were otherwise his secret, inaccessible to man.'[74]

It is precisely this fact that requires us to view the prophets as more than commentators on the social conditions prevailing in Israel or Judah at any given time. The function of prophecy is singular; it is to deliver the Word of God to man. Sometimes that word is one of blessing and encouragement, sometimes one of judgment and chastisement. Wherever it is heard, it is the authentic voice of Jehovah, and must be regarded as such. When the prophets denounce sin, they are delivering the authoritative word from Heaven on the issue, and not merely analysing prevailing or contemporary attitudes.

The theme of the prophetic understanding of sin is complex. Vos' summary is a useful treatment for our purpose. Under the heading 'The content of the prophetic revelation', Vos considers (a) The Nature and Attributes of Jehovah; (b) The Bond between Jehovah and Israel; (c) The rupture of the bond: the sin of Israel; and (d) The Restoration of the bond: the prophetic eschatology.[75] It is with the third of these themes (*Biblical Theology*, pp. 284-307) that we are concerned here.

Vos begins his analysis of this theme by stating that 'the early prophets predict clearly that the bond of the berith [covenant] will be suspended',[76] although it will not be 'irreparably broken off.'[77] The prophetic view, he claims, is to see sin as concrete, never abstract, dealing with apostasy and estrangement from God. Sin is to be seen, therefore, in the light of covenant theology, and is to be understood as constituting some kind of suspension of the ideal conditions in which the covenant normally operates.

Vos continues: 'The sin which the prophets condemn is largely collective national sin.... this is a collective treatment of sin [which]

is generically collective.'[78] There is solidarity of sin and of guilt. Consequently, says Vos, there is solidarity of punishment. Vos singles out Hosea as the prophet who most markedly works out the implications of individualism in relation to sin.

Vos states that the prophets first attack with unanimity the cultic ritual of the worship of Jehovah, from the 'corruptness of the priests (Micah 3:11)' to 'ritual flaw in the offering of leavened things' in Amos 4:4-5.[79] Clearly in these passages, as in Hosea 10:1, to which Vos refers in this connection, the emphasis is not on the sinfulness of the cultic ritual itself as much as on 'the sinful tendency back of it'.[80] What the audiences of the prophets failed to realise was that 'Not sacrifices but retribution will satisfy Jehovah'.[81] Isaiah is particularly ruthless in the absolute condemnation of these sins in holy things, and in making clear that 'not these sins in the abstract but some peculiar accompaniment of them rendered them unacceptable in Jehovah's sight'.[82]

Vos summarises the issue in these terms: 'We find, therefore, that in no passage of the four early prophets is the cult of sacrifice denounced as in itself and under all circumstances sinful...the cult as such is never declared sin.'[83] Sin attaches not to the cult, but to the sinful attitude on the part of those involved in it, and who thought that such formalism could satisfy the demands of God.

Secondly, Vos contends that 'Side by side with the ritual sin of Israel, its social sin falls under the prophetic condemnation'.[84] In a close analysis of this theme, Vos demonstrates that the condemnatory voice of the prophets in this connection is neither primarily economic or industrial, but theological and religious. Theocratic principles must take priority over financial or industrial ones. However, Vos is careful to point out that while 'The prophetic condemnation of the social sin of Israel does not have its deepest roots in humanitarian motives',[85] nevertheless 'the humanitarian element is not of course absent'.[86] Inasmuch as humanitarian elements enter into the situation, the whole problem, according to Vos, 'is raised to the religious sphere. For injustice is sin against God, and no consequences, however deplorable from the manward point of view, could equal the terrible significance of the religious fact to the prophetic consequence.'[87]

What matters at last, and what makes the social injustices so great, is what Vos calls 'the bearing of the wicked conduct upon Jehovah and His rights'.[88] Vos contrasts this fact, the fact that the prophets constantly keep the nature and being of God at the forefront of their discussion, with modern 'social' preaching, which gives priority to the social organism.[89]

Vos deals separately with the hamartology of Hosea and Isaiah, because, he says, they have made their own distinctive contribution to the biblical doctrine of sin as 'want of conformity to the ideal of marriage affection and loyalty',[90] and concludes:

> 'Because thus viewing sin from the one principle of unfaithfulness to Jehovah, Hosea reaches a profound conception of its character as a disposition, an enslaving power, as something deeper and more serious than single acts of transgression. It is a bent rendering its victims unable to reform.'[91]

Isaiah complements this picture by viewing sin 'as first of all an infringement upon the honour of God'.[92] It is offensive to men because it strikes at the glory and honour of God, slighting His authority and rebelling against His absolute right to command. Particular sins like drunkenness, pride and oppression are to be seen in this light.

Vos concludes his summary by contrasting the modern critical views concerning the prophetic doctrine of sin with the Bible's own testimony. According to the critics, the errors denounced by the prophets of the Old Testament were natural and unavoidable, part of the natural evolution of Israel's religious history. The prophets themselves, however, charge Israel with deliberate and wilful rebellion against the religion revealed to them at the Exodus, leaving them guilty before God. In Vos' view, therefore, the prophets are witnesses to the covenant between God and Israel, a covenant which is suspended in the sins of the covenant people, but which, as the prophets so eloquently declare, is never ultimately broken because of the supremacy of grace.

The Poetic literature (Psalms–Song of Solomon)

It is true to say that recent criticism of the Psalms has been approached from two different angles. One modern approach is typified by Artur Weiser in the SCM Commentary on the Book of Psalms. His general thesis is that underlying the Psalms is the culture and heritage of the Palestinian regions, where the tribes of Israel were to settle after the wanderings of the desert were over. Thus he says:

'Israel's political history and history of ideas developed as she borrowed those cultural forms and then tried to come to terms with their substance and to fill the alien forms with a new content, that is, with a new meaning which had its roots in and had developed out of her own traditions.'[93]

The final redaction of the Psalms is, on this theory, dated late in the history of Israel, although the traditions embodied in them may be early. According to Weiser, the relationship between cult and tradition is of such a nature that the cultus must be viewed as 'the sphere of life in which these traditions were preserved as a living force'.[94]

The evangelical approach (shared by some non-evangelical scholars) is different. Young sums up an alternative position thus:

'... we are mistaken when we regard the entire Psalter as designed for the usage of the Temple. That some Psalms were so used cannot be denied, but it is interesting to note that liturgical directions are lacking for many of the Psalms. The Psalter, rather, is primarily a manual and guide and model for the devotional needs of the individual believer.'[95]

In this connection too, Harrison is probably correct to say that

'It seems fairly certain that the psalmist was originally a lone composer who in some instances probably did not write with a view to forming a collection, or even having his meditations included as part of a collection of religious poetry.'[96]

Both Harrison and Young, *contra* the Weiser school, are agreed in viewing the Psalter primarily in individualistic terms, rather than through the eyes of a cultic editor.

Critical questions as to the authorship and compilation of the Psalms do not concern us here, since our concern is with the *content* of the Psalter, rather than its historical *context*. What is the teaching of the Book of Psalms as to the meaning and nature of sin? In this connection reference will be made to a useful, if little-known book of the nineteenth century, entitled *The Psalms: Their History, Teaching and Use*. The author, Dr. William Binnie, has not produced a commentary, but a book which gathers together the theology of the Psalter in a systematic way. The doctrine of sin is dealt with under the general heading of 'Personal Religion in the Psalms', and in a chapter entitled 'The Progress of Religion in the Soul'.

Binnie begins his investigation into the hamartology of the Psalms by referring to the giving of the Law at Sinai, where God showed His people '...the nature of sin, its sinfulness, its hatefulness to Him, and its certain fatality to them'.[97] He continues:

'Now, the Psalms are the Church's response to God's revelations. If, in the Law, God teaches the people the knowledge of sin, in the Psalter the people give expression to the convictions and feelings which that teaching has produced in them.'[98]

Binnie's position is, therefore, that the objectivity of the Law's demands are demonstrated in their subjective aspect in the Psalter, where sin, in its personal and intimate character is put in such clear relief.

Before moving to a detailed examination of the Psalms in this connection, Binnie draws attention to the fact of the 'deep sense of sin which is everywhere perceptible'.[99] Indeed, this observation might be as easily extended to embrace all the poetical books. There is no biblical poet who is not burdened with a sense of sin. Or, in Binnie's words,

'Sin, either as a present burden weighing down the soul, or as a burden that has been removed by the mercy of God, is a theme of perpetual recurrence.'[100]

Binnie also draws attention to Psalm 51, where David examines his sin in the matter of Uriah and Bathsheba, describing the king's anguished and penitential cries as 'the inevitable consequence of that living recognition of a Personal God, which... is such a characteristic feature of the Psalms'.[101]

However, Binnie is correct to draw attention to the fact that is is not simply the acts of sin, the concrete transgressions themselves, that occupy the attention of these biblical poets. Occasionally, says Binnie, 'we see them going deeper into the matter, and lamenting the deep corruption of nature out of which their transgressions flow as from a bitter poisonous fountain.'[102] He argues passionately against those who deny the doctrine of original sin, and concludes that the Psalms echo 'the whole substance of the doctrine of inborn depravity',[103] and draws attention to Psalm 14, which, he claims, evidences the fact that 'There must be in mankind a deep malignity of nature, an inborn ungodliness of heart'.[104]

From a discussion of these themes, Binnie goes on to discuss the evidence of the Psalms as to the divine remedy for the human condition in the provision of full and free grace. Of sin itself, however, the above establishes the thesis that the Psalms show evidence of remorse and repentance for actual sins, and also an awareness of the existence of original and inborn sin, thus throwing all hope of remedy and cure on to God alone. The poetry of the Old Testament, as with its historical and prophetic writings, highlights the twin themes of sin's ugliness before God, and God's gracious provision for man in his sin.

NOTES

1. H. J. Whitney *The New 'Myth'-ology*., p. 246.
2. Murray, J., *Collected Writings*, Vol 2, (1977), p. 47.
3. Aalders, G.Ch., *Genesis*, Vol. 1, Bible Student's Commentary, (1981), p. 99. Aalders goes on to show that even, for example, Roman Catholic scholars, who profess to accept the literal trustworthiness of the Bible, object to a speaking serpent story.
4. Idem.
5. Murray, op.cit., p. 49.
6. Idem.
7. Machen, J.G., *The Christian View of Man*, (1947), p.19.
8. Calvin, J. *Genesis*, (1984), p. 152.
9. Ibid., p. 153.
10. Idem.
11. Idem.
12. Kaiser, W.C., *Towards an Old Testament Theology*, (1978), p. 35.
13. Ibid., pp. 78-9.
14. Ibid., p.79.
15. Aalders, op.cit., p. 107.
16. Murray, op.cit., p. 72.
17. Hooke, S.H., *Middle Eastern Mythology*, no date, pp. 133-5.
18. Harrison, R.K. *Introduction to the Old Testament*, (1969), p. 557.
19. Idem.
20. For example, cf. Barthel, M. (tr. Mark Houson), *What the Bible Really Says*, (1982), p. 53: 'The Flood and Noah's Ark are not verifiable historical facts but episodes in a symbolic drama...'
21. cf. Ibid., p. 48.
22. Harrison, op.cit., p. 558.
23. Aalders, op.cit., p. 154.
24. Whitcomb, J.C., and Morris, H.M., *The Genesis Flood*, (1969), p. 18.
25. Robertson, O.P., *The Christ of the Covenants*, (1984), p. 113.
26. Ibid., p. 117.
27. Vos, op.cit., pp. 94ff.

28. Eichrodt, W., *Theology of the Old Testament*, Volume 2, english edition, 1967, p. 381.

29. Article on 'Law' in *New Bible Dictionary*, (1986), p. 683.

30. Young, E.J., *Introduction to the Old Testament*, (1983), p. 69.

31. Anderson, G.W., *The History and Religion of Israel*, (1965), p. 381.

32. Keller, W., *The Bible as History*, (1977), chapter 12.

33. Robertson, op.cit., p. 170.

34. Ibid., p. 171.

35. Hartley, J.E., article in *Theological Dictionary of the Old Testament*, Vol. 1, (1981), p. 404.

36. Whitney, T.N.M., p. 30ff.

37. Eichrodt, op.cit., p. 382.

38. Ibid., p. 383.

39. Ibid., pp. 383-4.

40. Ibid., p. 384.

41. cf. *New Bible Dictionary*, p. 683: 'The typical style [of casuistic law] is to start with "ki" or "im" ("if") and to give the transgression in the protasis and the legal verdict in the apodosis'.

42. Roberston, op.cit., pp. 173-4.

43. Ibid., p. 198.

44. Whitney, H.J., *Evangelism the Heartbeat of the Church*, (1987), p. 274.

45. Whitney, T.N.M., p. 144.

46. Bright, J. *A History of Israel*, (1981), p. 146.

47. Vos, op.cit., p. 203.

48. Ibid., p. 206.

49. Fairbairn, P., *The Interpretation of Prophecy*, (1964 reprint of 1856 edition), pp. 188-9.

50. Quoted in Hasel, G., *Old Testament Theology: Basic Issues in the Current Debate*, (1982), p. 97.

51. Eichrodt, Vol 1., op.cit., p. 512.

52. Ibid., p. 513.

53. Hasel, op.cit., p. 107.

54. cf. the Sinaitic code at Exodus 22:18: 'Thou shalt not suffer a witch to live', and the Chronicler's assessment of Saul's reign at 1 Chronicles 10:13: 'Saul died for his transgression which he committed against the LORD, even the word of the LORD which he kept not, and also for asking counsel of one that had a familiar spirit...'; the latter phrase refers to his consultation with a medium at Endor.

55. Eichrodt, Vol. 2, op.cit., p. 398.

56. Ibid., p. 410.

57. cf. 1 Kings 16:7 (Baasha), 19 (Zimri), 25 (Omri), 31 (Ahab); 2 Kings 3:3 (Joram), 13:2 (Jehoahaz), 10:11 (Jehoash), 14:24 (Jeroboam II), 15:8 (Zechariah), 15:18 (Menahem), 15:23 (Pekahiah) and 15:27 (Pekah), as those

of Israel's kings who walked in the ways of Jeroboam I.

58. It is a great pity that modern Old Testament historians like John Bright fail to acknowledge this, and examine and assess Israel's downfall in exclusively political terms. The *religious* reasons for the exile find little or no expression in the assessment of such academics. Especially telling is the fact that 2 Kings 17:21-23 is not listed in Bright's index of Scripture references.

59. Contrast Jotham king of Judah, who 'did what was right in the eyes of the LORD' (2 Kings 15:34), with his successor, Ahaz, who did not (2 Kings 16:2).

60. cf. 1 Kings 8:50: '... forgive your people, who have sinned against you.'

61. cf. Eichrodt, Vol 2, op.cit., p. 446.

62. Idem.

63. Ibid., p. 449.

64. Ibid., p. 450.

65. Robertson, op.cit., p. 255.

66. Kaiser lists five such elements: the promise of a great name, the 'planting' of Israel, setting up or establishing a seed, adoptive sonship, and the promise to be a God to the seed of His servant ('The Blessing of David: Humanity's Charter' in Skilton (ed), *The Law and the Prophets*, (1974), p. 309.

67. Ibid., p. 315.

68. Bright, op.cit., p. 259.

69. Ibid., p. 288.

70. Nicolson, W.B., *The Old Testament Church*, (1968), pp. 88-89.

71. Allis, O.T., *The Unity of Isaiah: A Study in Prophecy* (1977).

72. Ibid., p. 27.

73. Idem.

74. Mackay, J.L., 'Did the Prophets Prophesy better than they knew?', in *The Monthly Record of the Free Church of Scotland*, December, 1984, p. 260.

75. Vos, op.cit., p. 253.

76. Ibid., p. 254.

77. Idem.

78. Ibid., p. 285.

79. Ibid., p. 286.

80. Idem.

81. Ibid., p. 288.

82. Ibid., p. 289.

83. Ibid., pp. 292, 294. Vos makes the valuable point that one cannot say that 'the Mosaic legislation imposed no ritual demands upon Israel' (Ibid., p. 292). A moment's reading of the Old Testament will show this to be true; what the prophets are arguing against is that mere outward observance, and mere formalism, can do nothing to atone for objective guilt.

84. Ibid., p. 294.

85. Ibid., p. 295.

86. Idem.

87. Ibid., pp. 295-296.

88. Ibid., p. 296.

89. Vos puts it thus (Ibid., p. 297): 'What the prophets feature is the religious in the social; what many at the present time proclaim is the social devoid of or indifferent to the religious.'

90. Ibid., p. 297.

91. Ibid., p. 300.

92. Idem.

93. Weiser, A., *Commentary on the Psalms*, SCM Press, p. 23.

94. Ibid., p. 24. Scholars such as Gunkel and Eissfeldt share the same view.

95. Young, op.cit., p. 309.

96. Harrison, op.cit., p. 309.

97. Binnie, W, *The Psalms: Their History, Interpretation and Use*, c. 1870, p. 237.

98. Idem.

99. Idem.

100. Ibid., p. 238. Binnie cites such expressions as 'we have sinned with our fathers' (Ps. 106:6), etc.

101. Ibid., p. 239.

102. Ibid., p. 240. Binnie's observation is accurate even although his language sounds prosaic to modern ears.

103. Ibid., p. 241.

104. Ibid., p. 243. He also elicits the same teaching from Psalms 51 and 58.

Chapter 2

The New Testament

The Doctrine of Sin in the Teaching of our Lord

In discussing the teaching of the Lord on any subject-matter, it is usual to distinguish between the so-called Synoptic kerygma, and the kerygma of John.[1] However, this approach assumes too great a dichotomy between the writings of the Synoptic evangelists and the Johannine literature, a dichotomy which, if it exists at all, is one of *form*, and not one of *substance*. The presence of the 'dichotomy' is usually evidenced by drawing attention to the differences of style, vocabulary and diction, which, it is alleged, are everywhere apparent in a comparison of the Synoptic writings with those of John.

Two things must be borne in mind, however. There is as much stylistic and lexical variation within the Synoptic traditions themselves as there is between these traditions and the Johannine literature. Thus Merril Tenney reminds us in his *New Testament Survey* that 'Each Gospel was selective according to the purpose of the author, and is complete in the sense that it carries out his intent'.[2]

It is a mistake to assume that the resemblances between the evangelists which do eventually give rise to the Synoptic question have ended the discussion as to the marked differences between the Gospel writers themselves; questions of introduction and priority have still to be addressed.

The second consideration is the unity and compatibility of doctrinal emphasis which bind the Synoptic and Johannine literature together. Much current discussion gives the impression that both strands of writing are poles apart. But it is not so. The article on *hamartano* in the first volume of the *Theological Dictionary of the New Testament* discusses sin in both strands of writing separately, yet concludes that the same motif – Christ as victor over sin – is present both in the Synoptics and in John,[3] even if the motif is carried further in the Johannine writings.

The current study assumes the doctrinal unity of the four Gospels, and will be a synoptic study of the hamartology of Jesus in the widest sense, although the term 'Synoptic' is used with the narrower meaning of the first three Gospels.

The article in TDNT I makes two broad observations concerning the teaching of the Lord on the meaning of sin. The first is that '... Jesus did not speak of sin and its nature and consequences, but was conscious of its reality ... and acted accordingly'[4], and secondly, that 'in His acts and sayings He was conscious of being the Victor over sin'.[5] Grundmann, the writer of the article, suggests that the same victory motif is foundational to, and further developed by, John, where additional emphasis is placed on 'the overcoming of sin by atonement and the general human significance of this event'.[6]

The teaching of our Lord on this issue may be summarised under the following points. First, as G.E. Ladd reminds us, 'Jesus viewed all men as sinful.'[7] This is proven, he suggests, by the fact that the summons to repentance is addressed to all men. Summarising the Synoptists' position, Grundmann says that Christ knows 'that He is sent to those who live in guilt far from God in order to call them to God'.[8]

This thesis of the universality of sin in the teaching of Jesus finds its basis in Christ's own statement as to the whole meaning and substance of His mission, when He declares that He came not to call the righteous, but sinners to repentance (cf. Matt. 9:13; Mark 2:17). The whole mission of the Saviour is to be seen in this light. Grundmann draws attention to the parable of the Prodigal Son as a description of this mission. The parable, he suggests, 'shows us what Jesus understands by sin.... The event achieved through the coming of Jesus is recognition of this sin and conversion to God.'[9]

The best summary of this is probably that of George Smeaton, writing last century, who says: 'The Humiliation of the incarnate Son was primarily planned in connection with a remedial scheme, and is therefore a provision in the Divine counsels by occasion of sin.'[10] Smeaton is correct to see sin as the backdrop against which the 'remedial scheme' of the coming of Christ is painted. It is sin that occasions His coming into the world.

Second, as to the nature of sin, it is clear that sin is treated by Jesus with gravity and seriousness. Smeaton highlights the figurative language used by Christ to describe it, calling it darkness (John 8:12), trespass (Mark 11:25), debt (Matt. 6:12) and lies (John 8:44). These he sees as significant, since they are negative terms, and serve to establish the gravity of sin in comparative terms. Thus Smeaton: 'Nothing else therefore comes into consideration in estimating the enormity of sin but the infinite majesty, glory and claims of Him against whom we sin.'[11] Sin is to be viewed in the light of the God against whom the sin is committed.

It would be wrong, however, to suggest that it is only a negative picture which Christ paints of sin. In his sustained polemic against the representatives of an adulterated Judaism, Jesus says plainly that sin is servitude, and that those who are divorced from His truth are the slaves (*douloi*, John 8:34) of sin. Thus sin is not merely passive and privative; it is active and servile.

Thirdly, Jesus represents Himself as having the authority and the power to forgive sins. The Synoptists connect this with the healing miracles (as at Matt. 9, Mark 2, Luke 5 and 7), and (for example at Matt. 9:6) the Lord states the purpose of His healing the paralytic as 'that ye may know that the Son of Man hath power on earth to forgive sins'.[12] Interestingly, the miracle of healing is performed not so that the audience will be convinced of His ability to heal, but of His ability and authority to forgive. That this is so stated shows that the miracles have this apologetic function, and are declarative of the authority by which Christ alone can deal with sin.

Grundmann is further correct to state in this connection that such aversions on the part of Christ are to be regarded as eschatalogical, constituting, he says, 'the overcoming of sin and therefore the irruption of the divine lordship.'[13] In this connection Ladd's remark is apposite, when he defines 'eschatalogical salvation' as meaning 'not only the redemption of the body but also the restoration of communion between God and man that had been broken by sin'.[14] In this light must be viewed the many illustrations of the meaning of salvation employed by Christ (for example, the motifs of being gathered like sheep into the kingdom, drinking wine in the kingdom, the wedding feast etc.).

The fact of forgiveness, therefore, is firmly rooted in the climactic and radically eschatological nature of Christ's mission in the world. These are new beginnings, and this is the start of a new age dawning in the experience of mankind. The one sin that Jesus declares to be unforgiveable (Matt. 12:31ff.) shows that dogged resistance to His claims will, in the end, not prosper.

Fourth, in His teaching, Jesus shows that the means by which full forgiveness may be attained is His own vicarious and substitutionary death. He declares of Himself as the Son of Man that He came to give His life a ransom for many (Matt. 20:28; Mark 10:45). In an allusion to these words, Smeaton argues that this was the end served by the Old Testament sacrificial system (which he calls 'an education in sin'[15]), designed to make the Jewish mind familiar with 'the necessity of a sacrifice of atonement in order to avert punishment'.[16] The fact that both Matthew and Mark place these Son of Man sayings in the context of the prophecy of entry into Jerusalem, betrayal and death (Matt. 20:17-19; Mark 10:32-34) and the beginning of the fulfilment of the prophecy (Matt. 21:1ff. and Mark 11:1ff.) betrays an intimate connection between the ransom motif and the actual events surrounding the betrayal and condemnation of the Lord. The death is the ransom necessary for full forgiveness. On this point, Smeaton is worth quoting at length:

'... according to the tenor of our Lord's teaching, the incarnation was CONDITIONED BY SIN, and not necessary except on the supposition of redemption. The expiation of sin, the meritorious obedience to be rendered to the law, the vindication of divine justice, are the objects contemplated by the stupendous fact of the incarnation, the incarnation and the cross being inseparable.'[16]

Fifth, our Lord views the overcoming of sin and the application of His saving work as a work performed and accomplished in His people here and now. The eschaton has begun. Thus to the healed man he can say 'sin no more' (John 5:14). Grundmann, in the article in *Theological Dictionary of the New Testament*, sums this up under the concept of *krisis*. Referring to John 15:22-24, where Christ says that by His having come into the world there is no excuse for sin, he says that Christ shows the diabolical nature of sin, and the division that His coming has effected in the world of men. Those who do not believe die in their sin; those who receive His truth share His life. In the life of this latter category of people there predominates the rule of love.

In conclusion, reference ought to be made to Matthew 12:31-2 (and parallel passages in Mark 3:28-29 and Luke 12:10) concerning the specific sin of blasphemy against the Holy Spirit for which there is no forgiveness. The terms of Jesus' description of this particular sin make it clear that it belongs in a category of its own. The fact that the Synoptists mention it in the context of Jesus' power over the supernatural highlights the fact that this sin strikes at the very heart of the salvific and remedial purposes of Christ. Since our purpose here is not exegetical, it may be useful simply to note Alford's comment on the passage in Matthew:

> 'It is not a particular species of sin which is here condemned, but a definite act showing a *state* of sin, and that state a wilful determined opposition to the present power of the Holy Spirit.'[18]

These, therefore, are the salient features of the teaching of Christ with regard to sin: its universality, its nature and gravity, His own power to forgive, His means of doing so by a full and adequate ransom payment, and the application of it to His own people. The fact of an unforgiveable sin also forms part of the dominical hamartology.

The Doctrine of Sin in the Pauline corpus

One of the most perplexing questions which has faced New Testament scholarship in recent times is that of the relationship between Paul and Jesus, and in particular the question of the legitimacy of seeing the Pauline theology as a linear descendant of the Lord's own theology. There are, of course, other, separate difficulties which arise in connection with the apostle Paul, such as the fact that his letters are occasional, and give only a piecemeal view of his theology.[19] But the most important question which critical scholarship has had to face has been that of the origin of Paul's religion, and in particular its relation to Jesus of Nazareth.

This problem received thorough treatment in the James Sprunt lectures delivered at Union Theological Seminary, Virginia, in 1925 by J. Gresham Machen under the title *The Origin of Paul's Religion*.[20] Paying close attention to the facts both about the early life of Paul and the early history of the church, Machen concluded that 'Paul was a true disciple of the real Jesus',[21] and gave credence to his claim by comparing the teaching of Jesus with that of Paul. He discovered their doctrine regarding the kingdom of God to be similar, as also their respective teachings concerning the fatherhood of God, divine grace and the ethics of the Christian life. Machen concludes that 'the whole of Paulinism is based upon the redemptive work of Christ'.[22] Evangelical scholarship presumes the validity of this conclusion, and the essential unity that exists between the doctrine of the atonement in the ministry of Christ and in the theology of the apostle Paul.

Grundmann lays down as a 'presupposition... essential for an

understanding of what Paul says about sin'[23] that the Pauline
hamartology 'is oriented to the revelation of God in Christ...it is not
an empirical doctrine of sin based on pessimism. It is the judgment of
God on man without God as this is ascertained from the revelation of
Christ and revealed in full seriousness in the cross of Christ.'[24] This,
Grundmann suggests, leads to two propositions: first, that the Christ
Event bears upon man in his specific condition of sinnership, and
second, that it is this Event alone which can alter this state obtaining
in man's life and situation.

It is within this framework of the advent and work of Christ that
Paul's doctrine of sin is to be understood. This point has been well
made in an article by Prof. E. Donnelly, who quotes H. Ridderbos[25]
and G.E. Ladd[26] on the theme of Paul's doctrine of the kingdom to
establish his own thesis that 'in Christ the powers of the new age are
operative in the world'.[27] The fact of sin, demonic power and death
are to be viewed in coherence with this general aspect of Pauline
theology. Thus Paul's own definition of the Gospel as 'the power of
God unto salvation' means nothing if it does not mean that the new
age Kingdom has opened up the possibility of sin being dealt its
definitive death blow with the advent and saving work of Jesus Christ.

This view is shared by Donald Guthrie, whose summary of Paul's
doctrine of sin is a useful outline. He claims that 'of all the New
Testament writers, Paul approaches most to what might be called a
theology of sin'.[28] Arguing that the basis of this aspect of Paul's
theology is the same as the teaching of the Gospels, Guthrie examines
the vocabulary of the Pauline letters regarding the meaning and
definition of sin, and then lists the fundamental aspects of the Pauline
hamartology.

As far as the definition of sin is concerned, Guthrie highlights six
pictures or representations of sin in the letters of Paul. First, sin is
presented as a debt; not, says Guthrie, as something that can be settled
simply on the basis of man's accrual of merit before God, but the
opposite. Man's sin is a debt, the one obligation which he cannot
meet. It is the shortcoming he can never make good.

Again, Paul talks of sin as deviation. This is represented by the
word *parabasis*, used five times by Paul. Paul ties this closely to the
meaning and purpose of the law; Guthrie also makes the point that
'This particular view of sin makes no sense unless there is a recognized
standard by which the deviation can be measured'. The law, he says,

can identify the transgression, but it can do nothing to curb it or check it. It can define the parameters outside of which lies the wrath and curse of God, but it can do nothing to bring the outsider in. The law, of course, signifies more than merely the definition of sin; wedded to the weakness of the flesh, it leads to condemnation (Rom. 8:3), and outside of Christ it is actually the instrument that secures the state of sin and guilt in which sinful man is held (cf. Gal. 3:15ff.). It is clear that Paul uses the word *nomos*, law, in a variety of senses. The law of God defines sin, and is also the instrument of bondage for man in this condition.

Paul's concept of law and its meaning is integral to any exposition of his doctrine of sin. Prof. John Murray suggests that we can say five things about the law and its effects, based upon the theology of Paul: (1) It commands and demands, 'it propounds what the will of God is';[29] (2) It 'pronounces approval and blessing upon conformity to its demands';[30] (3) It condemns every behaviour which is contrary to its standards; (4) It exposes sin and gives conviction of it; and (5) It 'excites and incites sin to more virulent and violent transgression'.[31] Over against this, Murray posits two great negatives: in the teaching of the apostle Paul, (1) the law 'can do nothing to justify the person who in any particular has violated its sanctity and come under its curse';[32] and (2) 'It can do nothing to relieve the bondage of sin'.[33] The deliverance of the person in bondage to sin , defined and excited by the law, must come 'from an entirely different source'.[34]

Again, Guthrie notes Paul's idea of sin as lawlessness, *anomia*, sometimes translated 'iniquity'. In Titus 2:14 the apostle explicitly uses this word to describe the end for which Christ died: it was, he says, 'to redeem us from all lawlessness' (*hina lutrosetai humas apo pases anomias*). The word *anomia*, lawlessness, is used sparingly by Paul; it is John who gives expression to the sentiment that 'sin is lawlessness' in 1 John 3:4; nevertheless the idea is not alien in Paul. And it is interesting that, given the place occupied by the law in the whole question of the meaning and nature of sin, part of the apostle's definition concerns the fact that at last sin operates on an irrational plane where no law, no order, no logic obtains. Kept under by an accusing and condemning law, the sinner acts as if there were no law.

Guthrie also mentions that Paul regards sin as both external and internal; that is to say, for him sin concerns not only sinful acts, but sinful motives as well. The concept of sin is used both nominally and adjectivally – sin exists, and men do sinful things. Guthrie states that 'Paul shares with the contemporary Hellenistic world a fondness for producing lists of sins'[35] and refers to passages such as Romans 1:29-31; 13:13; Ephesians 5:3-5 etc. Whether the fact of such lists substantiates Guthrie's claim is, it seems to me, questionable; at the same time it is clear that sin is not abstract and impersonal, but specific and personal. It cuts right across personality, into the realm of thought as well as action, motive as well as deed.

Finally, Guthrie mentions two other concepts of sin found in Paul's writings: sin as a task-master (Rom. 6:16-17), keeping man in a state of bondage, and sin as the suppression of the truth (Rom. 1:18). Thus Paul paints a multi-faceted picture of the meaning of sin. This presentation accords fully with the tenor of the rest of the Word of God.

Guthrie goes on to discuss some specific areas relating to Paul's hamartology. He highlights, for example, the personification of sin in Paul's thought, sin as a tyrant, paying wages, sin as ever present. Again, he highlights Paul's doctrine of the universality of sin. This is the weight of Paul's argument in Romans 1-3, where he concludes all to be under sin. And Guthrie is quite correct to suggest that 'It is, indeed, on the basis of the universality of sin that Paul builds his doctrine of justification through Christ'.[36]

The consequences of sin in the teaching of Paul are twofold. First, mankind is exposed to the wrath of God. Leon Morris, writing in the *New Dictionary of Theology*, is correct when he maintains that 'In modern times, this is rarely emphasised'.[37] However, despite the many reinterpretations which abound in many theologies, it can hardly be maintained with any degree of plausibility that the wrath of God is a minor element in the hamartology of Paul. In one of his clearest definitions of the Gospel he maintains that in it the wrath of God is revealed from heaven (Rom. 1:18). It is the power of God to salvation not merely because of its demonstration of God's love, but on account also of its disclosure of God's wrath, and its provision of reconciliation. The ungodly are designated 'children of wrath' in Ephesians 2:3; and in both Ephesians 5:6 and Colossians 3:6, Paul talks of the wrath of God coming on the children of disobedience.

It cannot, therefore, be maintained that the wrath of God is used in an impersonal sense by the apostle as a picture of sin's 'inevitably... unpleasant consequences'.[38] The most renowned exponent of this aberrant view was C.H. Dodd, notably in his Commentary on Romans (1932); he was followed by Hanson in 1959, propounding the same thesis.[39] Dodd made a distinction between the Bible talking about the wrath of God, and what the Bible never says, that is, that God is angry with anyone. To Dodd and his followers, the Bible never attributes wrath to God, although it speaks of His wrath. The expression is, according to them, a pictorial representation of the inevitable unpleasant consequences of wilful wrongdoing.

This thesis, with its apparent embarrassment regarding the language and usage of Paul, can hardly be maintained. To talk of the wrath of God is as personal and attributive as to talk of God being angry. The distinction is a false one. The Bible knows of no just reason why God and anger should not lawfully be joined together. The clear and concise language of Prof. John Murray ought to guide all theological discussion in this area: 'It is unnecessary, and it weakens the biblical concept of the wrath of God, to deprive it of its emotional and affective character.'[40] This is exactly correct. The wrath of God is nothing other than 'the holy revulsion of God's being against that which is the contradiction of his holiness.... There is a positive outgoing of the divine displeasure.'[41]

It is important to note that for the apostle Paul, the wrath of God is not confined to a coming age or event. To be sure, there is such a thing as a 'wrath to come' (1 Thess. 1:10), from which the death and saving work of Christ has delivered all of God's people. But at the same time, Paul can talk of God as having judicially poured out His wrath on sinners in this present world, for example, by giving them over to reprobate mind and lifestyle (cf. Rom. 1:24). Ladd is correct to define this as 'a bit of realised eschatology.... Wrath expresses what God is doing and what he will do with sin.'[42]

The second consequence of sin is death, which Paul describes as the wages paid out by sin. The state of death is definitive as far as the condition of sinners is concerned – they are dead in trespasses and sins (cf. Eph. 2:1; Col. 2:13). The eternal state of the wicked will be one of death and perishing. This alerts us to the fact that death does not mean an end, or annihilation; as the consequence of sin, death is defined in terms of the distance which separates man from God, real now spiritually, and real hereafter eternally. In all of this, 'Paul is... under no delusion about the serious consequences of sin.'[43]

The final part of Guthrie's discussion concerns the origin of sin in man. His conclusion here is that 'It certainly would not be true to say that Paul expounds a doctrine of original sin, but there are indications that he may have held it'.[44] Although Guthrie concedes that the supreme evidence for a doctrine of original sin in Paul is the parenthetical passage in Romans 5:12ff., he is unwilling to hang too much on it since it is incidental to the teaching on justification. He will go as far only to allow that Paul saw mankind as '*affected* by Adam's sin, but gives no indication of how this worked out apart from the universality of sin and death'.[45]

This is undoubtedly the weakest part of Guthrie's discussion. Romans 5:12ff. shows clearly where sin originates, at the head of the stream of a lost humanity. Ladd is much to be preferred on this point:

> 'It is quite clear that Paul believed in "original sin" in the sense that Adam's sin constituted all men sinners... the entire race is one with Adam, and his sin and death is the sin and death of the entire race.'[46]

Or, as Murray puts it,

> 'The solidarity existing between Adam and posterity establishes a correspondence between that which is exemplified in the case of Adam himself and that which happens to the whole human race. Adam sinned, and death entered; in Adam all sinned and therefore death passed to all.'[47]

However, nowhere does the apostle suggest that the origin of sin in the Fall of the first man excuses mankind. Man's sin originates because of the Fall of the covenant head of the race, Adam himself; but his sin is his, and he alone stands culpable before God.

There is clearly a harmony between the doctrine of sin in the Pauline corpus of literature and the rest of the New Testament. Man outside of Christ is in a state of sin, of rebellion against God. His sin is many-sided; it leaves him the enemy of God, without strength, unbelieving and lawless. He requires a multi-faceted atonement which will satisfy God with respect to every aspect of his sin; the Pauline kerygma is one with that of John and the Synoptists, in declaring such a salvation as obtains in Christ for mankind in such a condition.

The Doctrine of Sin in the Rest of the New Testament
To conclude this brief survey of biblical teaching, it will be necessary to comment briefly on the General Epistles and on the Book of Revelation. The Epistle to the Hebrews poses unsolved and probably

insoluble problems as to its authorship and destination. Only its theological content makes clear that the writer is demonstrating to his readership the consummation of the Old Testament order in the advent and work of Christ, and the abrogation of Old Testament religion in its wake. Tenney suggests that 'The entire theme of the epistle is built around the word "better"... the new revelation in Christ has superseded the old; the coming of the substance has made the shadow obsolete.'[48]

In the teaching of the Epistle, the doctrine of sin forms a sub-section of the doctrine of atonement. Sin is why Christ died. Thus Hebrews 1:3 – He has purged sin; 2:14-15 – He delivers sinners from the snare of the devil and the captivating bondage of fear of death; 2:17 – He makes reconciliation for the sins of the people; 7:26-7 – He, the sinless one, offered up Himself as the supreme sacrifice for sins; 9:26-8 – He was offered once to bear the sins of many, and to put away sins by the sacrifice of Himself. The full exegesis of these passages requires us to go back to the religion and ritual of the Old Testament ceremonies, and particularly to the office and duties of the High Priest. Indeed, Ladd says that 'The central theme in the Christology of Hebrews is the High Priesthood of Christ',[49] and that the author's intention is to demonstrate the inadequacy of the Old Testament system for dealing with sin in its awful reality. The great and grand theme of the epistle is that Christ's service has rendered possible full salvation and freedom from the bondage of sin.

Thus while Hebrews gives no detailed definition of the meaning of sin and its consequences in the human family, it builds upon an already existing understanding of what sin is and has done to men. In particular, it builds upon the Old Testament understanding of sin by demonstrating that Christ has redeemed fully from that sin. At the same time, in view of the better thing that appears in Christ, the epistle shows the terribleness of final apostasy and ignoring what Christ has done for sin and sinners.

The epistle of James strikes its own unique note in the euphony of New Testament theology. This has led to various critical opinions as to the authorship and purpose of the letter, from Luther's designation of it as an epistle of straw, to modern claims that it cannot have been written by a Christian since the essentials of the Christian faith are allegedly missing from it.[50] Frederick Catherwood, however, is accurate when he says that James is not concerned with the problems arising at the intersection of great truths, but he rather deals 'with the

intersection of the great truths of faith and works'.[51] James is a study
in practical theology, and his lesson is simple:

> 'We are not saved by our own deeds but by Christ's sacrifice for our
> misdeeds. Yet no man whose deeds do not reflect Christ's law can claim
> to be a Christian.'[52]

James makes an interesting contribution to the New Testament
teaching on sin by giving an analysis of temptation. There is a blessing
for the person who endures temptation (1:12), which James defines
as being 'drawn away by... lust and enticed' (1:14). The chain of events
then runs like this (1:15) – there is lust, then sin, then death. Sin finds
a place between lust and death, the former as its point of origin and
the latter as its consequence.

James also stresses two other points. He assumes the existence of
a personal devil, who is himself a source of temptation, attempting to
wean the believer off the path of God's Word and truth. Again, James
does provide an interesting definition of sin at 4:17, where he says
that the person who knows what is good, and does not do it, 'to him it
is sin'. Such deliberate and wilful omission of the truth is blameworthy
and culpable because it is sin 'not through ignorance but in contempt'.[53]

The Petrine epistles emphasise in particular the eschatalogical
implications of sin. To be sure, 1 Peter emphasises much more than
this, particularly in the passages dealing with the atonement; for
example at 1:18-19, reference is made to redemption through the blood
of the Lamb, and, more explicitly, 2:24 refers to Jesus Christ bearing
our sins in His body on the tree. Again, 3:18 makes an explicit
connection between the death of Christ and sin when Peter states that
it was for (*peri*) sin that Christ died, in order to effect reconciliation
between sinners and their God. These passages accord both with
dominical and Pauline teaching.

But Peter reminds us too of the final consequences of man's
estrangement from God. 1 Peter 4:3 provides us with a list of some of
the sins of the Gentiles, which will all be laid bare in the day of
reckoning (4:5-6). Assuming the common authorship of the epistles,[54]
Peter, in his second letter, works this out more fully by foretelling, in
chapters 2 and 3, of the day when all the elements of the world will be
dissolved, the earth and the heavens being reserved against the day of
judgment (2 Peter 3:7). The Epistle of Jude deals with similar themes,

and we concur with Ladd that 'There is little of theological interest in Jude that is not found in 2 Peter'.[55]

The Johannine Epistles share a common authorship with the fourth Gospel, and in them, particularly in 1 John, there are very explicit and specific references to sin. John offers various definitions of sin, such as at 3:4, already referred to, where sin is defined as lawlessness. He also claims (reflecting his own recorded teaching of Christ in John 8) that to sin shows that we are the devil's children (3:8,10). John states in 2:1 that one of his purposes in writing is that men and women will not sin. But he also knows that a full provision has been made for sinners in the atoning work of Christ the Advocate. The blessings of that salvation are to be appropriated along the path of repentance and confession (1:9), where the blood of Jesus can cleanse from all unrighteousness.

Like many of the New Testament epistles, the letters of John answer a specific situation, that of false teachers and false theologians springing up in the early New Testament churches. The fundamental error John is attacking is that of denial of Jesus Christ and His incarnation; in presenting a full-orbed view of the atonement, John also shows us something of the meaning and reality of sin as both culpable and curable.

Finally, mention must be made of the testimony and teaching of the Book of Revelation. It need hardly be said that this New Testament document poses problems of interpretation on a level very different to that of other writings. The question of authorship is by no means settled either; testimony both ancient and modern has disputed the Johannine authorship. However, we agree with the statement of Carson, Moo and Morris, that 'it is not clear that the person who wrote the fourth Gospel could not also have written Revelation'.[56] With the Apocalypse, questions of genre require to be settled before questions of interpretation can be broached. Tenney outlines four schools of interpretation: the Preterist school, which sees the book as a symbolic account of events at the time of its composition; the Idealist school, which sees Revelation as a symbolic picture of the struggle between good and evil; the Historicist school, which holds that the events of the book outline the whole course of the church's history; and the Futurist school, which regards the events in the book as entirely eschatological.[57] Coupled with this is the problem of interpreting the millenium of Revelation 20, and the resultant theories of pre-, a- and post-millenialism. Much of one's understanding of the Book of Revelation depends on the position one takes on these two questions of interpretation.

Two things are clear as to the meaning and teaching of this last book of the canon. First, the fact that the revelation comes to John in a definite historical situation, together with the fact that the book is prefaced by letters to churches in particular geographical localities, tells us that the Book of Revelation is of relevance to the present experience of the Church. Neither absolute historicism nor exclusive futurism can be tolerated. The guiding line at all times must be that the Apocalypse is rooted in the historical fact of the church in the world, with some things to say about the future. Hendriksen, therefore, is right when he says that 'In the main, the purpose of the Book of Revelation is to comfort the militant Church in its struggle against the forces of evil'.[58]

Secondly, the dominant theme of the book is the glory of a victorious Saviour. From the beginning of the book, where John is confronted with a glorious vision of the exalted Christ (1:13ff.), to the end, with its triumphant vision of 'the throne of God and of the Lamb' (22:3), the glory of Christ is paramount.

These twin themes must be borne in mind when we ask the question – what is the doctrine of sin herein presented? The broad answer is that Revelation sees sin as a power which troubles the church in various different ways. However, the sovereignty of God in Christ gives hope, for at last the sin question will vanish in the Heavenly Jerusalem:

> 'Throughout the prophecies of this wonderful book Christ is pictured as the victor, the conqueror.... He conquers death, Hades, the dragon, the beast, the false prophet, and the men who worship the beast.'[59]

It is in the Book of Revelation that we are given the clearest eschatology of sin.

Ladd summarises the teaching of the book under three headings. First, he underlines the teaching with respect to the problem of evil.[60] Ladd himself represents the teaching of Fuller Seminary by taking what he defines as a 'moderately futurist' view of the Book of Revelation. Where this becomes unworkable is in his assertion that 'The Revelation foresees a short period of terrible evil in history at the end time'.[61] In actual fact, the book portrays the incessant presence of sin in the life of mankind which is a *sine qua non* of the Christian philosophy of history. The martyrdoms of Revelation 7:9-17, for example, Ladd posits as being entirely in the future; whereas Buis gives a far more balanced view by asserting that

'... there is no exegetical reason for referring it to some special period at the end of the world; but rather it speaks of the fact that there is a certain degree of tribulation for all Christians while on earth, although in some periods of history, for example at the time of the early church, that tribulation is greatly accentuated'.[62]

The point is that sin is arrayed against the people of God, as the great enemy of a militant church. And behind all that is transacted on the stage of human history is the ongoing struggle of the Beast, warring against the Lamb (cf. 15:1ff.). It is this great spiritual battle which leaves the church suffering in the world.

Secondly, Ladd draws attention to the presentation of the wrath of God in the Book of Revelation. This is referred to both as the wrath of God (16:1) and the wrath of the Lamb (6:16). Revelation declares nothing if it does not declare a judgment to come, and the visitation of wrath on those who had the mark of the Beast and worshipped him (16:2). God's minute record of human experience testifies infallibly to the sinfulness of sin, and calls for its most severe penalties (21:11ff.). Sin cries to God and is heard.

Thirdly, Ladd highlights the fact that the Book of Revelation presents a new kingdom, a new creation. The Beast – sin – having been conquered forever, a new situation obtains, and a new day dawns. The meaning of the millenium bears upon this question of Christ's kingdom, and in particular on that aspect of the question which concerns the possibility of temporal sovereignty on earth prior to eternal sovereignty in Heaven. Suffice it to note that sin in all its forms will be eradicated from the final state of the redeemed people of God, whose robes are white in the blood of the Lamb (7:14). There will be no night, no curse, no stain, no defilement. Another list of sins meets us at the end of the Book, at 22:15 – outside the city are sinners; inside are saved sinners, who have a right to the tree of life, and who may 'enter ... the gates into the city' (22:14).

NOTES

1. cf. for example, Ladd's *Theology of the New Testament*, (1987), esp. chap. 16 pp. 215-222 ; and also TDNT I, sv *hamartano*, both of which take this approach.

2. Tenney, M., *New Testament Survey*, (1982), p. 133.

3. cf. TDNT, ibid., p. 304: 'Jesus as Victor over sin – this is the Synoptic kerygma derived from the story of Jesus' with the statement of p. 305: 'In the Christ kerygma of John we again see the fact of the overcoming of sin by Christ as it is first displayed in the picture of the historical Jesus presented by the Synoptists.'

4. TDNT I, p. 303. Grundmann cannot, however, avoid noting some definitions, such as that sin is 'guilt towards God' (Idem.).

5. Idem.

6. Ibid, p. 306.

7. Ladd, op.cit., p. 155.

8. TDNT I, p. 303.

9. Ibid, p. 303.

10. Smeaton, G., *The Doctrine of the Atonement*, (1871), p. 20.

11. Ibid, p. 21.

12. It ought to be pointed out, in the light of recent debate over the Son of Man sayings, that a verse such as this also shows that this designation is not generic but specific, and applies uniquely to Christ as a self-designation.

13. TDNT I, p. 304.

14. Ladd, op.cit., p. 74.

15. Smeaton, op.cit., p. 24.

16. Ibid, p. 25.

17. Smeaton, op.cit., p. 41.

18. Alford, H., *The Greek Testament*, Vol I, (1874), p. 130.

19. Morna D. Hooker, in chapter 1 of her *Pauline Pieces*, summarises some of these difficulties for us. In addition to the two cited, she asks questions such as – what role was played by Paul's opponents in the shaping of his theology? Is the New Testament obsessed by Christocentricity? Is Paul confined to thought patterns familiar to him? Is the canon distorted? How much is authentic Paul and how much has been interpreted? An evangelical view of the text will deal with these questions in a manner which will do justice to the inspiration of the biblical text and the integrity and unity of Scripture.

20. Republished by Eerdmans: Michigan, 1976. For all that the orginial lectures were delivered some 70 years ago, this work remains an important evangelical contribution to Pauline studies.

21. Machen, op.cit., p. 142.

22. Ibid, p. 169.

23. TDNT I, p. 308.

24. Idem. The Christocentric character of Paul's doctrine of sin cannot be overemphasised.

25. 'The governing motif of Paul's preaching is the saving authority of God in the advent and work, particularly in the death and resurrection of Christ.... It is this great redemptive-historical framework within which the whole of Paul's preaching must be understood' (Ridderbos, H., *Paul: An Outline of his Theology*, p.39, quoted in Donnelly, E., 'Paul: Kingdom Theologian', *Reformed Theological Journal*, Vol 2: November 1986, p. 19.

26. 'The centre of Pauline thought is the realisation of the coming new age of redemption by the work of Christ' (Ladd, op.cit., p. 374).

27. Donnelly, art.cit., p. 20.

28. Guthrie, D., *New Testament Theology*, (1985), p. 200.

29. Murray, J., *Principles of Conduct*, (1957), p. 184.

30. Idem.

31. Ibid, p. 185.

32. Idem.

33. Idem.

34. Ibid, p. 186.

35. Guthrie, op.cit., p. 203.

36. Ibid, p. 206. cf. also the observation by D.L. Smith that 'Paul is particularly emphatic on the universality of sin and death, as well as the universal accessibility of salvation and life' (Smith, D.L., *With Wilful Intent: A Theology of Sin*, (1994), p. 310. Prof. Smith also states that 'Paul was closer to being a systematic theologian than any of the other New Testament writers. And he is closer to a theology of sin than the others as well. But many of the themes he espouses in his teaching are common to all the evangelists' (Ibid., p. 288).

37. *New Dictionary of Theology*, (1988), p. 732.

38. Idem.

39. For a discussion and critique of this, see Morris, L., *The Apostolic Preaching of the Cross*, London: Tyndale press, 1955, pp. 102-6.

40. Murray, J., *The Epistle of Paul to the Romans*, (1960), p. 35.

41. Ibid., pp. 35-36.

42. Ladd, op.cit., p. 407.

43. Guthrie, op.cit., p. 209.

44. Idem.

45. Ibid., p. 213.

46. Ladd, op.cit., p. 403.

47. Murray, op.cit., p. 186.

48. Tenney, op.cit., p. 359. On the concept of 'better', cf. Ladd, who says that 'The idea of perfection is one of the repeated themes of Hebrews' (op.cit., p. 578).

49. cf. Ladd, op.cit., p. 578. cf also G. Smeaton, op.cit., pp. 333-4: 'Christ is not compared to every Jewish priest accomplishing the service of God in the daily ministration, but to the High Priest in his call, his qualifications, and peculiar ministry, as he entered the holiest of all on the great day of atonement.'

50. See *New Bible Dictionary*, op.cit., pp. 550-1.

51. Sir Frederick Catherwood, MEP, writing the foreword to John Blanchard's commentary on James, *Truth for Life*, England: Walter Books, 1982, p. 9.

52. Ibid., pp. 9-10.

53. J. Calvin, Commentary ad.loc.

54. This is no small assumption to make, but to date no conclusive evidence has been forthcoming to convince us not to make it. E Green's conclusion is, at least, workable: 'There is nothing that forbids us to entertain the Petrine authorship' (article on 2 Peter in *New Bible Dictionary*, p. 923.

55. Ladd, op.cit., p. 607.

56. D.A. Carson, D.J. Moo, L. Morris, *An Introduction to the New Testament* (1992), p. 471.

57. Tenney, op.cit., pp. 387-9.

58. Hendriksen, W., *More than Conquerors*, (1974), p. 46.

59. Ibid., p. 8.

60. Ladd, op.cit., pp. 624ff.

61. Ibid., p. 624.

62. Buis, H., *The Book of Revelation*, (1974), p. 46.

Conclusion

The foregoing has attempted to set forth the Bible's teaching concerning sin, at the various stages of biblical revelation. The main points of the Bible's doctrine can be summarised as follows.

1. The world was originally good as created by God. Sin was no part of God's universe, and the result was that the world and everything in it was good, was holy, and was dedicated to God. Perfection and stability grew out of a unique and a special relationship between Creator and creature.

2. Sin entered the human race, with consequences both for man and the creation, as a result of one act of disobedience. The reason that act had such far-reaching consequences was that Adam acted not simply on his own behalf, but as a representative of humankind. His sin is our sin because the whole human race was 'in' him, to be sprung from his loins; in the language of the older divines, Adam was a covenant or federal head.

3. The presence of sin immediately called forth a response from God. This was in terms of divine judgment upon man for his sin, resulting in estrangement from God. A state of war was declared, where hitherto there had been peace.

4. The word of grace woven into the divine judgment was the one hope extended to man, an indication of the fact that man's deliverance from his own sin rested upon the grace and activity of God alone. There could be no security, and no deliverance from the grip of sin, except the power of divine, sovereign, merciful grace.

5. With the 'calling out' of a people to serve Him in the world, the Lord gave laws to Moses for Israel, in which sin was codified by the commandments and prohibitions laid down in the decalogue. There was now a measure given by which sin could be judged, and a standard by which guilt could be established. The law was given to a people in covenant relationship, and provided covenant means of redemption and release. Nevertheless it externalised sin, as a reminder to the covenant community that sin meant more than a subjective disintegration. It issued in a particular relationship and standing before God.

6. The prophetic ministry of the Old Testament continued to apply the demands of God's law to the chosen people, bringing home to

them that in each stage of history the race stood under God's condemnation, and the only hope of salvation rested upon God's covenant mercy and grace.

7. The personal religion of the Psalms highlights individual need and responsibility. There may be collective sin, and there may be universal sin, but for each individual there remains personal sin and debt before the holiness of God. The psalmists are aware of their own, individual needs, and their own need particularly of cleansing and redemption.

8. The coming of Christ into the world represents the advent of the great prophet, the last prophet, onto the stage of human history. He builds upon the foundation of law and prophets, declaring that he came to fulfil these and not to destroy them. But the revelation advances, for He claims alone to have the power to forgive sin, and He has come to lay down His life in order to deal with sin. He is the God against whom the race has transgressed, and His claim is that He alone can deal with that transgression.

9. The epistles of the New Testament are a commentary on the Gospel narrative, and bring home to the readers the universality of sin and condemnation and death, and the hope that there is alone in Jesus Christ. The New Testament letters deal with the need for individual and corporate repentance and reformation, and draw attention to the definitive work of Calvary in making atonement for the sins of the world.

10. The Book of Revelation, the great denouement of God's designs of Providence and Grace, show us the final outworking of the sin story. There is at last a world with no sin, where the inhabitants are freed not only from the penalty and power of sin, but freed from its very presence. The Judge has given final judgment, and sin is dealt a death blow. There is now no more sin, death or curse. Paradise is restored, never more to be lost.

Section 2

The Reformed
Doctrine of Sin

Introduction

The late Philip E. Hughes, one of the leading evangelical students of Reformed theology this century, summarises the Reformation for us in the following terms: 'The Reformation of the sixteenth century was fundamentally a return to the biblical creation-fall-redemption ground-motive.'[1] He fills out this assertion by stating that

> 'The Reformation was indeed a great spiritual and therefore a great intellectual and social liberation of man's being... it penetrated, evangelically, to the very centre of man's being and basic need as a fallen and sinful creature severed from the meaning of his existence.'[2]

The spiritual movement known as the Reformation represented a movement away from the medieval theology by which all things depended upon the Church. It was only in consequence of the Church's teaching and the Church's sacramentalism that sin could be understood, first, and absolved consequently. The Reformation returned to a Bible-based, Christ-centred and Spirit-empowered Christian life, to a dynamic theology rooted firmly in the Word of God.

As far as the Fall of man into sin is concerned, it is true that

> 'The Reformation took its stand upon the Scriptural Fall as total...[it] sets forth the biblical concept of the whole man as the object of God's concern.... The historic Fall affected the whole man.'[3]

There can be no doubt that the Reformation meant, among other things, the crossing of a Rubicon of biblical scholarship. For centuries, the plain truths of Scripture had lain dormant and interred under layers of ecclesiastical tradition. In the sixteenth century, however, God raised up men who were not afraid to challenge the vain conversation of the fathers, and to preach the whole counsel of God. It is no simplistic truism, therefore, to aver that

> 'The Protestant Reformation produced a theology that was a massive reassertion of the centrality of God, the glory of his sovereignty, and the primacy of his grace in the salvation of humanity through Jesus Christ.'[4]

The discussion of this chapter will seek to demonstrate these theses. The most consistent historical outworking of the biblical doctrine of sin is to be found in the reflection of theologians of the Reformed school of thought. The Reformed doctrine of sin, which finds its expression in the original writings of the Reformers, as well as in subsequent authors, safeguards the salient features of the Bible's teaching in this whole area (as outlined in the previous chapters). The following discussion summarises and critically evaluates the Reformers themselves, notably Calvin and Luther, followed by a summary of their theological successors, the Puritans,[5] and finally will look at the thought of Charles Hodge in the nineteenth century, and two outstanding twentieth-century contributors to this area of thought: G.C. Berkouwer and J. Murray.[6] Biographical profiles, as well as summaries of their major writings, will be given in each chapter.

NOTES

1. Hughes, P.E., *Christianity and the Problem of Origins*, Presbyterian and Reformed, 1967, p. 8.
2. Ibid., p. 9.
3. Whitney, H.J., *The New Infallibility* (hereinafter T.N.I.), pp. 8-9.
4. Jones, R.T., writing in the *New Dictionary of Theology*, IVP, p. 565.
5. This is an important emphasis, because, as shall be seen, it has been fashionable to deny any concrete or substantial connection between the makers of Reformed thought on the one hand, and the Puritans on the other.
6. These two representatives are chosen in order to show something of contemporary Reformed opinion.

Chapter 3

John Calvin and
the Problem of Sin

BIOGRAPHICAL DETAILS

1509	10 July – Born Picardy, France
1532	Published a Commentary on Seneca's *De Clementia*
1536	Settled at Geneva, and became pastor, but left on account of ecclesiasical conflicts there. Published first edition of his *Institutes of the Christian Religion,* which was to grow considerably by the time it reached its final edition in 1559.
1538-1541	Pastoral work in Strasbourg with Martin Bucer
1541-1564	Ministry in Geneva; major publications come from this period.

Between 1540 and 1564, Calvin published Commentaries and Sermons on almost every book of the Bible. Some of his work remains unpublished.

Gerald Bray says of Calvin that in him 'we find a balance between the text, its meaning and its application which has seldom, if ever, been equalled in the life of the church' (*Biblical Interpretation: Past and Present*, 1996, p. 204). His great contribution to the movement we call the Reformation is that he drew the attention of men to the Word of God, and gave the movement its emphasis on *sola scriptura* – the Bible alone.

Further Reading
The Life of John Calvin by Theodore Beza (published in a modern translation by Evangelical Press, 1998)
Calvin's Wisdom: An Anthology Arranged Alphabetically by J. Graham Miller (Banner of Truth, 1992)

Although Martin Luther precedes John Calvin chronologically, there is no doubt that it is Calvin who is the dominant figure in the area of Reformation theology. Jean Calvin (1509-64) was French by birth, and received his early training in Paris, with a view to his entering the priesthood. His theological studies were followed by a period of training for the legal profession. His first major work, a commentary on Seneca's *De Clementia*, showed his thorough-going humanism at the time of its writing in 1532. It was not a success, and Jean Cadier is probably correct to suggest that the lack of enthusiasm for this project 'may well have been of some importance in closing for Calvin the road of secular philology and opening before him that of theology and commenting on Holy Scripture'.[1]

It was not, of course, merely his failure in secular humanism that led John Calvin to a life's work in theology and evangelism, but a profound change in his own life. Of this change, little detail is given us in the extant works. Cadier suggests that 'Calvin was always very reticent on the details of his conversion',[2] and apart from a reference in the Preface to his Commentary on the Psalms (1558)[3] and a letter to Jacques Sadoletus (1539), a Roman Cardinal, there is little autobiographical material in his writings.

However, other evidence[4] suggests that Calvin's sudden conversion took place around October-November 1533, at which point he identified himself with the Reformed cause, and became a fugitive as a result. The important point for us to note here is that 'For Calvin, conversion had meant a break with his previous studies, and... a break with the humanism which had hitherto been the aim of his life'.[5] Wendel, however, goes on to say that Calvin 'remained no less humanistic in method and in his particular type of intellectual outlook'.[6] By this he means that Calvin continued to show great admiration for the ancient philosophers, particularly Erasmus and his school, but came now to see their limitations. While this may be true, it can hardly be said that his method is totally humanistic. If one thing stands out in Calvin's works, it is the biblical nature of his theological studies. If Wendel's assertions are qualified to mean that Calvin, after his conversion, became a *biblical* humanist, with his humanism governed by biblical principles and teachings, then we can accept the statement.

Calvin's *Institutes of the Christian Religion*

This 'biblical humanism' can be seen quite clearly in Calvin's *Institutes*. The first edition of this monumental work was published in Basel in 1536, scarcely three years after Calvin's conversion. The *Institutes* went though several editions until its final edition in 1559. The work itself is divided into four sections: Book I deals with the subject of God the Creator, Book II with God the Redeemer, Book III with the way we receive the grace of Christ, or God the Holy Spirit, and Book IV with the Church. The pages of the *Institutes* handle two themes: the knowledge of God and the knowledge of ourselves. The development of these themes has led to a great deal of theological debate and discussion; in this section we can touch only upon the main emphases of Calvin's doctrine of sin.

The discussion of sin in the *Institutes* opens up for us the second theme mentioned, that is, the knowledge of ourselves. Book I has emphasised the salient features of the biblical revelation about God; now Calvin turns to look at some features of biblical anthropology, and turns his attention at the beginning of Book II to a discussion of the Fall of man as the first element in our getting to know ourselves.

It is interesting that this is Calvin's starting-point in the quest for self-knowledge and self-understanding. Although he makes the point that man was created in an elevated position of sinlessness and perfection, true knowledge consists in an acknowledgement and understanding of what sin has done to us, and where it has left us. There is a change in our orientation now with regard to the omnipresent God; where once there was perfect harmony between man and his Maker, there is now alienation and estrangement. It is this condition that confronts us in the present, and requires to be addressed. Calvin is under no illusion but that a remedy must be found for this sin problem if life is to have any meaning or value.

In order to examine this more thoroughly, Calvin suggests that 'it will be necessary to attend to the peculiar nature of the sin which produced Adam's Fall' (*Inst.* II.i.4). The change which occurred in man's relation to God is for Calvin rooted in the *peccatum originale*, the first, original sin. In II.i.4 Calvin agrees with Augustine that pride is involved, but he says we must go further. Sin is not simply to be regarded as some kind of moral defect, but as something which is grounded in radical and total unbelief. Eve's fall, says Calvin, 'obviously had its root in disobedience' (II.i.4). In his commentary on Genesis 3:16, Calvin says that 'the woman is led away...through unbelief' (*per infidelitatem*). The emphasis in Calvin, therefore, is that the first sin of our original parents was the child of unbelieving and apostate defection from God. Or, to put it otherwise, 'Infidelity was at the root of the revolt', and man 'did his very utmost to annihilate the whole glory of God'.

In II.i.5, Calvin examines the twofold consequence of Adam's Fall. First, the image of God in man was 'effaced', and was robbed of its 'ornaments', wisdom, virtue, justice, truth and holiness. Sin affects man in such a way as that 'in the whole of his being no rectitude remains' (*in tota natura nulla rectitudinis gutta superest*).[7] The second consequence of the Fall is that 'in regard to human nature, Adam was not merely a progenitor, but, as it were, a root, and that accordingly, by his corruption, the whole human race was deservedly vitiated' (II.i.5).

Calvin often refers to the Pelagian/Augustinian debate in this regard, and seeks to demonstrate how irrational and unscriptural the Pelagian view of man is. Calvin continues the idea of Adam's first sin as the 'root' of every other sin by stating that 'from a corrupt root corrupt branches proceeding, transmit their corruption to the saplings which spring from them' (II.i.6). This means that guilt attaches to fallen human nature as soon as it is formed; man, from the point of origin, is a sinner before God.

To summarise, Calvin defines original sin as 'a hereditary corruption and depravity of our nature, extending to all the parts of the soul, which first makes us obnoxious to the wrath of God, and then produces in us works which in Scripture are termed works of the flesh' (II.i.8). Calvin is concerned to guard against the fallacy that this means guilt for someone else's sin; he explicitly states in II.i.8 that 'This is not liability for another's fault'; our ruin, he is at pains to stress, 'is attributable to our own depravity' (II.i.10).

In chapters ii-v of Book II of the *Institutes*, Calvin explores the meaning of original sin in relation to the will of man, and the extent to which sin has enslaved it. Calvin spends a great deal of time evaluating the opinions of others regarding free will, before coming to an interesting discussion on the intellect and will of man. These, he says, labour under the defect of being confined to earthly things, and not knowing enough about heavenly things to make God fully known to us. Calvin insists that man needs divine help at every stage of his educational and volitional development. Calvin sums up the matter thus:

> 'When the will is enchained as the slave of sin, it cannot make a movement towards goodness, far less steadily pursue it.... Nevertheless there remains a will which both inclines and hastens on with the strongest affection towards sin; man, when placed under this bondage, being deprived not of will, but of soundness of will' (II.iii.5).

Or, as Dr. Neisel paraphrases it, man has freedom to choose sin, but no freedom to leave it.[8] The exercise of this choice is, says Calvin, voluntary and free.

From this discussion, Calvin proceeds in II.iv to propose that the only remedy for this condition of enslavement is the power of the grace of God. At this point also there is a discussion on the nature and purpose of God's law, which, says Calvin in II.vii.7, is a mirror in which we see our impotence, our iniquity and the curse which we are under. The more it declares God's righteousness, the more it shows us our own guilt before God. This matter leads Calvin into an exposition of the work of Christ as our Redeemer and Mediator.

It ought to be pointed out that Calvin does allow for man, even depraved by sin, a measure of ability in the lower realm of temporal things. For example, in II.ii.13, he comes to deal with the ability of man in such things as 'policy and economy, all mechanical arts and liberal studies'. Calvin's position is that 'Since man by nature is a social animal, he is disposed, from natural instinct, to cherish and preserve society; and accordingly we see that the minds of all men have impressions of civil order and honesty'. Man frames laws for the good of society in spite of the sin within. Similarly, reading the works of worldly authors, he says, shows that the human mind, 'however much fallen and perverted from its original integrity, is still adorned and invested with admirable gifts from its Creator' (II.ii.15). Indeed, says Calvin, 'we cannot read the writings of the ancients... without the highest admiration; an admiration which their excellence will not allow us to withhold.'

All who encourage the myth that Calvin was a slayer of the arts and a denier of all that is good in culture and society, should read his doctrine of sin! There it is evident that the modification which sin has brought into human thinking and philosophy does not compromise the beauty of art forms or the truth contained in and expressed through the secular arts. Indeed, Calvin tells us that we cannot help admiring these things. They evidence, he says, 'some remains of the divine image distinguishing the whole human race from other creatures' (II.ii.17). The problem is that they tend to the glorification and pride of man, who, in sin, is incapable of seeking God. It remains, therefore, true, that 'To the great truths, What God is in himself, and what he is in relation to us, human reason makes not the least approach' (II.ii.18). It is the twin realisation both of the sovereignty of God and the depravity man that makes the gospel indispensable for the rectification of our human condition.

Calvin on Romans

Calvin's biblical exegesis formed a major part of his ministry and was an indispensable element of the success of the Reformation. He has a thorough-going biblical methodology which ties doctrine to Scripture and allows Scripture to speak for itself. For an example of his treatment of Scripture, we will turn to some statements in his Commentary on Romans. This was one of the earliest of his works, published first in 1539.

In his summary of the argument of the Epistle, Calvin says that 'the Apostle proceeds to do two things – to convince men of iniquity, and to shake off the torpor of those whom he proves guilty'. The gospel is addressed to man in his self-sufficiency and native self-righteousness, and this false basis for hope and confidence must be demolished. In Romans 1 Paul states that there is a revelation of God in the works of creation, but that men have taken that revelation and discarded its evidence. This, says Calvin, is not the work of philosophers; the native rejection of God on the part of man, he says, 'is not learned in the schools, but is innate, and comes with us, so to speak, from the womb' (on Rom. 1:22). In the same way as the notion of God is 'innate', the rejection of God is also 'innate'. Man, *qua* man, has an idea of God; man, *qua* sinner, rejects the God whom he knows to exist.

Moreover, ignorance of God through sin cannot be made good through any study or science: 'empty is the man in whom there is not the knowledge of God' (on Rom. 3:11). Left to itself, man's nature would become the seed bed of every kind of vice and iniquity. Even although the vices enumerated in Romans 3:10-18 'are not found conspicuously in every individual, yet they may be justly and truly ascribed to human nature' (on Rom. 3:18). Apart from the grace of God at work in the heart, every individual has the potential, according to Calvin, to perform the worst vices.

The deep-seated and deep-rooted nature of sin is expressed by Calvin in his treatment of Romans 5:12ff. There he says that 'Paul distinctly affirms that sin extends to all who suffer its punishment... to sin in this case, is to become corrupt and vicious; for the natural depravity which we bring from our mother's womb, though it brings not forth immediately its own fruits, is yet sin before God and deserves his vengeance....' The corruption of man's nature is itself culpable and blameworthy; man, in Calvin's view, is responsible to God for what he *is* as much as for what he *does*. The law, which shed its own light on the sin of man, did not add to man's lostness, but did cast light on the consequences of his being in that condition: 'all became miserably lost immediately after the Fall of Adam, though their destruction was only made manifest by the law' (on Rom. 5:13). The corruption of man's nature through the Fall of Adam does not mean that Adam is responsible for our sin. Calvin is at pains to stress that 'by Adam's sin we are not condemned through imputation alone, as though we were punished only for the sin of another; but we suffer his punishment, because we also ourselves are guilty; for as our nature is vitiated in him, it is regarded by God as having committed sin' (on Rom. 5:17). Or, to put it otherwise, 'in order to partake of the miserable inheritance of sin, it is enough for thee to be man, for it dwells in flesh and blood.'

This, says Calvin, does not mean that man is forced by sin to act contrary to his will. 'We are,' he says, commenting on Romans 7:14, 'so entirely controlled by the power of sin, that the whole mind, the whole heart, and all our actions, are under its influence. *Compulsion I always except, for we sin spontaneously, as it would be no sin, were it not voluntary.* But we are so given up to sin, that we can do willingly nothing but sin; for the corruption which bears rule within us thus drives us forward.' Sin is therefore a power on the human heart and will; but it could not be sin if the act performed by the moral agent was not free. The level of freedom Calvin permits to the will is discussed below.

The law of God shows us what our sin is, and points us in the direction of life. But, says Calvin, 'the corruption of our nature renders the law of God in this respect useless to us; for while it shows us the way of life, it does not bring us back who are running headlong into death' (on Rom. 8:3).

And at last, the doctrine of sin serves to show us the glory of the method of justification found by God in Christ. And as Calvin has it, 'to be justified, according to Paul, is to be absolved by the sentence of God, and to be counted just.... Hence God will allow no accusation against us, because he has absolved us from all sins' (on Rom. 8:34). This is the only hope, the gospel hope – that Christ died for our sins according to the Scriptures.

Calvin's *Sermons on Galatians*

A great deal of Calvin's biblical exposition has come down to us in the form of sermons. Calvin made it his practice to preach systematically through portions of Scripture; his forty-three sermons on Galatians, for example, were preached between November 1557 and May 1558. We can take them as an example of his biblical expository work, which was to play such a major role in the formation of Reformation life and work, for he was nothing if not a theologian of the Word. In the words of one commentator, 'He applied the methods of humanistic scholarship to the Bible to find out the exact meaning of the words of a text, and the circumstances of the history involved.'[9] His approach to biblical hermeneutics is best summed up in his own prayer, at the conclusion of lecture 36 on Jeremiah: 'O grant, that being ruled by thy Spirit, we may surrender ourselves to thee, and so acquiesce in thy Word alone, that we may not deviate either to the right hand or to the left, but allow thee alone to be wise, and that acknowledging our folly and vanity, we may suffer ourselves to be taught by thy Word.'[10]

In a sermon on Galatians 1:3-5, on 'The Blood that Cleanses', Calvin paints a devastating picture of man in sin. He says:

'On the one hand, God, by virtue of the fact that he has made us, accepts us and calls us his own. However, on the other hand, since we have become corrupt and evil, he hates us and we have become his enemies. Indeed, there is, as it were, a mortal conflict between us, until we are accepted for the sake of the Lord Jesus Christ.'[11]

Only by the saving work of Christ can there be deliverance from this condition:

'We will never understand that our sins condemn us in God's sight, unless we know that we need to be put right with him... we are totally corrupt and there is only wickedness in us; it follows therefore, that God must hate us. However, if he hates us, woe unto us, for we are damned. This is why we need to be justified before we can be pleasing to God.'[12]

The sin that corrupts our nature demonstrates itself in sinful, wicked practice. Calvin deals with this in his treatment of the 'works of the flesh' (Gal. 5:19-23) in a sermon on 'The Spirituality of the Law'. 'The appearance of fruit,' says Calvin, 'enables us to assess the condition of the tree.... Just as the tree is known by its fruit, the sin that reigns in us and in our nature is seen by the works that we produce... we have to return to the fact that our lives declare, loud and clear, the kind of people we are.'[13] In some people, Calvin argues, some sins are more apparent than others. He also takes issue with Roman Catholic, medieval exegesis which identified 'flesh' with man's sensual appetites; Calvin reminds his hearers that ambition and pride are equally works of the flesh, along with sexual impurity and lust. And even although there is 'some degree of decency' in the lives of many unregenerate men, it still remains the case that 'the heart of man is a deep pit of iniquity'.[14]

Calvin views the law of God has having been given in order that men could be 'doubly convicted of their sins before God and realise that their hypocrisy, self-flattery, desire to hide behind excuses, and other such sins, are vain and to no avail'.[15] By the law comes the knowledge of sin, and through it 'God awakens us... and leads us to acknowledge our desperate condition... the law reveals just who we are, and sets before us the judgment of God'.[16] It is this awareness of who we are that makes us seek Christ. It is of God's goodness that the law has been given, even with its judicial and condemnatory force. The promise of savlation ought to have been enough to lead man to seek God; but man's sin revealed itself in the stubbornness of his heart, and his misuse of God's gifts. 'Of necessity,' therefore, argues Calvin, 'he deals harshly with us, and exposes what we are truly like, to alarm us so that we might run to him for grace.'[17]

Again, therefore, as in the *Institutes*, Calvin's doctrine of sin in the sermons is to be viewed as a foil to the greater presentation of the glorious mercy in Christ. 'We can only be happy,' he says, 'if God overlooks all our deeds and blots out all our sins. This joy is ours if God is gracious to us, no longer considering what we are by nature –

poor, condemned sinners – and accepting us, not as we are in our own persons, but for the sake of His only Son.'[18]

The emphases of the biblical exposition, the Commentaries and the *Institutes* are of a piece. Man is alienated from God through sin. There is personal dysfunction as a result of sin, but the real problem is objective, one of status and not merely one of condition. Our standing before God is affected by the sin and unbelief of our hearts; the function of the law is to show us ourselves, and to drive us to Christ for the mercy and salvation He alone can give. There can be true happiness in the human heart only when the blood of Calvary is applied to the human condition.

Reprobation and Responsibility

Calvin grounds his theology in the absolute sovereignty of God in Christ. Overarching his doctrine of man is his doctrine of God; every human action and every human condition is subject to the sovereign laws of a sovereign God.

Calvin is undoubtedly of the view that election is not universal. The sovereign election of God is distinguishing and discriminating. So he states at *Inst.* III.xxi.7:

> 'We say, then, that Scripture clearly proves this much, that God by his eternal and immutable counsel determined once for all those whom it was his pleasure one day to admit to salvation, and those whom, on the other hand, it was his pleasure to doom to destruction. We maintain that this counsel, as regards the elect, is founded on his free mercy, without any respect to human worth, while those whom he dooms to destruction are excluded from access to life by a just and blameless, but at the same time incomprehensible judgment.'

Calvin's doctrine of election has been the subject of much scholarly debate; it seems clear, however, that he is insisting here on a divine decree that inalienably fixes the end (pre-destinating) of all men. Those whom God elects in Christ will be admitted to salvation; those whom God dooms to destruction are excluded from that same salvation, although the Gospel is to be preached to all.

Much of our difficulties revolve around the apparent discrepancy of these statements. If the Gospel presses for a response by all either to accept or reject the Saviour, what place is there for a divine decree at all? On the other hand, if the number of the saved, as well as the number of the damned is fixed unalterably, what point is there in gospel preaching?

Calvin's own formulation of the doctrine is important. Election, he says, is founded on mercy. That is, it builds upon the mercy displayed in the Gospel, and focuses upon those for whom the Gospel is good news, that is, mankind in sin. On the other hand, reprobation, the passing by of the non-elect and their being pre-destined to destruction, Calvin says is grounded upon judgment. Calvin views reprobation as a judgment upon man in sin. The decrees of God fall upon an estranged race. The wonder is not that any are lost but that any are saved. Mercy flowers in election to life; judgment issues in reprobation and damnation. This is the awe-inspiring decree. It may be hard doctrine to modern ears; but there is no injustice in it. How could there be good news for man enslaved in sin were it not that God, rich in mercy to all who call on Him, elected some to everlasting life?

Calvin answers those who rebel against such teaching by reminding his readers that any doctrine of Scripture will excite unbelief to mockery and scorning. At this level, predestination holds no more difficulty for man in sin than the doctrine of the Trinity or the doctrine of creation (III.xxi.4). Calvin seems at one point to take refuge in what he calls 'believing ignorance' (III.xxi.5), the fact that there are some things even believers can never know. There can never, however, be any discrepancy between divine, sovereign grace in election (and divine, sovereign judgment in reprobation) and the preaching of a full and free Christ. For at last 'The refusal of the reprobate to obey the word of God when manifested to them, will be properly ascribed to the malice and depravity of their hearts, provided it be at the same time added, that they were adjudged to this depravity, because they were raised up by the just but inscrutable judgment of God, to show forth his glory by their condemnation' (III.xxiv.14). The secret things of election and reprobation belong to God; while the revealed things of the Gospel and its gracious offer of pardon, which guilty sinners need, belong to us (cf. Deut. 29:29).

Summary and evaluation

In order to evaluate the hamartology of Calvin, we would do well to consider William Cunningham's maxim concerning him, that '[he] derived his system of doctrine from the study of the sacred

Scriptures'.[19] Calvin's scheme of thought is nothing if it is not biblical. The great Reformer was not afraid to challenge the most fundamental tenets of traditional Romanism where these did not accord with the teachings of the Word of God. This grew out of no polemical spirit, but fundamentally out of the clarity and accuracy of his scriptural exegesis. Warfield suggests that it was Calvin's humanistic training that gave him an 'acute philological sense and the unerring feeling for language which characterize all his expositions'.[20] Calvin has rightly been called 'the creator of genuine exegesis'.[21]

Calvin's legacy to the Christian church in her understanding of the meaning and nature of sin was to emphasise the radical and all-pervasive power of sin in human life. Beginning with the fundamental tenet of the sovereignty of God, Calvin saw sin as the fundamental expression of anti-theism. This was more than a denial of God; it was a deliberate volitional orientation of rebellion against the God of Creation and Providence. Sin derives its seriousness from the God against whom every act of iniquity and rebellion is committed. Calvin, as we have seen, defines sin in terms of revolt against the authority of God. There is unashamed rebellion. The sinful tendency in man derives both its meaning and its objectivity from the God who demands the contrary. Boettner correctly states that 'Calvin stressed the principle of the sovereignty of God, and developed a principle which was more objective and theological'.[22]

The corollary of this was that for Calvin, there is no area of man's being that is not corrupt. This corruption is not accrued but derived. It is there from birth. The doctrine of original sin is, in Calvin, the key to knowing ourselves.

William Cunningham, whose work on Reformation theology remains unsurpassed, reminds us of the context of Calvin's teaching. Stressing the glory and prevenience of God in the work of salvation, Cunningham reminds us that popery had perverted the teaching of the Bible as to the nature of salvation, giving man a great part in saving himself. He continues:

'This perversion of the way of salvation was most congenial to man's natural inclinations and tendencies... and if it were to be dealt with at all, it would require the strongest appliances – the most powerful and thorough-going influences – to counteract it, to drive it out and to keep it out. And this was what Calvinism, and Calvinism alone... was adequate to effect.'[23]

Cunningham reminds us of the polemical edge of Calvin's work. He stresses the fact that God raised Calvin at a time when a superstitious salvation by works was holding men in the grip of sin and bondage. Calvin's emphasis is on the supreme fact that there is nothing man can do to effect release for himself from a bondage such as this.

But by stressing this, Calvin almost forgets that sin is no definition of human nature *per se*, and this must be underlined. To be sure, it is a *sine qua non* of our understanding of ourselves now; but the definition of human nature as it originated from the hand of God finds little expression in the *Institutes*. Calvin is more concerned, due to the polemical stance he is taking, to emphasise the biblical doctrine of total depravity as the backdrop against which he will paint his brilliant picture of the sovereign, divine work of salvation effected in Christ.

Bearing this in mind, we must aver the scripturalness of Calvin's doctrine of original sin, in its twofold aspect: total corruption on the part of the individual and transmission by imputation. Cunningham elsewhere warns against the fallacy of those who insist that this hallmark of Calvinism was in fact no part of Calvin's own teaching.[24] Cunningham makes the point here that in fact the sinful acts of men are more incomprehensible to us when, for example, we disallow the fact of imputation as a possible explanation for these. The doctrine of imputation will be examined later in connection with the contribution of Prof. John Murray.

To bring this brief summary of Calvin's hamartology to a conclusion, it is important to stress the point emphasised in his writing that sin has brought about a radical change in the will of man. Calvin is not clear on the nature and function of the will before the Fall, but he is in no doubt as to the effect of the Fall upon the human will. This, according to Cunningham, became a hallmark of Reformed thought: the fact that the Reformers 'ascribe to man freedom or liberty of will – full power to will and to do what was spiritually good before the Fall; and denied it to him after he had fallen.'[25]

Wendel agrees with this, when he states that in Calvin's thought 'the will in particular, can no longer strive for anything but evil'.[26] He reminds us of the importance of distinguishing between the will in itself, and a good or bad will:

'In his state of integrity, Adam's will was not only at his own disposal; he could also direct it towards good or towards evil. But since the Fall, 'it is certain that man has had no free will to do good without the help of the grace of God.'[27]

It is this fact, says Calvin, that makes us responsible for our own sin and for no-one else's.

Cunningham has an interesting discussion in his *The Reformers and the Theology of the Reformation* on Calvin's doctrine of free will. He mentions the distinction in Luther's thought between freedom of will in the 'lower realm', that is, in political and civil matters; and freedom of will in the spiritual realm. Cunningham suggests that while something of this distinction is operative in Calvin, 'he did not regard it as of much importance in a theological point of view.'[28] And even although Calvin was willing to grant man a freedom in the things of culture and politics which he could not concede to man in the area of his relation to God, he could not grant him, even in those lower realms, a 'liberty of indifference', or acknowledge that his will was 'a self-governing power'.[29] A.N.S. Lane puts it thus:

> 'Calvin was himself prepared to accept the term "freewill" (*liberum arbitrium*) if it was used not in the sense of "a free choice of good and evil" but to mean that man acts wickedly by will and not by coercion.'[30]

In Calvin's soteriology, only grace can destroy the power of sin in which man's will is enslaved. In commenting on Romans 6:18, Calvin says that

> '... no-one can be a servant to righteousness except he is first liberated by the power and kindness of God from the tyranny of sin.... What are then our preparations by the power of free will, since the commencement of what is good proceeds from this manumission which the grace of God alone effects?'

So Lane, in discussing this theme, says that, according to Calvin, grace brings with it 'a total transformation and renewal of our wills'.[31] True freedom of will must be precipitated by grace, which does not destroy the will, but destroys the sin which held it in bondage.

NOTES

1. Cadier, J., (tr. D. Johnson), *John Calvin: The Man God Mastered*, (1960), p. 32

2. Ibid., p. 38.

3. In which Calvin says that at first he was given over to the superstitions of the Papacy, but by 'a sudden conversion', God renewed his heart.

4. For which see Cadier, op.cit., chapter 4, and also Wendel, F., *Calvin*, (1959), Chapter 1 Part III.

5. Wendel, op.cit., p. 44.

6. Idem.

7. This is Neisel's translation in *The Theology of Calvin*, 1980, chapter 5.

8. Neisel, op.cit., chapter 5.

9. *New Dictionary of Theology*, p.121.

10. Quoted in J.G. Miller, *Calvin's Wisdom*, (1992), p.10.

11. J. Calvin *Sermons on Galations* (Banner of Truth reprint, 1997), p.21.

12. Ibid., p.179.

13. Ibid., p.537.

14. Ibid., p.545.

15. Ibid., p.313.

16. Ibid., p.315.

17. Ibid., p.316.

18. Ibid., p.280.

19. Cunningham, W., *The Reformers and the Theology of the Reformation*, (1862), p. 341.

20. Warfield, B.B., *Calvin and Augustine*, (1980), p. 9.

21. The phrase belongs to Diestel and is quoted by Warfield, Idem.

22. Boettner, L. *The Reformed Doctrine of Predestination*, (1932), p. 368.

23. Cunningham, op.cit., p. 341.

24. See for example, his chapter on 'The Doctrine of the Fall', in his *Historical Theology*, Vol 1, (1870), p. 504.

25. Cunningham, *Ibid.*, p. 578.

26. Wendel, op.cit., p. 188.

27. Ibid., p. 189, quoting from the *Inst.* 2.6.

28. Cunningham, *Reformers,* pp. 487-8.

29. Ibid., p. 488.

30. Lane, A.N.S., 'Did Calvin believe in Free Will?', *Vox Evangelica*, XII, 1981, p. 79.

31. Ibid., p. 81.

Chapter 4

The Hamartology of Martin Luther

BIOGRAPHICAL DETAILS

1483	Born Eisleben, Germany
1501-5	Educated at Leipzig and Erfurt
1506	Began teaching in Wittenberg
1507	Ordination
1517	Publication of the Ninety-Five Theses
1512-18	Publication of important works, such as lectures on Psalms, Romans, Galatians, Hebrews
1520	Excommunicated; the break with Catholicism was marked by the publication of three important Reformation works: *Appeal to the Christian Nobility of the German Nation, The Babylonian Captivity of the Christian Church*, and *The Liberty of a Christian*
1522	Return to Wittenberg
1525	Married Catherine von Bora; publication of *The Bondage of the Will*

Alister McGrath calls Luther 'the most creative of the reformers', most of whose writings, he says, 'were produced in response to some controversy' (*Christian Theology: An Introduction* (1994, p.64)

Further Reading
Here I Stand by R. Bainton (1983)
Martin Luther and the Birth of Protestantism by J. Atkinson (1982)
Luther: Theologian for Catholics and Protestants, edited by G. Yule (1985)

The life of Martin Luther has been linked with 'the birth of Protestantism'.[1] After training at Erfurt, where he secured both a Bachelor and a Master degree in the Arts, Luther entered an Augustinian cloister at Erfurt. It was there, in 1507, that there occurred the famous incident when Luther, celebrating his first mass at the time, was struck by the unapproachable majesty of the God whom he served as a priest. It was in Wittenberg, some eight years later, while preparing some lectures on Romans that Luther experienced a conversion experience, in which his soul was flooded by the power of the Evangel. This, combined with a growing disillusionment with the power usurped by the Roman Church, led to the nailing of his 'Ninety-Five Theses' to the door of the Castle Church in Wittenberg on October 31st 1517. This event, precipitated by the growing sale of indulgences by the Roman Church for the forgiveness of sins, invited controversy, and was intended as such. In a very real sense, therefore, they were his first hamartalogical statement, for in them Luther 'denied the power of the Pope over purgatory for the remission of either sin or penalty'.[2] According to the Luther scholar James Atkinson, writing on 'Martin Luther' in the *New Dictionary of Theology*, these theses sparked off the Reformation movement. In his book on Luther, Atkinson makes the interesting comment: 'This theology [of the theses] was not new, but it was the first time it had been used in criticism of the practice and theology of the Church of the day;'[3] what Luther actually subsequently proposed was 'an independent scheme of reform'.[4]

The break with Medieval Catholicism took place in 1520, with the publication of three significant works, *Appeal to the German Masses*, *On the Babylonian Captivity of the Church* and *The Freedom of a Christian*. The remaining twenty-six years of his life were lived in constant dispute with ecclesiastical authority, and in propagating the truth. In 1525 he published what is probably his greatest work, *The Bondage of the Will*, an important document in the effort to trace his teaching on the doctrine of sin.

If it is true that Luther was the father of the Reformation movement, then it is true that Luther's discovery of biblical hamartology precipitated the whole movement. Nor is this an exaggerated claim to make; for, as Iain Siggins puts it, 'The Reformation, in its earliest and simplest form, was a protest against the present state of penitential practice.'[5] In other words, the doctrine of sin opened the door to the whole of the Reformation movement. Hamartology paved the way for a radical return to biblical Christianity. This was expressed last century by William Cunningham in the following terms:

> 'The leading service which Luther was qualified and enabled to render to the church, in a theological point of view, was the unfolding and establishing the great doctrine of justification, which for many ages had been grossly corrupted and perverted....'[6]

Our inquiry as to the precise teaching of Martin Luther in this whole area will focus on his biblical prefaces, *The Bondage of the Will*, and some of his other writings.

Atkinson tells us that the nature of the reformation which Luther precipitated was due in part to the discovery 'that the true evangelical theology had been smothered under a human scholasticism which was no more than idolatrous intellectualism'.[7] He goes on to demonstrate that for Luther this approach meant a radical break with the humanism which undergirded the tenets of radical and Medieval Catholicism:

> '... as early as 1517 Luther knew that Erasmus' humanism and Christian ethic was not the real strong meat of evangelical, theological Christianity, and that his own emphasis on Christ, grace, revelation, sin, redemption, the servile will, and all those doctrines that were once again to ring across the world, would one day make an unbridgeable breach between the two men.'[8]

There can, therefore, be no doubting the assertion of Basil Hall, that the emphasis on these long-forgotten doctrines of biblical Christianity arose from Luther's view of 'the centrality of Christ for grasping the meaning of Scripture'.[9] Hall is also correct, therefore, to assert that 'It is this nexus of Scripture as showing forth Christ as gift and of the word of God as God's speech and act... which form central themes for Luther's theological development from 1513-1519 – indeed they remained so all his life'.[10]

It is this emphasis on Christocentric exegesis that opens the door for Luther's unyielding stress on the doctrines of the faith. Thus, in his *Preface to the New Testament* (1522) he states that:

> '...the Gospel... is a good story and report, sounded forth into all the world by the apostles, telling of a true David who strove with sin, death and devil, and overcame them, and thereby rescued all those who were captive in sin, afflicted with death, and overpowered by the devil.'[11]

In this light he develops the theme of the New Testament as fulfilling the promises and prophecies of the Old, as in the protoevangelium of Genesis 3:15. Luther has this to say on this point:

> 'Christ is the seed of this woman, and He has trodden upon the devil's head, i.e. sin, death, hell, and all his power, for without this seed, no man can escape sin, death or hell.'[12]

It is clear, therefore, that a biblical doctrine of sin is fundamental and radical in Luther's presentation of a biblical doctrine of salvation.

In his *Preface to the Romans* (1522), Luther offers a definition of sin. He is worth quoting at length:

> 'Sin, in the Scripture, means not only the outward works of the body, but all the activities that move men to the outward works, namely, the inmost heart, with all its powers.... And the Scriptures look especially into the heart and have regard to the root and source of all sin, which is unbelief in the inmost heart. As, therefore, faith alone makes righteous...so unbelief alone commits sin, and brings up the flesh, and produces pleasure in bad external works, as happened to Adam and Eve in Paradise.'[13]

Like Calvin, Luther stresses the unbelief which is at the heart of sin in its many forms. He also stresses the heart, of which he says that it is the seat of all that motivates man to sin and disobedience.

The same emphasis is found in Luther's Commentaries on Scripture. Commenting, for example, on Galatians 1:3, he describes Christianity as being summarised in the two words 'grace and peace'. These deal with the effects of sin in human life: 'Grace releaseth sin, and peace maketh the conscience quiet. The two fiends that torment us are sin and conscience. But Christ hath vanquished these two monsters, and trodden them under foot.... Grace containeth the remission of sins, peace, a quiet and joyful conscience. But peace of conscience can never be had, unless sin be first forgiven.' Luther, in the same section of the Commentary, has a sustained polemic against the ritualism and consequential sacerdotalism of the Roman Church: 'Much less is sin taken away by the works and inventions of men, as wicked worshippings, strange religions, vows, and pilgrimages... the justiciaries and merit-mongers, the more they labour and sweat to bring themselves out of sin, the deeper they are plunged therein, for there is no means to take away sin, but grace alone.'

The law Luther sees as having been brought in to 'reveal and increase sin'; yet, he says, 'is it not against the promises of God; yea, rather, it confirmeth the promises; for as concerning his proper work and end, it humbleth and prepareth a man (so that he use it rightly) to sigh and seek for mercy' (on Galatians 3:20). Luther describes the order in which such experiences take place: man feels, by the law witnessing against him, that he hates God, and God's good and holy law. He confesses that there is no good in him, and acknowledges himself to be miserable and under damnation. When man has confessed his sin, 'his time is accomplished and ended; and now is the time of grace, that the blessed seed may come to raise up and comfort him that is so cast down and humbled by the law' (ibid).

In all of this, it must be remembered that Luther is speaking as a reactionary; his works all have a markedly polemic edge. It is also true that his own personal life underwent radical re-formation and profound conversion. But this does not detract from the truth of what he is saying. The traditions which had for centuries alleged to have had the power to deal with sin were now being openly challenged in the light of the Word of God. Grace alone could deal with this: 'When Luther by his careful exegesis of Romans discovered the profundity of Paul's understanding of sin, the need for a deeper understanding of grace was forced upon him.'[14] And this point, Yule suggests, is what lies at the heart of Luther's exegesis of the epistle to the Romans.

Atkinson calls the epistle to the Romans 'the theological textbook of reformed theology, the charter of the Reformation,'[15] and there is no doubting the part that true exegesis of this work was a major factor in the spread of the Reformed faith. F.F. Bruce is worth quoting on this point. He says:

'In November 1515, Martin Luther...began to expound Paul's Epistle to the Romans to his students, and continued this course until the following September. As he prepared his lectures, he came more and more to appreciate the centrality of the Pauline doctrine of justification by faith.'[16]

He continues: 'The consequences of this new insight which Martin Luther gained from the study of Romans are writ large in history.'[17]

Atkinson summarises for us the salient features of Luther's Commentary on Romans which go some way to outlining for us the doctrine of sin as taught by Luther. On Romans 5:14, Luther reminds us of the importance of a correct starting-point: 'Not as scholastics define it but as Paul and Christ teach it; the loss of all uprightness and of the power of all our faculties of body and soul, of the whole inner and outer man.'[18] Atkinson's correct comment on this is that 'It is not a matter of how a man stands in his own eyes or in the opinion of his fellows, but of how God sees him'.[19] Such a condition as prevails in the experience of fallen man, says Luther, 'proves that whatever good work we effect, there remains in it that concupiscence toward evil and nobody is free from it, not even an infant a day old.'[20]

Alongside this emphasis on the totality of sin's power, there is also an emphatic repudiation of obedience to the law as a sufficient means of salvation. This is not to say that Luther repudiates obedience to the law. The whole is summed up in the following terms: 'Paul does not argue that faith alone justifies apart from the works proper to it, but that faith alone justifies apart from the works of the law.'[21]

In this way Luther's exegesis of Romans both demolishes the possibility of a salvation based upon man's works, and opens the door for a firm assertion of the need of man in sin for such a salvation as God has provided.

It is perhaps in *The Bondage of the Will* that Luther's hamartology finds its fullest and most considered expression. Considered by many as his greatest work, *The Bondage of the Will* was an answer to Erasmus, who in 1524 published *The Freedom of the Will*, an attack on Reformation teaching, particularly on total depravity. Luther's answer came a year later, in which he wrestled with the problem of the will in relation to the decrees of God, and considered the problem of God's commanding man to do the good which he is unable, because of his sin, to do. In *The Bondage of the Will*, Luther expounded the thesis that

> 'The Augustinian view of the total depravity of man, that man in his totality – body, soul, mind – is a fallen creation, is the best empirical explanation of it all, and basically biblical. Man is corrupted, tainted, impure, in all he thinks, says and does.'[22]

In *The Bondage of the Will*, Luther argues that freedom of will can be truly predicated of God alone: 'free will is plainly a divine term, and can be applicable to none but the divine Majesty only.'[23] Indeed, Luther goes so far as to say that theologians should refrain from using the term 'free-will' when speaking of human ability, and should apply it only to God.

The message of the book is clear; man in a state of sin cannot please God. The argument of Erasmus was that if the law commanded something to be performed by us, it necessarily follows that we have the capacity to choose to obey that law. On the contrary, argued Luther: 'the words of the law do not prove the power of free will, but shew what we *ought to* do, and what we *cannot* do.'[24] Similarly, he argues, when Paul speaks in Romans 3 of none seeking God, 'that ignorance and contempt, most undoubtedly, are not in the flesh, that is (as you – Erasmus – interpret it) 'the inferior and grosser affections', but in the most exalted and most noble powers of man, in which righteousness, godliness, the knowledge and reverence of God ought to reign, that is, in the reason and in the will; and thus in the very power of free-will, in the very seed of good, in that which is most excellent in man.'[25]

As James Montgomery Boice reminds us, Luther viewed this debate as crucial: he 'plunged into the subject zealously, viewing it as an issue upon which the very truth of God depended.'[26] The Fall of man into sin was not merely a casual 'stumbling', but a complete plunging of his nature into sin and rebellion against God. The answer to the problem lies not in a partial ability on the part of man; 'As to myself,' Luther says, 'I openly confess that I should not wish Free-will to be granted to me, even if it could be so, nor anything else to be left in my own hands, whereby I might endeavour something towards my own salvation.'[27] The need of man is to confess his sin and come to God, to rest alone in Christ; there can be no combination of the positions that Christ is sole Saviour and man part-saviour.

Perhaps the best summary of Luther's hamartology is expressed by Atkinson in the following passage:

'The reformers were not obsessed with sin; they treated it with the seriousness of Christ.... [They] all taught this bondage of the will in all matters pertaining to salvation and righteousness. All that they now enjoyed was the direct gift of the grace of God, and on Him, not on themselves, they depended. They feared God and nobody and nothing else.'[28]

At last, this is the hallmark of the doctrine of sin in the leading men of the Reformation – it is fearless and bold. It grows out of natural and exact biblical exegesis. And it describes man accurately – tainted with the corruption of sin and impoverished in the whole of his relationship to God.

NOTES

1. This is the subtitle of Atkinson's work on Luther (2nd edition, 1982).

2. Bainton, R., *Here I Stand*, 1983, p. 81.

3. Atkinson, J., *Martin Luther and the Birth of Protestantism*, (1982), p. 152.

4. Idem.

5. Iain Siggins on 'Martin Luther and the Catholic Preachers of his youth' in *Luther: Theologian for Catholics and Protestants*, (ed.) S. Yule, 1985, p. 70.

6. Cunningham, W., *The Reformers and the Theology of the Reformation*, op.cit., p. 64. In an interesting discussion, Cunningham goes on to point out that Luther's obsession with this doctrine tended to an imbalance in his presentation of the truth, and 'led him to view almost every topic chiefly, if not exclusively, in its relation to forgiveness and peace of conscience... and this fostered a certain tendency to exaggeration and extravagance in his doctrinal statements' (Idem.).

7. Atkinson, op.cit., p. 80.

8. Ibid., p. 89.

9. Basil Hall on 'Hoc est corpum meum' in Yule (ed.), op.cit., p. 117.

10. Ibid., p118.

11. Luther, *Biblical Prefaces*, p. 440.

12. Idem.

13. Ibid., p. 450.

14. George Yule on 'Luther's Christology' in Yule (ed.) op.cit., p. 91.

15. Atkinson, op.cit., p. 108.

16. Bruce, F.F., *Romans*, Tyndale NT Commentaries, IVP, 1983, p. 59.

17. Idem. Bruce continues: 'There is no telling what may happen when people begin to study the Epistle to the Romans. What happened to Augustine, Luther, Wesley and Barth launched great spiritual movements which have left their mark in world history' (Ibid., p. 60).

18. Atkinson, op.cit., p. 117.

19. Idem.

20. Idem.

21. Ibid., p. 119, on Rom. 3:19-20.

22. Ibid., p. 234.

23. M. Luther,*The Bondage of the Will* (tr. H. Cole) (1976), p. 76.

24. Ibid., p. 164.

25. Ibid., p. 334.

26. J.M. Boice *Foundations of the Christian Faith*, (1986), p. 210.

27. *Bondage*, p. 384.

28. Atkinson, p. 234.

Chapter 5

Summary of the Reformation Emphases

Calvin and Luther stand out as the unparalleled giants of Reformed exegesis and theology. It was through their efforts that the wave of spiritual revival which today we call the Reformation swept across Europe. But theirs were not the only voices adhering to the Reformation cause. Men like Melancthon, Bucer, Zwingli, and many others were also spreading the truth. It would be doing a great disservice to such men to exclude them even from the most summary chapter on the Reformed doctrine of sin. In dealing with the subject of Luther's *Bondage of the Will*, Boice makes the point that 'John Calvin, Ulrich Zwingli, Martin Bucer and all the other leading Protestant Reformers were one with Luther in these convictions'.[1]

Heinrich Heppe's *Reformed Dogmatics* has long been acknowledged as an invaluable resource for discovering the kernel of Reformed thought. This volume appeared in London in translation in 1950. In it, Heppe summarises, by quoting from the original sources, the salient teaching of the Reformation on a variety of theological chapters. Two chapters are given over to the doctrine of sin. Chapter 14 of the *Reformed Dogmatics* deals with 'The Violation of the Covenant of Works', and deals with Adam's sin, in which and by which, communion with God was lost, and Adam and his posterity fell, liable now to punishment and death.

In Chapter 15, Heppe summarises passages from the original writings of the Reformation which define sin and its meaning. This chapter is divided into 42 heads, and these summarise the doctrine of sin in the Reformation writings. Heppe's points are as follows:

1. The immediate fruit of the violation of the covenant of works is the misery of sin.
2. The meaning of *peccatum* (sin) is 'to wander'.
3. Sin is discrepancy, *anomia* (lawlessness), *actio* (action) and *res* (it is a thing, possessing objective reality); it is also volitional.
4. Sin is a contradiction not merely of God's law, but of His holiness.
5. This man performs by an act of will.

6. '...sin is in the first instance a privative or *privatio institiae*, a lack of harmony in human being and action towards the holiness and law of God.'[2]

7. Effects of sin are *macula* (stain) and *reatus* (guilt).

8. Sin is establishment in a state of guilt.

9. The cause of sin is not God.

10. The cause of sin is in the fact of man's liability to change.

11. Sin in the human race originates in Adam's Fall.

12. Sin is the natural condition of fallen man.

13. Original sin is not only the absence of original righteousness, but corruption of human nature in every area and part of the soul.

14. 'Inherited sin includes two things: imputed sin and inherent sin.'[3]

15. Corruption rests on actual disobedience and is itself sin.

16. Corruption includes the defect of original good, and the succession of evil to its place.

17. Appetitive faculties now have an anti-God tendency.

18. Man is not free from concupiscence until death.

19. The subject of original sin is the whole body and soul of man.

20. We must not confuse concupiscence and original impulses.

21. 'Concupiscence then is not the substance of human nature but an accident of it.'[4]

22. Concupiscence is a positive evil.

23. There is such a thing as *propagatio peccati*, the transmission of sin. Every human is born in a condition of sin.

24. Sin is inherited and appears as actual sin.

25. We must reject the distinction between venial and mortal sins. Every sin renders a man 'condemnable for eternity'.[5]

26. There are divisions of sins, such as inward/outward, omission/ commission, sins *per se* (prohibited by God's law) and *per accidens* (not prohibited but not good), sins deliberate and accidental etc.[6]

27. There are sins which must be labelled sins of weakness, or of an erring conscience, or against knowledge. There are also sins which may be besetting (perpetrated through free will, with no resistance to the temptation), or non-besetting. There are also sins remissible and irremissible.

28. The sin against the Holy Spirit can only be committed by a person rejected totally by God.

29. The only person who can commit this sin is 'the man who has known Christ through the gracious working of the Holy Spirit and experienced His blessed fellowship, yet falls away from Christ and becomes the enemy of Christ and His kingdom'.[7]

30. This sin leads to persistent blindness.

31. It can never be known to us who are guilty of this sin.

32. '...the irreversibility of the sin against the Holy Spirit is founded on the fact that Father and Son from eternity had resolved not to allow the

benefit of the work of redemption to those who committed this sin'.[8]

33. Death is the punishment for sin – in its temporal, spiritual and eternal aspects.

34. Spiritual death is spiritual impotence.

35. The will of fallen man is always a free will.

36. By common grace, man can produce an ordinary morality.

37. Fallen man cannot grasp the gracious favour of redemption when it is offered to him.

38. The will of man is free only to evil.

39. Enslavement by sin is itself a punishment for sin.

40. The death of the body is also a punishment for sin.

41. The peak of man's misery in sin is the eternal death, which consists of an eternal separation from the society and blessedness of God (*poena damni*) and eternal suffering (*poena sensus*).

42. For God's elect people, corporeal death is not really a punishment for sin, but a discipline which will issue in greater blessing.

Heppe fills out these points in detail and with clarification. He also attributes these emphases to different writers of the Reformation. The list above is intended to show the thoroughness of treatment accorded this doctrine in Reformed dogmatics, and to show the clarity of thought with which the issue is grasped. The conclusion to which this cursory survey of Reformed teaching leads us is that

'All the magisterial Reformers took a sombre view of the radical effects of sin and rejected the medieval doctrine that man's natural gifts were only partially affected by the Fall. On the contrary, man's will had become enslaved through sin.'[9]

It is this insistence on the radical nature of sin that demonstrates the biblical nature of the theology which issued from the Reformation.

NOTES

1. J.M. Boice, *Foundations of the Christian Faith*, (1986), p. 211.

2. Heppe, H., *Reformed Dogmatics*, (1950), p. 323.

3. Ibid., p. 331.

4. Ibid., p. 338.

5. Ibid., p. 349.

6. Heppe adds that 'with special emphasis the Reformed dogmaticians stress the sin of fornication' (Ibid., p352)

7. Ibid., p. 358.

8. Ibid., p. 359.

9. *New Dictionary of Theology*, op.cit., p. 566.

Chapter 6

Sin and the Puritan Tradition

BIOGRAPHICAL DETAILS

Thomas Goodwin

1600	Born Norfolk
1613	Enrolled at Christ's College, Cambridge
1620	Converted
1628	Became lecturer at Trinity Church, Cambridge
1632	Ordained a vicar in Trinity Church
1634	Became Independent
1639	Pastored in Netherlands for a year
1640	Returned to England as Independent minister
1650	Appointed President of Magdalen College, Oxford
1680	Died February 23rd.

Richard Sibbes

1577	Born Suffolk
1610	Graduated from Cambridge
1610	Preacher at Cambridge
1616	Preacher at Gray's Inn, London
1624	Master of Katherine Hall, Cambridge
1635	Died July 6th.

John Owen

1616	Born Oxfordshire
1642	Moved to London; published *A Display of Arminianism*
1646	First preached before Parliament
1647	Published *The Death of Death*
1651	Made Dean of Christchurch, Oxford
1652	Made Vice-Chancellor of Oxford University
1660	Ejected from the University; moved to Stadhampton
1683	Died August 24th

Further Reading:
Among God's Giants by J.I. Packer (1991)
A Guide to the Puritans by R.P. Martin (1997)
John Owen on the Christian Life by Sinclair B. Ferguson (1987)
The Puritans: Their Origins and Successors by D.M. Lloyd-Jones (1987)
Worldly Saints: The Puritans As They Really Were by Leland Ryken (1990)

In order to demonstrate the continuing influence of Reformed theology in the western world, it is necessary to look at the hamartology of the Puritan writings. *The New Dictionary of Theology*, in its article on 'Puritan theology', reminds us that

> 'Though "Puritan" was initially a term of abuse, historians use it for those concerned for the further reform of the Elizabethan and Stuart Church of England, because of their particular religious experience and commitment to Reformed theology. Their faith was shaped by their struggle with popular religious culture and Roman Catholicism.'[1]

The term was abusive then, and probably still is; as Alister McGrath says, 'the modern popular stereotype of the movement is still that of a bleak and dreary moralism.'[2]

Our interest here is to establish the link between the specific Puritan theology and the theology of the Reformers, which we have been studying above. This connection has been made explicit by Reformed scholars in modern times. For example, in his work on the theology of John Owen, giant among the Puritans, Sinclair Ferguson comments that although Owen makes his own emphases as he gives expression to the doctrine of the plan of salvation, 'he finds himself in harmony with earlier reformers such as Calvin and Bucer, and is happy to admit it.'[3] It would, however, be too simplistic to maintain that this principle could be applied unconditionally to the whole of Owen's theology, and Ferguson does the church a great service by asking continually of Owen's theology 'to what extent he managed to remain faithful to the biblical and theological insights of the Reformation, and the exposition of Calvin in particular'.[4]

Ferguson does not hesitate to highlight the differences of emphasis and expression which are to be found in a comparison of Owen and Calvin, Reformation theology and Puritan theology; but in a sentence which is concerned in the immediate context with the doctrine of prayer, Ferguson states a principle which can in fact be written over the whole, not only of Owen's theology, but of Puritan thinking, that '...its antecedents are to be found especially in the teaching of Calvin'.[5]

The point has been made explicit in Paul Helm's, *Calvin and the Calvinists* (1982). Helm's monograph is a critical response to an earlier work published by Oxford University Press and written by the successor of Dr Martyn Lloyd-Jones in Westminster Chapel, Dr R.T. Kendall. In Kendall's work, *Calvin and English Calvinism to 1649*, the thesis of a radical cleavage between Reformed and Puritan thinking is pursued relentlessly throughout. Kendall's view is summarised by Helm thus:

> 'He claims that the central figures of Puritanism such as William Perkins and William Ames derived their theology not from Calvin but from Theodore Beza, Calvin's successor in Geneva. He holds that there is a fundamental shift in outlook between Calvin and Beza, and consequently that the whole of the Puritan tradition... was set on the wrong, anti-Calvinistic track. According to Kendall, the Westminster divines, without realizing it, became virtually Arminian in many respects.'[6]

This, as Helm correctly observes, is a very serious charge against Puritanism. It is to aver that the Puritans 'were in fact undoing the work of the Reformation;'[7] and this, at last, 'affects a proper understanding of Scripture and of the whole nature of the Christian message.'[8] As Iain Murray has observed, 'much more than a dictionary is needed to evaluate Puritan theology: the starting point has to be the New Testament.'[9] It is this single point that demonstrates conclusively the direct linear descent of the Puritans from the theology of the Reformation. It was Bible-based and God-honouring. The Puritan doctrine of sin must be examined in this light.

Before coming to examine the Puritan hamartology, it may be asked – what was Puritanism, and who were the Puritans? This question is the starting-point for Jim Packer's work *Among God's Giants*. He summarises the meaning of the word 'Puritan' in this way:

> 'Puritanism I define as that movement in sixteenth- and seventeenth-century England which sought further reformation and renewal in the Church of England than the Elizabethan settlement allowed. 'Puritan' itself was an imprecise term of contemptuous abuse which between 1564 and 1642... was applied to at least five overlapping groups of people – first, clergy who scrupled some Prayer Book ceremonies and phrasing; second, to advocates of the Presbyterian reform programme broached by Thomas Cartwright and the 1572 Admonition to the Parliament; thirdly, to clergy and laity, not necessarily nonconformists, who practised a serious Calvinistic piety; fourth, to 'rigid Calvinists' who applauded the Synod of Dort, and were called doctrinal Puritans by other Anglicans who did not; fifth, to MPs, JPs and other gentry who showed public respect for the things of God, the laws of England and the rights of subjects.'[10]

This lengthy quotation does have the merit of pointing out the complexity of the subject. Puritanism is not simple to define; the *New Dictionary of Theology* says that historians employ the word 'for those concerned for the further reform of the Elizabethan and Stuart Church of England, because of their particular religious experience and commitment to Reformed theology'.[11]

Puritanism was, in fact, a popular movement of revival. The great Scriptural doctrines were handled and applied to everyday life, and were published in a way that made them accessible to the Christian public. Who could not know about the horror of a burden of sin after reading Bunyan's *Pilgrim's Progress*, for example?

In order to understand the Puritan doctrine of sin, brief references will be made to Goodwin, Sibbes and Owen on this theme. If the choice of these men requires justification, it can be found in the *New Dictionary of Theology* statement that these were 'formidable expositors', whose 'power as preachers, leaders and theologians gave Puritan theology both popular influence and scholarly depth'.[12] Following this, a brief summary of the Puritan emphases will be made.

Thomas Goodwin

Thomas Goodwin (1600-80) became a vicar in the Church of England in 1632, but resigned two years later after becoming convinced of the rightness of independency.[13] Becoming president of Magdalen College, Oxford, he, along with Owen, made a counter-attack against those who criticised the anti-Puritan attitude in many quarters. Goodwin's doctrine of sin is adequately summarised in Volume 10 of his works, entitled 'An Unregenerate Man's Guiltiness before God in respect of Sin and Punishment'.

A glance at the contents of Goodwin's work will show that it follows in the vein of the teaching of the Reformation theologians, emphasising the fact of the imputation of Adam's sin, of total corruption of nature, the defilement of the conscience by sin, and of sin's guilt and punishment. Goodwin begins, interestingly enough, with a discussion of the meaning of Romans 5:12-14, a passage which, as we shall see, will be crucial in any assessment of modern treatments of sin. Goodwin, in the flowing language typical of the Puritan period, highlights Paul's assertion that death reigned after sin entered into the world (on Rom. 5:14) – 'Other monarchs,' says Goodwin, 'never subdued all; some outlaws and nations were not overcome; here not a man but falls under it',[14] and the universal fact of death establishes for Goodwin the universality of sin.

Goodwin underlines the fact of the participation of all men in the sin of the first man. Sin passes to others, he suggests, either by example or by a partaking in the sin itself. We are not sinners because we followed Adam's example (and Goodwin is quick to highlight the corollary of this – that neither are we forgiven and cleansed by following the example of Christ), but because of our natural descent from him. The head of the race having been corrupted by sin, every descent by ordinary generation (and hence not Christ) is corrupted in the stream of issuing humanity. This leads to the corruption of total human nature – the effects of sin are to be considered holistically, according to Goodwin:

> '... an act of sin, or transgression of the law, though it be a transient thing, yet by whomsoever it be committed, it hath a permanent effect and consequent, and leaves behind it a depravation of God's image, and an inherent defilement and corruption; and though it comes out from the soul, yet it casts defilement into it.'[15]

Goodwin is alert to the objections men will raise regarding the total corruption of man by sin. Objectors, he says, will appeal (a) to the apparent goodness of some unregenerate men as furnishing evidence against the corruption of their natures, and (b) to the apparent light of conscience in the ungodly as furnishing proof that they are not devoid of good. Goodwin's two-fold approach is that man's nature and constitution are so tainted and infected by sin that they are modified by sin in all of their actions; and that the light of conscience is but a shadow of the goodness inherent in God's law, and owes its being to the creative input of God among His creatures. It is the work of God's sanctifying grace that takes to do with the gradual, and, eventually, total removal of the stain of sin: 'every part in Christ being sanctified with a law of life, was to take away the law of sin in every part of us.'[16]

The corruption of sin also leaves man spiritually bankrupt and impotent, says Goodwin. This is not to say that the man in sin does not know the truth; what he lacks is the grace to use it: 'an unregenerate man hath only the notion of these things, without the warmth or life, or knowing how to make use of them; but a believer hath both.'[17] Goodwin moves on to deal with the practical consequences of sin and its corrupting influences in the life of man. Man is necessarily misguided by a depraved reason. Such a reason could never affect man for the good. There is a religious reason, he suggests, for wickedness: 'there is in the hearts of all men a secret unbelief of the very first principles of true godliness; and not only so, but contrary sayings and dictates of the heart, which are the foundation of all corruption in their lives.'[18]

Goodwin underlines the fact of original sin, and refutes the Roman Catholic theologians who underemphasise the fact of original sin by asserting that it is not a fit object of repentance. He is strikingly accurate in his analysis of this kind of theology:

> '... they load not men's consciences at all with repentance or humiliation for original sin, as having been sufficiently removed by baptism; so as that (i.e. original sin) comes not within the compass of any confession that is to be made either to a priest for absolution, nor of a repentance before God.'[18]

Appealing to Psalm 51:5,6, Goodwin demonstrates the scripturalness both of original sin and the practice of repenting of it. This original sin Goodwin sees as consisting of two parts: '(1) Guilt of Adam's act, and (2) Inbred corruption.'[19] Goodwin goes on to trace this in the development of man, who, he says, becomes guilty of both of these at conception, and continues guilty of the act of Adam's sin, 'and the inherent corruption did withal grow greater all along the time he was warmed in the womb',[20] and then the original sin comes to the light of day as man grows to maturity and adulthood.

To be sure, Goodwin acknowledges that man in sin can perform good deeds and acts. The image of God has been defaced, but its relics remain, 'lest men should be devils upon earth'.[21] Yet man, for all his 'morality and civility', is unable to know true happiness until he finds Christ for his soul, and the happiness there is to be had in Him. All else lies under the wrath and displeasure of God: 'that his wrath shall break in upon the sinner... is the most proper effect of all other of the demerit of sin, God being stirred up and provoked thereunto by sin.'[22]

Of this punishment by God of sin, Goodwin makes the following observation:

'...if justice will have its perfect work, and bring its suit against the sinner unto the ultimate issue, it is requisite God himself put his immediate hand to the execution, otherwise this work of justice will not be perfect.'[23]

Punishment of sin is perfectly executed by God Himself, whose holiness is violated by it, according to Goodwin. He is emphatic that whatever punishment man (for example, in his conscience) might feel having sinned against God, God alone can perfectly punish. That is why, he suggests, the Bible talks of God taking vengeance – 'the demerit of sin is such, as it exciteth vengeance to it.'[24] This alone will satisfy God's justice.

Goodwin brings his work to a conclusion with the following exhortations: 'Let us be firmly persuaded of the reality of this wrath to come – Let us adore and fear the greatness of God, and be moved to turn to Him – Let us consider what it is to die, and what the state of the other world is – Let believers learn highly to value that salvation which Christ obtains for them.'[25] Thus ends an exhaustive tome in which the Reformed emphases are highlighted by Goodwin. He shows in the extensive treatment which he affords his subject that he is following in the stream of Reformed theology as taught by Calvin and Luther (above).

Richard Sibbes

Our second example of Puritan thought is Richard Sibbes (1577-1635). In many ways Sibbes was foundational to Puritan thought – he was influential in shaping the theology of Goodwin, for example, and it was through his writings that Richard Baxter came to faith in Jesus Christ. Sibbes came from Suffolk. Of his father it has been said that '[he] was by his trade a wheel-wright, a skilful and painful workman, and a good, sound-hearted Christian'.[27] Sibbes studied at St John's College, Cambridge, from which he graduated MA in 1602, and BD in 1610. He lectured in Cambridge until 1615, when, through the infamous labours of Archbishop Laud, he was deprived of this post, and became Preacher at Gray's Inn, London. In 1626 he became Provost of Trinity College, Dublin, and then Master of Catherine Hall, Cambridge. Sibbes became heavily involved in controversies over church government, and at times this alienated him from his Puritan contemporaries, like Goodwin. Sibbes passed away on 5th July 1635, aged fifty-eight.

The *New Dictionary of Theology* is correct to state that Sibbes' writings are 'practical rather than systematic'.[28] Packer lists Sibbes' *Bruised Reed* of 1630 under what he terms 'Evangelistic books' of the Puritan period,[29] books, he says, which deal with 'sin and redemption, repentance and faith, conversion and regeneration'.[30] And, in accordance with our present thesis, Packer states that the 'extremely rich exploration' by the Puritans of these great doctrines demonstrates that they are 'children of the Reformation'.[31] The practical consequence of this is that to discover Sibbes' position on any doctrine demands a thorough search of his works. Here, again, the most cursory summary will suffice.[32]

In a sermon on Matthew 26:28 entitled 'Sin's Antidote' (vii, 263-79), Sibbes states that 'sin as it is is a breach of the law' (vii, 265). The law, as given by God, binds all men with a twofold bond: what Sibbes calls 'a bond of duty', and 'a bond of misery', that is, the curse pronounced by the law itself on the person who disobeys and thus dishonours the majesty of God. This sin has pervaded the whole course of man's behaviour; if we are to know, says Sibbes, 'the whole breadth and depth of sin', we must realise that not only are *our* natures loathsome, but so also the nature of every man and woman born into the world. To maintain otherwise 'springs from ignorance of the spreading of original sin' (i, 64). Or, to put it otherwise, 'man is a trader in sin.... For it is not one act that denominates a sinner, but the constant practice of his life' (i, 400).

Sibbes clarifies this in a sermon entitled 'The Spiritual Jubilee' (Romans 8:2; v, 225-48). In it he states that 'We are under sin', and asks – 'What sin?' His answer to this is that we are under a three-fold sin:

> '1. We are under the sin of our first father... we all sinned in the loins of Adam our first parent; and the guilt of that first sin lies upon us. 2. ...There is another sin that is derived and springs from that first sin; which is the deprivation of the image of God, the privation of our nature. We call it original sin, whereby we are stripped of that good we had in our first creation, and have the contrary image, the image of Satan stamped upon us... 3. And then we are under actual sins, which are so many bonds to tie us fast under sin.... Every sin doth, as it were, tie us faster to damnation, and keeps us faster under the bondage of sin.... This is the miserable state of man' (v, 227).

Sin such as this is, according to Sibbes, the object of the hatred of God, and its nature as guilt calls forth the wrath of God. This point is clear in the following quotations:

> 'Sin and death are an adamantine chain and link that none can sever. Who shall separate that which God in his justice hath put together? If sin go before, death will follow. If the conception go before, the birth will follow after; if the smoke go before, the fire will follow. There is not a more constant order in nature than this in God's appointment: first sin, and then death and damnation after' (v, 235).

> '...where there is a falling into sin, there will be a falling into misery and judgment' (ii, 256).

It is only by grace that a man can understand the meaning of sin. Sibbes is insistent that 'God opens the heart and eyes of his children to see and feel what sin is' (vi,169). The corollary of this is that 'the Christian soul, once stung with sin, flies to the free mercy of God for ease' (vi,173). On this point, that God prepares for conversion by giving the sinner such a sight of his sin as will drive him to Christ, Packer is worth quoting at length:

> 'The occasionally voiced suggestion that there was something legalistic in their stress on the need for a "preparatory work" of contrition and humbling for sin before men can close with Christ is quite false: the only point they were making... was that, because fallen man is naturally in love with sin, it is psychologically impossible for him to embrace Christ whole-heartedly as a Saviour, not just from sin's penalty but from sinning itself, until he has come to hate sin and long for deliverance from it. The "preparatory work" is simply the creating of this state of mind. On the whole the Puritan account of conversion as a work of man turning to God which is also a work of God turning man to himself, seems to mirror exactly what the New Testament says.'[33]

Sibbes' sermon on 'Sin's antidote', quoted from earlier, is quite a masterly treatment of how God forgives sin. He highlights the fact that the justice of God is to be satisfied prior to the obtaining of mercy on the part of the sinner: 'Justice must be fully satisfied, that mercy may be fully and comfortably manifested... there is no man that receives this mercy in the forgiveness of his sins till justice be satisfied even to the utmost' (vii, 207). This Christ has achieved in His self-offering, having discharged the debt and satisfied the holiness of God.

Sibbes spells out the achieving of this in a brilliant passage from a sermon entitled 'The Church's Riches':

> '[Jesus Christ] took upon him likewise our sins, so far as there is anything penal in sin in respect of punishment.... He took upon him our nature, that he might become sin for us; he took upon him the guilt as far as guilt is an obligation to punishment... Christ took the communion of our nature, that he might take the communion of our punishment, not of our fault...'

In this way, Sibbes underlines the Reformers' teaching regarding Christ as the substitute for the sins of His people.

As has been stated, Sibbes' works were intensely practical. We shall conclude this brief view of his hamartology by quoting from a sermon in Vol. ii on 'The Returning Backslider':

> '...let us labour for the forgiveness of our sins, that God would remove and subdue the power of them, take them away, and the judgments due to them, or else we are but miserable men, though we enjoyed all the pleasures of the world... [a man] has no comfort, so long as he knows his sins are on the file, that God in heaven is not at peace with him...Therefore, it being so miserable a case to want [i.e. lack] assurance of the forgiveness of sins, it should make us be never an hour quiet till we have gotten it, seeing the uncertainty of this life, wherein there is but a step betwixt hell, damnation and us' (ii, 264).

Sibbes is nothing if he is not practical. He has a theology which is thoroughly biblical and thoroughly Reformed. And he has one which he does not intend to leave in a closet, but one which is to be the life of the child of God. Sin to Sibbes is a dreadful thing, which brings guilt and punishment. To be a Christian is to hate the dreadful monster of sin.

John Owen

The greatest Puritan theologian of the seventeenth century was undoubtedly John Owen (1616-83). He has been called 'the great systematic thinker in the Puritan theological tradition';[34] Packer says of him that '[he] was one of the greatest of all English theologians. In an age of giants, he overtopped them all. C.H. Spurgeon called him the prince of divines.... Owen was a theologian of enormous intellectual energy.'[35]

Owen was the son of a Puritan vicar, and was born in Oxfordshire in 1616. He graduated MA from Oxford in 1635, and was converted shortly afterwards. He left the University in 1637, to return (after a period in the pastoral ministry) as Dean of Christ Church in 1651, and Vice-Chancellor the following year. A major voice in the whole debate over church government characteristic of the period, Owen's legacy to Reformed thought has been monumental, and here it is possible only to mention briefly the important emphases of his teaching.

Students of Owen are fortunate in having a rich compendium of his thought and teaching in Sinclair Ferguson's work, *John Owen on the Christian Life* (1987), and Ferguson's work will serve as the frame for our study of Owen. Owen's study of sin and its effects is dealt with particularly in Volumes III and IV of his writings, volumes which deal with the Person and Work of the Holy Spirit. Unregenerate man is characterised by darkness, depravity and death, the result of sin affecting the mind, the will and the soul respectively.[36] This darkness, says Owen, is alienating:

'The darkness of sin clouds man's view of the nature of the gospel and the necessity of faith... [it] produces a real aversion to God, filling it with enmity against him and with desires that are antagonistic to him, as well as with prejudice against spiritual realities.'[37]

Owen's conclusion on this theme is that

'... we do conclude that the mind in the state of nature is so depraved, vitiated and corrupted, that it is not able, upon the proposal of spiritual things unto it in the dispensation and preaching of the gospel, to understand, receive, and embrace them in a spiritual and saving manner, so as to have the sanctifying power of them thereby brought into and fixed in the soul, without an internal, especial, immediate, supernatural, effectual, enlightening act of the Holy Ghost...' (III,281-2).

Owen's concern in Vol. III, Chap. 4 is to show the effect of sin in the fact of death. He defines the spiritual death of the unregenerate in terms of (a) the absence of the principle of life, (b) a cessation of all acts of true obedience to God, and (c) a lack of power to perform these acts.[38] This, as Ferguson points out, is the backdrop to Owen's teaching on grace as sovereign and effectual.

Owen's teaching on the effects of sin is summarised under five heads: (1) Sin is original; corruption is at work from the earliest moments of life. (2) The power of sin grows proportionately with the passing of the years, so that as children grow into youth and adolescence, the effects of sin are the greater; to quote Owen, 'The same principle and habit of mind, carried over unto riper age and greater occasions, bring forth those greater sins which the lives of men are filled withal in this world' (III, 340). (3) From this, there proceeds the performing of 'actual sins'. (4) 'As men grow up in the state of nature, sin gets ground in them and upon them, subjectively and objectively' (III, 342). With the developing of the mental processes, men increase in their capacity for sin, while objectively, greater occasions for sin present themselves to men. (5) 'A course in, and a custom of, sinning with many ensues' (III, 343). Only the goodness of God restrains this inherent evil in man.[39]

Ferguson summarises Owen's position thus:

> 'Here, then, is the "experimental" aspect of man's depravity and death in sin. It is delineated at length by Owen, because the magnitude of regeneration is measured by the fact that grace delivers, renews and alleviates man from all he has known by way of bondage, darkness, death and corruption under the dominion of sin.'[40]

It will be sufficient to end this summary of Owen's teaching with some comments on his view of the ongoing conflict between the believer and his sin. Ferguson introduces this to us thus:

> 'It is an axiom for Owen that while the presence of sin can never be abolished in this life, nor the influence of sin altered... its dominion can, indeed must be destroyed if a man is to be a Christian.'[41]

Or, as Owen puts it:

> 'As every drop of poison is poison, and will infect, and every spark of fire is fire, and will burn; so is every thing of the law of sin, the last, the least of it, – it is enmity, it will poison, it will burn; Grace changeth the nature of man, but nothing can change the nature of sin' (VI,177).

Sin has a 'usurped' dominion over man, a dominion in which the mind of the unregenerate is enmity towards God. But the axiom for Owen is that grace and sin cannot share the same throne; they cannot both have dominion. Owen explores the symptoms of sin's dominion, and in doing so is superbly pastoral. Owen reflects the emphasis of the New Testament that the believer is under grace, and not under law.[42]

For all that grace has dethroned it, sin continues to dwell in the heart of man – its presence is still real and influential: 'the power of sin remains where the dominion has been banished.'[43] It is there as a law, strengthening man in his performance of wicked deeds; it is still enmity towards God, affecting the believer's affections, making him weary towards the works of faith, and his mind, weakening him in the practice of meditation. To this end, it is deceitful, and requires to be watched against. In his superb thesis on the mortification of sin, Owen puts it like this:

> 'I shall discharge him from this duty who can bring sin to a composition, to a cessation of arms in this warfare; if it will spare him any one day, in any one duty,... let him say to his soul, as to this duty, "Soul, take thy rest." The saints, whose souls breathe after deliverance from its perplexing rebellion, know there is no safety against it but in a constant warfare' (VI, 12).

Breward has written that 'The intellectual strength and coherence of [the Puritan] theological tradition is increasingly recognized by historians, despite its eclipse during the heyday of liberal theology'.[44] This is undoubtedly true, and much research requires to be done. Breward is indubitably correct to maintain that the Puritan theologians were indeed men of intellectual strength, whose teaching must be taken seriously in any study of historical theology. And Breward has crystallised for us the relevance of the Puritans for our concerns at present, namely the wide cleavage that separates Puritan theology from liberal thought, of which Neo-orthodoxy is an example. Both claim to evolve out of the Reformation, but both cannot. They are too distinct in themselves to be compatible, despite their respective claims to have originated from a common source. It is the Puritan emphasis which most markedly and faithfully brings the Reformed teaching forward, by a faithful adherence to the Scriptural truths of that movement. What Packer writes of Owen could be said of Puritan theology as a whole, that it is 'constantly and consciously near the centre of seventeenth-century Reformed thought throughout'.[45]

The best summary of the Puritan hamartology is probably that offered by Packer in the following words:

'Knowing God, the Puritans also knew man. They saw him as in origin a noble being, made in God's image to rule God's earth, but now tragically brutified and brutalised by sin. They viewed sin in the triple light of God's law, lordship, and holiness, and so saw it as transgression and guilt, a rebellion and usurpation, and as uncleanness, corruption, and inability for good. Seeing this... the great Puritans became great pastors.'[46]

As such, their theology is characterised both by its faithfulness to the biblical teaching, and its adherence to the Reformed position.

A Twofold Influence

The foregoing has attempted to crystalise the salient features of the Reformed doctrine of sin in its two most formative stages, the theology of the Reformers and the thought of the Puritans. Historical theology bears testimony to the fact that there was a profound influence exercised by this particular theology on both sides of the Atlantic, first in that it led to the Westminster Assembly of 1644-49, and secondly, that it led to a significant contribution to American theology, particularly through Jonathan Edwards.

The Westminster Assembly was convened by an act of Parliament in 1643, following the abolition of episcopacy, with the remit to advise Parliament on matters of religion and worship. The resultant documents, most notably the Westminster Confession of Faith and the Shorter Catechism, have been the foundation for Scottish and American Presbyterianism. Their significance for our purpose is that they stand in the stream of the Reformed thought we have been considering above. Williston Walker states that the two Westminster documents just named 'have always ranked among the most notable expositions of Calvinism'.[47] Sinclair Ferguson, writing on the historico-theological influences on the Westminster Confession, correctly highlights the strategic importance of the federal principle, which, he suggests, was brought to maturity in Calvin's Institutes, where it was 'recognised as the theological key to the Scriptures;'[48] and Prof. Torrance, writing in the same volume on the strengths and weaknesses of the Westminster theology, also highlights this federal scheme which was 'expounded by the great Puritans like William Perkins... whose powerful influence is seen in the Westminster divines....'[49] There is a consensus of opinion, therefore, that, whatever might be the merits or otherwise of the Westminster Assembly, its doctrinal and theological emphases accord with Reformed and Puritan thought.

This point has been made explicit by Reformed theologians elsewhere. The Moderator of the 1979 General Assembly of the Free Church of Scotland stated in his moderatorial address that 'the Confession... is historic Calvinism at its best'.[50] Similarly, Professor John Murray writes that the Confession gave Reformed thought 'fuller and more precise definition'.[51] David Wright states that '[The Westminster Confession] purveys a developed, so-called 'scholastic' Calvinism, reflecting the influence of Puritan covenant theology...'[52]

Murray goes on to delineate the significance of this for our present study:

'All true theology is realistic; it takes the data of revelation and the facts of life seriously. At no point does a theology governed by sentiment rather than by facts quibble with the teaching of Scripture more than on the subject of sin. The Confession is not afraid to enunciate the doctrine of total depravity.... Less than this is not a true transcript of the biblical teaching...'[53]

Chapter VI, therefore, of the Westminster Confession – accepting as it does the literal Fall of Adam, and the Fall of all men in him, with the consequence of total corruption in every aspect of man's life and behaviour, this sin imputed to all of Adam's seed as the source of actual sins, calling forth the wrath of God, and remaining in the believer – can be seen to accord with the principles of the Reformed and Puritan doctrine as already delineated. This teaching met with resistance in England within twenty years of its formulation, but was accepted north of the border and became the confession of classic Scottish Presbyterianism.

The other major significance of Reformed and Puritan thought lies in the impetus it gave to American theology. The persecuting principles of Charles I and Archbishop Laud, both one in their aversion to Calvinistic principles both in religious thought and its practice, led to the emigration of many Puritan preachers and families to America. This movement began around 1628, and grew over the next twenty or so years under the leadership of Puritan giants such as Winthrop, Cotton and Mather. Walker summarises:

'These early congregationalists of New England did not differ theologically from their Puritan brethren in Great Britain – they welcomed the appearance of the Westminster Confession, adopted it in substance, and stressed the federal or covenant theology'[54]

These were the origins of Reformed and Puritan thought in American theology, of whom the great representative is the eighteenth-century theologian, Jonathan Edwards.

The thought of Jonathan Edwards has been ably assessed in Iain Murray's biography.[55] Summarising Edwards' theological position, Murray writes that 'The high degree of importance which Edwards came to attach to Calvinistic belief was to have far-reaching consequences for his whole ministry'.[56] Murray goes on to demonstrate this particularly by reference to the position Edwards took on church order, and the opposition he met from men of Arminian persuasion in New England in the 1730s. Murray's thesis of a noticeable decline in theological orthodoxy in the mid-eighteenth century is ably defended, and cannot be ignored in any study of American theology in its subsequent stages. The *New Dictionary of Theology* says that

'Although the New England theologians all called themselves Calvinists, they did not share entirely similar beliefs.... To an unusual degree, Edwards brought together penetrating insight into religious experience, sophistication in the use of current philosophy, and firm commitment to Calvinistic convictions. His books such as *The Freedom of the Will* (1754) and *Original Sin* (1758) defended divine sovereignty in salvation over against contemporary views arguing for autonomous moral action.'[57]

Edwards' Calvinism might be questioned in the light of his assertion as follows: 'I utterly disclaim a dependence on Calvin, or believing the doctrines which I hold, because he believed and taught them; and cannot justly be charged with believing in everything just as he taught.'[58]

For all his disclaimer, Edwards' *Freedom of the Will* clearly demonstrates his Calvinistic mode of thought. More a philosophical answer to John Locke than a theological treatise notwithstanding, his work concludes:

'It is easy to see how the decision of most of the points in controversy between Calvinists and Arminians depends on the determination of this grand article concerning the freedom of the will requisite to moral agency; and that by clearing and establishing the Calvinistic doctrine in this point, the chief arguments are obviated, and the contrary doctrines demonstratively confirmed.'[59]

He shows how he has demonstrated the

> 'total depravity and corruption of man's nature, whereby his heart is wholly under the power of sin, and he is utterly unable, without the interposition of sovereign grace, savingly to love God, believe in Christ, or do any thing that is truly good and acceptable in God's sight'.[60]

Murray summarises Edwards' argument thus:

> 'Man's utter incapacity to do spiritual good does not arise out of a physical lack of faculties, but altogether out of the wrong moral disposition of those faculties. In this way he explains how man, though totally corrupt in his nature, is still a responsible free agent.'[61]

This accords with what we have already discovered to be the essence of Reformed hamartology.

Edwards' great contribution to the Reformed doctrine of sin was in his last work, published in 1757, *The Great Doctrine of Original Sin Defended*. It set out to provide a biblical explanation for the universal phenomenon that 'Man has a universal tendency to disregard God and to disobey His law'.[62] Murray reminds us of the pastoral concern of Edwards in this work: 'He saw superficial views of the gravity of human corruption as the primary cause of the neglect of commitment to a supernatural redemption.'[63] Murray quotes from Edwards' Preface:

> 'I look on the doctrine as of great importance. For if the case be such indeed, that all mankind are by nature in a state of total ruin, then doubtless, the great salvation by Christ stands in direct relation to this ruin, as the remedy to the disease. The whole gospel must suppose it and all real belief, or true notion of that gospel, must be built upon it.'[64]

A study of Edwards' theology in its historical setting will clearly show his adherence to the Reformed doctrine of sin. His insistence on man's moral inability to turn to God is cardinal to this doctrine. And what is interesting in a study of Edwards' life and thought is that in his own day there were many theologians of a very different (Arminian) persuasion who lent to subsequent generations of evangelists the idea that regeneration occurs by a mere act of a person's will. Edwards recognised this as evidencing an impoverished view of sin and its effects. His Principalship of the then young Princeton had the effect of making Princeton a hallmark of true, biblical, Reformed scholarship. So Murray:

> 'Edwards' hopes that the New Jersey village would long remain a centre for true Christianity were abundantly fulfilled. The most dependable reflections on Edwards' theology almost all came from such men as Hodge, Miller and Atwater – all teachers at Princeton Theological Seminary – and it remained so right down to B.B. Warfield who died in 1921. For upwards of a century-and-a-half, the place to which Edwards gave so much thought, and where his dust was to lie, remained a foremost preserver and propagator of historic Christianity.'[65]

It is clear, therefore, that the hamartology of the Reformation and of the Puritan period clearly influenced subsequent theological tradition on both sides of the Atlantic, and was instrumental in the continuance of this tradition. It remains now to note some ways in which this Reformed doctrine of sin was carried along in the stream of nineteenth- and twentieth-century theological reflection.

NOTES

1. *New Dictionary of Theology*, p. 550.
2. A. E. McGrath, *Christian Theology: An Introduction* (1994), p.73.
3. Ferguson, S.B., *John Owen on the Christian Life*, Edinburgh: Banner of Truth, 1987, p. 30.
4. Ibid., pp. 187-8.
5. Ibid., p. 224.
6. Helm, P., *Calvin and the Calvinists*, (1982), pp. 5-6.
7. Ibid., p. 9.
8. Ibid., p. 10.
9. Murray, I.H., 'New England Puritans', in the *Banner of Truth* magazine, issue 179-80, 1978, p. 74.
10. Packer, J.I., *Among God's Giants*, Kingsway, 1991, p. 41.
11. *New Dictionary of Theology*, p. 550 on 'Puritan Theology'.
12. Ibid., p. 551.
13. cf. Lloyd-Jones' emphasis in his book *The Puritans* (Banner of Truth, 1987), pp. 258-9: 'The Puritan is primarily concerned about a pure church, a truly Reformed church – if we fail to put this doctrine of the church in a central position, we are departing from the true Puritan attitude...'
14. Goodwin, Works, Vol X, p. 5.
15. Ibid., p. 49.
16. Ibid., p. 130.
17. Ibid., p. 151.

18. Ibid., p. 224.

19. Ibid., p. 325.

20. Ibid., p. 398.

21. Idem.

22. Ibid., p. 419.

23. Ibid., p. 518.

24. Ibid., p. 522.

25. Ibid., p. 523.

26. Ibid., p. 549. This is the chapter introduction to Vol X, Bk Xiii, Chap. IX.

27. 'Memoirs of Richard Sibbes, D.D.,' in *The Complete Works of Richard Sibbes*, Vol 1, (1973), p. xxvii. His parents were Paul and Johan; the word 'painful' in the quotation is synonymous with 'laborious', 'hard-working'.

28. *New Dictionary of Theology*, p. 551.

29. Packer, op.cit., p. 47.

30. Idem.

31. Ibid., p. 48.

32. References will be given thus: i 100 will mean Vol 1 of the Collected Works, which were originally published in 7 vols, 1862-4.

33. Packer, op.cit., p. 48.

34. *New Dictionary of Theology*, p. 552.

35. Packer, op.cit., pp. 251, 253.

36. Ferguson, S.B., op.cit., p. 37.

37. Ibid., p. 38; cf., Owen, Vol 2, pp. 257ff.

38. Ibid., p. 38.

39. See also Ferguson's summary, Ibid., pp. 38-41.

40. Ferguson, Ibid., p. 41.

41. Ibid., p. 125.

42. Ferguson says that 'The Pauline doctrine of the law is thus understood by Puritan theology' (Ibid., p.129).

43. Ferguson, Ibid., p. 131.

44. *New Dictionary of Theology*, p. 552.

45. Packer, op.cit., p. 253.

46. Ibid., p. 34.

47. Walker, W., *A History of the Christian Church*, (3rd ed), (1970), p. 414.

48. Ferguson, S.B., 'The Teaching of the Confession', in Heron, A.I.C. (ed.), *The Westminster Confession in the Church today*, Edinburgh, 1982, p. 37.

49. Torrance, J.B., 'Strengths and Weaknesses of Westminster Theology', in Heron, Ibid., pp. 48-9.

50. Quoted in *The Monthly Record of the Free Church of Scotland*, July/Aug 1979, p.133.

51. Murray, J., *Collected Writings*, Vol 1, (1976), p. 317.

52. *New Dictionary of Theology*, p. 156.

53. Murray, op.cit., p. 319.

54. Walker, op.cit., p. 433.
55. Murray, I.H., *Jonathan Edwards: A New Biography*, Banner of Truth, (1987).
56. Idem.
57. M.A. Neill, writing in *New Dictionary of Theology*, p. 458.
58. Edwards, J., Preface to *Freedom of the Will* (1877).
59. Ibid., p. 404.
60. Ibid., p. 406.
61. Murray, op.cit., p. 426.
62. Ibid., p. 429.
63. Idem.
64. Idem.
65. Ibid., p. 462.

Chapter 7

Sin in the Theology of Charles Hodge

BIOGRAPHICAL DETAILS

1797	Born Philadelphia, USA
1816-19	Studied at Princeton Theological Seminary
1821	Ordained
1819-20	Instructor, Original Languages of Scripture, Princeton
1822-40	Professor of Oriental and Biblical Literature, Princeton
1840-54	Professor of Exegetical, Didactic and Polemic Theology, Princeton
1878	Died, Princeton

Further Reading:
Princeton Seminary: Faith and Learning 1812-1868 by David B. Calhoun (1994)
   Princeton Seminary: The Majestic Testimony 1869-1929 by David B. Calhoun (1996)
   Charles Hodge: Systematic Theology (abridged editon), edited by E.N. Gross

---

In the Preface to a volume of theological essays published from Princeton Seminary in 1856, Dr. Patrick Fairbairn wrote: 'For an exact and discriminating knowledge of the peculiar doctrines of Calvinism... the Essays under consideration could not easily be surpassed'.[1] So generous was Fairbairn in his praise that he went on to state of the authors that 'on them, the mantle, not merely of Edwards, but of Calvin himself, seems peculiarly to have fallen'.[2]

One eminent theologian of the Princeton tradition of the nineteenth century may be cited in support of Fairbairn's thesis that Princeton represented the continuance of a truly Reformed hamartology. He is Charles Hodge (1797-1878). An eminent graduate of Princeton, Hodge was offered the post of assistant-teacher of Biblical literature and exegesis within a few months of graduating, and he became professor

119

some two years later, around 1822. His sons, A.A. Hodge and Caspar Wistar Hodge, and his grandson, Caspar Wistar Hodge jnr., were all to become professors in worthy succession to Charles. A man of wide learning and ability, it has been said of Hodge: 'By deep study he arrived at the settled conclusion that the doctrinal standards of the Reformers and Puritans were the truth, and in 1872 at his jubilee, when multitudes were elsewhere confounding novelty with truth, he boldly declared – "I am not afraid to say that a new idea never originated in this seminary".'[3]

In his treatment of the doctrine of sin in his magisterial *Systematic Theology*, Hodge stated that the definition of sin presupposes 'the existence of a personal God of infinite perfection, and... the responsibility of man'.[4] Definition of sin, he argues, is based primarily on the statements of God's Word, and secondarily on the facts of our own moral nature. Drawing on these, Hodge elsewhere defines original sin in these terms:

'1. What the Scriptures teach on this subject is the entire and universal corruption of our nature. 2. That this innate, inherent, hereditary corruption manifests itself in all forms of actual sin, as a tree is known by its fruits. 3. That regeneration consists in creation of a new principle, a germ of spiritual life, and not in the absolute destruction and removal of this inherent corruption. 4. That consequently in the renewed there are two conflicting principles, sin and grace, the law of sin and the law of the mind. 5. That this remaining hereditary corruption, as modified and strengthened by our actual sins, is what is meant by indwelling sin.'[5]

Hodge took up a stout defence of Augustinian, as opposed to Pelagian theories of sin and its origin and extent. His statement of the Protestant doctrine of sin fell under five main sections. First, he emphasised that sin is a specific evil. Every man knows, according to Hodge, 'that sin is not simply limitation of his nature, nor merely a subjective state of his own mind, having no character in the sight of God'.[6] In view of the Neo-orthodox emphasis on subjectivity as the criterion for truth, it is important to underline the classical Reformed insistence on the objective nature of sin and guilt. In the thinking of Hodge it is underlined that sin has 'a specific character of its own and includes both guilt and pollution'.[7]

Secondly, sin has a relation to the Law. This bears upon man's moral character, which, as such, leaves him subject to the law of what is morally right. If man knows that he ought to do one thing, or that he ought not to do something, it is because of the setting of a standard, a rule of law, which binds the conscience of man. This rule, says Hodge, is revealed in man's natural constitution, in the Decalogue, in the Mosaic code, and in the whole Bible.

Thirdly, sin is related to the Law of *God*. The nature of sin derives from the fact and existence of a superior moral Being, 'whom we know to be infinite, eternal and immutable in His being and perfections'.[8] In relation to the Law of God, Hodge discusses the extent of the law's demands, underlining the biblical principle that the law demands complete perfection, 'the entire conformity of the moral nature and conduct of a rational creature with the nature and will of God'.[9] Hodge qualifies this by asserting the Bible's own disclaimers, (a) that there can be no perfection in this life, and (b) that no man can achieve merit through his good works. Moreover, the extent of obedience required shows that sin is not confined merely to volitional acts, but goes deeper still, to the 'first impulses' of evil. All our evil dispositions are condemned by the holy law of God. Hodge's position here is summarised in his statement that 'there is sinfulness as well as sins'.[10]

Fourth, sin is defined in terms of its lacking the conformity to the law of God which the Bible demands. Hodge defines this as follows:

> 'The want of conformity to the divine law which constitutes sin is the want of congeniality of one moral nature with another, of the dependent and created nature with the infinitely holy nature, which of necessity is not only the sum, but the standard of all excellence. Herein is sin: that we are not like God.'[11]

Fifthly, Hodge asserts that sin includes the guilt and pollution which relate it to the justice and holiness of God respectively.

Under the heading 'The Effects of Adam's Sin upon His Posterity', Hodge deals with the nature of the injury done by the sin of Adam to those who were and are descended from him. Hodge follows the theology of the Westminster Confession by taking a federal, or covenant view of the nature of Adam's sin and its relation to mankind. In an article on the theology of Charles Hodge, G.W. Grogan, former principal of the Bible Training Institute, Glasgow, argued that this whole question of original sin was 'The chief centre... of Hodge's interest in man'.[12] Grogan points out that this whole question was at the frontier of much theological debate in America in the nineteenth century. Various historical influences were to be seen in the differing perspectives adopted. Some argued a position akin to Augustine, who said that Adam was the human race in its entirety, so that when he sinned, all sinned. No imputation is necessary in this case. Hodge, on the other hand, followed Cocceius and Turretin, in arguing for a covenant view. Grogan maintains that Hodge inferred this from the parallel drawn between Adam and Christ in Romans 5. Thus Grogan:

> 'It was [Hodge's] conviction of the vital importance of the covenant of grace which made him so insistent on the covenant of works. It was the logic of Scripture that he felt to be at stake.'[13]

According to Hodge, the relation sustained by Adam to mankind in his sinning against God opens up for us the facts of (1) the imputation of Adam's first sin, (2) the corruption of nature derived from him, and (3) the inability of fallen man to perform spiritual good. On imputation, Hodge espoused a doctrine of the immediate imputation of Adam's sin to all mankind, so that not only sinfulness, but the penalty of God against sin is attributed to all men in the wake of Adam's Fall. So Hodge:

> 'Men... stood their probation in Adam. As he sinned, his posterity came into the world in a state of sin and condemnation. They are by nature the children of wrath. The evils which they suffer are not arbitrary impositions, nor simply the natural consequences of his apostasy, but judicial inflictions.'[14]

The ground of such imputation is, says Hodge, a twofold union between Adam and his posterity, a union which was natural, in that he is the natural father of all living, and the sin which so corrupted his nature becomes then the natural constitution of his progeny; and, above that, there is the divine arrangement by which God deals with Adam as the representative of the race, the federal head of his posterity. The sin of Adam, says Hodge, thus becomes the judicial ground of the condemnation of all men. Hodge demonstrates that this representative principle is markedly biblical, and that it is especially taught in Romans 5:12-21.

Hodge summarises the Protestant doctrine of original sin under five statements: 1. Corruption of man's nature affects the soul. 2. It consists in the loss of original righteousness, and the consequent entire moral depravity of our nature. 3. It is truly sin, involving both elements of guilt and pollution. 4. It retains its character as sin even in the regenerated. 5. It renders the soul spiritually dead, and man unable to do any spiritual good in the sight of God.[15] Hodge argues these points from the facts of sin's universality in the world, from the entire sinfulness of men, witnessed supremely in the universal rejection of Christ, in the earliest manifestations of sin in the life of children, in the explicit statements of Scripture to this effect, and in the fact of the universality of death.

In dealing with the fact of inability, Hodge is careful to safeguard the Protestant doctrine from being falsely represented. 'The doctrine of man's inability,' he is jealous to state, 'does not assume that man has ceased to be a free moral agent. He is free because he determines his own acts. Every volition is an act of free self-determination.'[16] Man's inability is to be seen particularly in the spiritual realm, respecting 'the things of the Spirit'. Hodge's statements exemplify the biblical position regarding sin as holding dominion over man, and the sinner in bondage to sin in every area of life and experience.

Before passing from Hodge's hamartology, it must be noted that on at least one aspect of his teaching Hodge did not command the universal assent of his Reformed brethren. In a review of Hodge's *Systematic Theology*, R.L. Dabney argued that on the question of whether imputation of Adam's sin was mediate or immediate, Hodge followed a line which could not be supported by the writings of the Reformers. Dabney disagreed with Hodge that

> '...in the order of causation, the imputation of the guilt of Adam's first sin upon men precedes, transferring that guilt upon them conceived as at first otherwise innocent and guiltless; whereby a privative moral corruption of soul is by God visited on Adam's children as the penalty of imputed guilt, and, in the first instance, of it alone.'[17]

This is the doctrine of immediate imputation, as taught by Hodge, that the mode of imputation of the sin of Adam to his posterity is by the immediate transference of guilt, God rendering guilty a seed otherwise innocent; and, consequent upon that transference of guilt, a corruption of soul and total inability follow as God's punishment.

Dabney dismissed this as being 'not the peculiarity of the Reformed doctrine, but an exaggeration into which a few of its distinguished names have been betrayed'.[18] Some twenty pages of text are filled by Dabney in order to demonstrate his thesis that the distinction between mediate and immediate imputation is a false one, opening the way for extremes which have no place in Reformed thought. The fact of the matter is that '[man] enters existence corrupted, as he enters it guilty. He enters it guilty as he enters it corrupted.'[19]

The fact of such disagreement between Dabney and Hodge highlights the possibility of intra-confessional debate, of difference of opinion within the Reformed camp itself. John Murray in his work *The Imputation of Adam's Sin*, in which he favours immediate imputation, argues that the theology of men like Jonathan Edwards, whom Dabney cites to support his own thesis, has often been misrepresented, and that it is too simplistic to allege that he propounded the doctrine of mediate imputation.[20] Murray shows how the lines of New England theology followed a logically consistent course. He also emphasises the point that the restricted question in the whole debate is whether the involvement of Adam's posterity in his sin was directly based on the relation sustained by Adam with his seed, or whether it was mediated through the inheritance of a corrupt nature from Adam. Murray follows Hodge in arguing that the union between Adam and his seed contemplated in Romans 5:12-21 forces the conclusion that imputation was immediate.

Our conclusion must be that the doctrine of imputation remains a salient feature of the Reformed doctrine of sin, even although the mode of imputation requires precise definition.

NOTES

1. *Theological Essays reprinted from the Princeton Review*, (1856), p. iii.
2. Ibid., pp. iii-iv.
3. Article entitled 'Charles Hodge (1797-1878)' in *The Banner of Truth* (10th issue), 1958, p. 14. cf. also John Leith's comment that 'Hodge had no doubt that his theology and that of the Reformers was the same', in *Introduction to the Reformed tradition*, Edinburgh: St Andrew Press, (1978), p. 126.
4. Gross, E.N., *Charles Hodge: Systematic Theology* (abridged edition), 1988, p. 276.
5. Hodge, C., *Princeton Sermons*, (1879), p. 94.
6. Gross (ed.), op.cit., p. 284.
7. Idem.
8. Ibid., p. 285.
9. Ibid., p. 286.

10. Ibid., p. 287.
11. Ibid., p. 288.
12. Grogan, G.W., 'The Theology of Charles Hodge', in *The Monthly Record of the Free Church of Scotland*, March 1979, p. 63.
13. Ibid., p. 63.
14. Gross (ed.), op.cit., p. 291.
15. Ibid., p. 297.
16. Ibid., p. 308.
17. Dabney, R.L., *Discussions*, Vol 1, Banner of Truth reprint, pp. 254-5.
18. Ibid., p.258.
19. Ibid., p. 281.
20. Murray, J., *The Imputation of Adam's Sin*, (1959), chapter 3, esp. p. 62.

Chapter 8

The Twentieth Century:
John Murray and G. C. Berkouwer

BIOGRAPHICAL DETAILS

John Murray

1898	Born Sutherland, Scotland
1923	Graduated MA, Glasgow
1927	Graduated from Princeton Theological Seminary
1930	Begins teaching in Westminster Theological Seminary
1937	Ordained in the Orthodox Presbyterian Church
1964	Retires from Westminster
1967	Married Valerie Knowlton
1975	Died in Scotland

Gerrit Berkouwer

1903	Born Holland
1936	Published *Karl Barth*
1940	Began lecturing in the Free University of Amsterdam
1945	Appointed Professor of Dogmatics at the Free University
1952-75	Published his 18-volume *Studies in Dogmatics*

Further Reading
The Collected Writings of John Murray, published by the Banner of Truth Trust, in 4 volumes
Studies in Dogmatics, by G.C. Berkouwer, published by Eerdmans.

Our first example of twentieth-century Reformed thinking on the doctrine of sin is John Murray, late professor of Systematic Theology at Westminster Seminary, Philadelphia, U.S. A. In a very real sense, Prof. Murray can be seen as bringing the old Princeton theology into the twentieth century, because Westminster Seminary, where Murray taught for over 35 years, was established by evangelical scholars from Princeton. In the struggles over biblical authority and inerrancy in the late 1920s, they believed that the Princeton of that era had ceased to be the Princeton of Alexander and Hodge. Murray's work spans almost the first forty years of Westminster's existence, from 1930 to his retirement in 1966.

The *New Dictionary of Theology* has rightly described Murray as 'An eloquent and thoughtful advocate of the classical orthodoxy of the Westminster standards'.[1] His biographer writes of him, in connection with John Murray's work alongside Gresham Machen, the founder of Westminster, that 'Murray became the foremost spokesman for the need of a full-strength commitment to Reformed theology'.[2]

The following aspects of his hamartology show Murray to be indeed an exponent of the theology which characterised the Reformation theologians and the Puritans after them.

In *The Imputation of Adam's Sin*, Murray states that although modern theology (Brunner is cited as an example) is hospitable to the notion of solidarity in sin and guilt, nevertheless, he says:

> '...we must see that the recognition of and the emphasis upon solidaric or corporate sin and guilt in our present day theology are not to be interpreted as identical with the classic protestant doctrine of the imputation of Adam's sin.'[3]

In particular, Murray attacks the appeal of modernism to the apparently mythical Fall of Adam as descriptive and expressive of solidaric unity in sin. Murray is deeply aware of the fact that although modern theology is in some degree accommodative of the biblical insight, nonetheless in its nature and expression, he maintains that it is something other than orthodox biblical faith.

Murray's commitment to the Reformed hamartology is grounded in his belief in the literal interpretation of the opening chapters of Genesis.[4] In his discussion of 'Creation Ordinances' in *Principles of Conduct* (1957), Murray reminds us that the Fall of Adam and Eve into sin is directed against a specific command on the part of God. Murray continues:

'We may properly infer that transgression of commandment is the principle of sin and obedience to commandment the principle of integrity. Obedience to commandment is the subjective condition of virtue and commandment is the objective criterion. Disobedience to commandment is the subjective condition of sin and commandment its objective criterion.'[5]

Sin, for Murray, is grounded in the facts of specific commandment and of actual transgression. It is, he argues, exegetically untenable to view the opening chapters of Genesis as anything other than literal truth. And the message these chapters relate is of the factualness of overt transgression on the part of Adam and Eve as the foundation for sin, corruption and guilt on the part of all who are descended from them.

Murray devotes a chapter in Volume 2 of his Collected Writings to 'The Nature of Sin'. He underlines five aspects of biblical hamartology. First, he emphasises the reality of sin. It is not illusory, and it is not enough to describe sin as privation or negation. Sin, he says, 'is a positive something... not simply the absence of something.'[6] This point he argues elsewhere:

'Far too frequently we fail to entertain the gravity of this fact. Hence the reality of our sin and the reality of the wrath of God upon us for our sin do not come into our reckoning.... And sin, if reckoned with at all, is little more than a misfortune or maladjustment.'[7]

Moreover, Murray saw the shift away from orthodox biblical thinking in the light of this modern emphasis on an impoverished view of sin and its effects. Our thinking, he declares, 'must be revolutionized by the realism of the wrath of God, or the reality and gravity of our guilt, and of the divine condemnation,'[8] if we are fully to appreciate the central fact of the gospel, the justifying act of God's grace.

In an article on 'The Theology of the Westminster Confession of Faith' (Collected Writings, Vol. IV), Murray underlines this last fact by declaring that 'our concept of salvation is, therefore, conditioned, by our view of the gravity of that to which salvation is directed'.[9] Further:

'The stress upon the wrath of God [i.e. in the Westminster Confession] is worthy of particular attention. The liability of sin finds its epitome in God's wrath and any confession that overlooks or suppresses the reality and implications of God's wrath stands condemned, not only as failing to assess the gravity of sin and of our relation to God because of sin but also as failing to construe aright the salvation which faith appropriates and which is central in the Christian confession.'[10]

Central to biblical hamartology, and central to a Reformed concept of sin, is, according to Murray, an awareness of the realism of the fact of transgression.

Again, Murray underlines the specific nature of the evil of sin. He cites disease, calamity and death as examples of evils, but states that there are aspects to sin as evil which these others do not have. The reason for this is that sin, according to Murray, is a condition in which man finds himself. Symptomatic of this condition, and consequent upon it, are facts such as disease, calamity and death. So Murray, in commenting on Romans 3:23, which describes universal sinfulness under the concept of having failed of the glory of God, says that the verb 'to lack', 'to be destitute of', 'refers to a condition, not to an action.'[11] Not but that there is action in sin; Murray's point is that sin cannot be understood except in terms of the specific condition in which it has placed man.

Third, Murray highlights that sin is moral evil. 'It is recognized as something that ought not to be.... It is a violation of the category of ought.'[12] In particular, this means violation of the law of God, without which the word 'ought', and all morality, can have no meaning. It is this law which binds the conscience of man with a 'principle of all-inclusive obligation to God'.[13]

This fact of the pervasiveness of God's law means that the supreme standard by which sin is to be judged is the giving of a command on the part of God. 'We owe devotion to God in every phase and department of life,' says Murray.[14] And although circumstances may vary the degree of opprobrium attached to any of our sinful actions, 'the law by which sin is to be judged is not variable'.[15]

Fifthly, sin involves *macula* and *poena*, stain and guilt. The first of these refers to the fact that 'Man is totally unholy. All his functions and exercises are unholy because they lack conformity to the will of God.'[16] The latter refers to liability to punishment. Murray follows Reformed theologians in distinguishing between demerit (*reatus potentialis*) and the judgment of demerit (*reatus actualis*), but rejects the distinction between *reatus culpae* and *reatus poenae* ('the guilt of sin' and 'liablity to punishment') as improper, making a distinction where none exists. Nonetheless, the fact of sin as objectively considered means that we cannot neglect the fact of guilt:

'We may find a great deal of emphasis upon the undesirability of sin, the unfortunateness, the odiousness, ugliness, disgustingness, even filthiness of sin, without any truly Christian assessment of sin as lawlessness, pollution and guilt.'[17]

Murray makes these general conclusions on the doctrine of sin:

'...sin involves both guilt and pollution. It is this doctrine of sin that supplies the basis for the doctrine of salvation on both its objective and subjective sides. Guilt involves our liablity to the divine wrath and curse. It is with that that salvation on its forensic and objective side deals. Pollution deals with the defilement of sin and is formulated under total depravity and inability. This is the presupposition of salvation on its subjective, internal and ethical side.... If we eviscerate guilt, we eviscerate Christianity in its objective accomplishment; if we deny original sin we eviscerate Christianity in its subjective application and fruition.'[18]

The conclusions to which Murray comes with respect to his doctrine of sin can be demonstrated to be grounded in the biblical framework which we outlined in the preceding chapters, and are unashamedly Reformed in their allegiance to the theology of the Westminster Confession.

G.C. Berkouwer

Our final study in this section on Reformed hamartology is the thought of G.C. Berkouwer (b. 1903), the famous Dutch theologian and Professor of Dogmatics in Amsterdam. Berkouwer's studies have included the relationship between faith and salvation, the Roman Catholic church, and the theology of Karl Barth. Barth's theology has been subjected to criticism by Berkouwer in two volumes, *Karl Barth* (1936) and *The Triumph of Grace in the Theology of Karl Barth* (1954, 1956). Although the latter volume showed a markedly increased sympathy with Barth's dogmatic position, 'incisive criticism was by no means lacking'.[19]

Berkouwer's hamartology is displayed in his magisterial volume on *Sin* in his series on *Reformed Dogmatics* (English Translation 1971). The massive size of the volume represents the fact that the English translation brings together the two Dutch volumes from which this work has been translated, the first of which constitutes Part 1 (The Origin and Knowledge of Sin), and the second Part 2 (The Essence and Spread of Sin).

Chapters 1-5 deal with the origin of sin, the question '*unde malum?*', 'whence evil?'. Berkouwer qualifies this question in the first chapter with the statement: 'We are of the opinion that an explanation for sin is truly impossible... the riddle of sin is... *sui generis.*'[20] However, Berkouwer realises that the question of sin's beginning (rather than of sin's origin) is raised on the pages of the Word of God, and he devotes his discussion to an exegesis of primary passages.[21] For Berkouwer it is axiomatic that *Deus non est causa, auctor peccati* (God is not the cause, or the originator of sin). The biblical *a priori* is the holiness of God. Confession of sin he calls the 'existential application' of this principle. This is not to say that God is not sovereignly involved in the question of sin and its effects in human life. Thus there is a level at which 'There can be no reason for sin in God's creation,'[22] and a level at which God is sovereignly in control in the affairs of creation. Murray commends these emphases in Berkouwer.

Knowledge of sin, says Berkouwer, is given in the Law of God, by which God's sovereign election of Israel was made visible and manifest to them. He warns against a false dichotomy between law and Gospel, stating that 'Metanoia (repentance, conversion) has everything to do both with the law and the Gospel'.[23] This is one aspect of Berkouwer's critiques of Barth; for, whereas Barth stresses the triumph and priority of grace, Berkouwer is concerned that there is a 'radical antilegalism' in his thought. Berkouwer wishes to restore the law to its rightful place in biblical soteriology.

Chapters 8 and 9 deal with sin in its essence and gravity. Berkouwer is insistent that the essence of sin is that it 'eliminates every alibi and is completely inimical to God';[24] it is always against God.[25] Berkouwer also reminds us of the multiplicity of biblical terms to denote this fact, and reminds us of the deep-seated and personal nature of sin. It is not, he says, a 'peripheral phenomenon'.[26] The story of the Fall, which he accepts as literal history, shows the nature of sin and its reality; in the narrative 'we find the aspects of temptation, disobedience and transgression against the explicit commandment of God.... No definition is now given of sin, and yet our sin is laid bare in the reality of an act.'[27] A critique of Barth follows at this point.

For all that the Bible is insistent on the terrible nature of sin as it is, there is also gradation; Berkouwer cites passages from Leviticus to show that the Bible distinguishes motives and intents. The fact

now is that in the post-Christ era, where full light has been given on
the nature of sin as seen through the cross of Jesus Christ, man is
fully responsible, without any excuse:

> '...within the crescendo of history it is more and more evident that sin can
> be called in this new situation a deliberate act against the light which has
> now arisen and the cross of God's atonement'.[28]

This is not to minimise the gravity of sin at any stage of human history.

Berkouwer gives close attention to the Roman Catholic distinction
between mortal and venial sin. With Calvin he rejects this distinction
as 'little more than a smooth palliative "to soothe our sluggish
consciences".'[29] Such compartmentalisation is neither biblical nor
Reformed. Berkouwer's position is that in Reformed thought there is
'a staunch protest against a quantitative, categorical, atomistic and
abstract view of man's sin'.[30] This leads to a discussion of the Sin
against the Holy Spirit; Berkouwer follows Heppe in identifying the
contours of this sin 'in a radical and total, blatant and wilful apostasy'.[31]

Much emphasis is placed in Chapter 11 on the fact of God's wrath,
which is not of 'an irrational or an incomprehensible kind. It is not a
capricious vehemence.... Nor is it an enigma.'[32] God's wrath, maintains
Berkouwer, is a personal reaction on the part of God against man's
sin. No contradiction obtains between love and wrath on the part of
God; because, as Berkouwer puts it, 'God's mercy does not imply a
toleration of man's sin.'[33]

Chapters 12-14 are engaged with the 'problem of an alien guilt',
the fact of our connection with Adam and the biblical doctrine
regarding original sin. Murray is true to say in this connection that
'Both Realism and Federalism are subjected to critical examination
and rejected as offering adequate accounts of racial solidarity in Adam.
Berkouwer is not successful in providing a fruitful alternative.'[34]
Berkouwer seems to follow Bavinck in urging a common guilt in
Adam, but in rejecting realistic and federalistic theories as a means of
explaining it. His conclusion, rather weak, is that 'the doctrine of
original sin is first of all a confession of our guilt.'[35] This subject of
confession is discussed thoroughly.

Berkouwer's treatment concludes with a chapter on the end of sin.
He underlines the tension that there is between new life in Christ and
remaining, indwelling sin. His concluding affirmation is that the
Protestant Reformed documents boldly declare an immediate end of

sin at the point of departure from this life to be with Christ.

John Murray gives this work a glowing review. Berkouwer has succeeded in conceptualising the orthodox, biblical doctrine of sin in a thorough discussion. But Murray's review ends 'with a question mark'. This concerns, he says:

> '...the omission of a chapter or, at least, section, on the aftermath of damnation for the godless. It is true that any sensitive soul trembles at the thought of everlasting destruction from the presence of the Lord and from the glory of His power.... But it is, nevertheless not easy to understand this hiatus in a volume of such proportions on the subject of sin, and more particularly, when so much space is properly devoted to the wrath of God as his judgment upon sin.'[36]

Murray's point is an important one, for the Reformed witness to the teaching of Scripture has always included a reference to the final judgment of the wicked.

NOTES

1. *New Dictionary of Theology*, op.cit., pp. 447-8.
2. Iain H. Murray in Murray, J., *Collected Writings*, Vol. 3, p. 57.
3. Murray J., *The Imputation of Adam's Sin*, (1959), pp. 5-6.
4. See discussion of Murray's position in Chapter 1 of this thesis, under 'Sin in the Mosaic Epoch of Revelation'.
5. Murray, J., *Principles of Conduct*, (1957), p. 40.
6. Murray J., *Collected Writings*, Vol. 2, (1977), p. 77.
7. Murray, J. *Redemption, Accomplished and Applied*, (1961), p. 117.
8. Ibid., p. 118.
9. Murray, J., *Collected Writings*, Vol. 4, p. 253.
10. Idem.
11. *Commentary on Romans*, Vol. 1 ad. loc., p. 112.
12. *Collected Writings*, Vol. 2, op.cit., p. 77.
13. Ibid., p. 78.
14. Idem.
15. Ibid., p. 79.
16. Ibid., p. 80.
17. Ibid., p. 81.
18. Ibid., pp. 88-9.
19. *New Dictionary of Theology*, op.cit., p. 89.
20. Berkouwer, G.C., *Studies in Dogmatics: Sin*, (1971), p. 16.
21. Berkouwer's ability in this regard earned the following high praise from John Murray: 'in respect of exegesis, biblical theology, historical theology,

and dogmatic theology, this work is unexcelled' (review in *Westminster Theological Journal*, 35.2 (1973), p. 227).

22. Berkouwer, op.cit., p. 136.
23. Ibid., p. 195.
24. Ibid., p. 241.
25. Ibid., p. 242.
26. Ibid., p. 265.
27. Ibid., p. 269.
28. Ibid., p. 290.
29. Ibid., p. 306.
30. Ibid., p. 307.
31. Ibid., p. 344.
32. Ibid., p. 359.
33. Ibid., p. 397.
34. Murray, art.cit., p. 230.
35. Berkouwer, op. cit., p. 465.
36. Murray, art.cit., p. 231.

Summary of Section Two

In a sermon delivered at Randwick Presbyterian Church, Australia, in 1977, entitled 'Theology for Today', Dr. Harold Whitney stated that a return from the irrationalism of Neo-orthodoxy to a sound theological system which can be built on, requires a theology which is 'biblical, reformed, evangelical and contemporary'.[1] In the previous chapters we have sought to outline the biblical parameters of our study, and the parameters of Reformed hamartology. We have sought to apply Dr. Whitney's principle that 'We stand by the Bible of the Reformers and the sense in which it is interpreted in the Westminster Confession of Faith'.[2] Through representative theologians of the Reformed tradition, beginning with Calvin and Luther, through the Puritans, who were, 'doctrinally the "literal and lineal descendants of John Calvin",'[3] men like Owen and Sibbes, and their descendants like Edwards in the eighteenth century, Hodge in the nineteenth and Murray and Berkouwer in the present, we have seen the salient features of Reformed hamartology, and underlined the fact that it is in this stream that the biblical system is most closely adhered to.

The Reformation emphasis of *sola scriptura*, the Bible alone, led to a biblically oriented and Christ-centred approach to the whole question of the human condition as it has been affected by sin. It spawned a great deal of exegetical activity and material, and led to a re-discovery and re-affirmation of the truths of the Word of God. It accepted the Bible as literal truth, inerrant revelation, and infallible wisdom. It grounded the church's doctrine on the church's Bible, leaning on Scripture to formulate dogma.

This was partly a reaction to the Medieval Catholic system, which proffered a system of ecclesiastical ritual and machinery to deal with sin. The Church could sell indulgences in order to atone for sins both in this life and beyond the grave. The Scriptural emphasis upon the free grace of God in Christ cut the gordian knot of ecclesiastical jurisdiction in the affairs of men's sins, and drew the attention of men and women to the teaching of Scripture, with its emphasis on grace alone.

The Reformation was also, however, a movement of the Spirit of God, which gave dynamism and power to the Reformers in their work.

There is no doubt that the hand of God was upon men such as Calvin, Luther and Zwingli; their doctrine grew out of the Bible and was firmly moulded by their own experiences of saving grace. The doctrine of man in general, and the doctrine of sin in particular, with their emphases on man's total estrangement from God and total corruption of heart, became the backdrop against which the Reformers painted their picture of the salvation achieved by Christ and applied by the Holy Spirit.

The question of succession to the Reformers remains for some a matter of academic debate. Who maintained their work and witness? For some, Calvin is good, but Calvinism is bad. Some have maintained that the successors of Calvin, most notably Theodore Beza, introduced concepts alien to Calvin's own thought, such as an over-emphasis on contractual federalism. Yet the only way to approach this question is to return to the sources; and when we do that, we see that the Reformation theology has been taught by men like the Puritans, like the Hodges, like John Murray. God has preserved His truth in a stream of witness that continues to ground the thinking of men and women in the infallible statements of the Word of God.

That is not to say that there can be no development of thought or of insight. The Holy Spirit still guides into the truth. And in proportion as that truth is faithfully sought out, faithfully taught and faithfully preached, men will discover that they are sinners, and will seek the refuge of Calvary's blood.

The same gospel that swept across Europe in Reformation revival and renewal, is able still to bring sinners in need and contrition to the cross of Calvary. Whether the modernist gospel grounded in the thinking of Barth, Bultmann and Brunner can achieve this is the subject of the following pages.

NOTES
1. Whitney, H.J., *Evangelism the Hearbeat of the Church*, (1987), p. 273.
2. Idem.
3. Ibid., p. 308. Whitney is quoting partly from Prof. John Fiske of America.

Section 3

The Neo-orthodox
View of Sin

Chapter 9

The Doctrine of Sin in
the Theology of Karl Barth

BIOGRAPHICAL DETAILS

1886	Born Switzerland
1911	Pastor in Safenwil
1921	Teacher at Gottingen and Munster
1930	Teacher at Bonn
1935	Teacher at Basel
1968	Died

Major Publications
Church Dogmatics (massive theological work written over many years, and unfinished at the point of his death); Commentaries on *Romans* (1921), *1 Corinthians* (1924) and *Philippians* (1928).

There appears to be a two-fold consensus of opinion about Karl Barth which is common to almost every assessment of his theology. The first is in respect of his genius and significance. In writing in the *New Dictionary of Theology*, Prof. J.B. Webster designates him 'The most significant theologian of the twentieth century'.[1] Similarly, when Paul Schrotenboer made a critical review of the first volume of Barth's *Church Dogmatics* in the *Westminster Theological Journal* for May 1957, he opened his article with the words: 'Almost forty years ago the star called Karl Barth shot up to sudden and great brilliancy. It was no momentary illumination, for its brilliance has continued right up to the present.'[2] There can be no questioning the massive intellect that lay behind the *Church Dogmatics*; for sheer brilliance Karl Barth is matched only with difficulty.

The second point that is made by scholars, and which follows from the first, is that Barth has shaped much of modern theology.

Consequently, any theological position must be measured in terms of proximity or otherwise to that of Barth. Whitney is ready to acknowledge this in his work *The New Heresy*. He declares at the outset that

> 'So much has been written by so many about the theology of Karl Barth that it seems almost a work of supererogation to attempt to say anything more. At the same time, anyone who has a serious interest in theology today, seems under an obligation to make his own assessment of this theologian.'[3]

Similarly, John Webster, in an article on Continental Theology, writes: 'To be a systematic theologian in Germany involves taking a stance on Barth's work, however critical that stance may be.'[4]

In this connection Donald Bloesch makes a very apposite remark. In his book, *The Evangelical Renaissance*, in which he evaluates the resurgence of evangelicalism in the 1970s, he makes the point that 'Those who call themselves 'evangelical' in the Anglo-Saxon countries generally regard the late Karl Barth with suspicion.'[5] He sounds a warning note to those who do not appreciate Barth's genius and influence:

> 'While openly questioning much of what Barth says, we think that it is possible to appreciate some of his novel and daring formulations of the age-old truths of the Bible... we believe that Barth must be taken with the utmost seriousness by any theologian of Reformed persuasion.'[6]

In the following chapter an attempt will be made to examine and assess the work of Barth, and to take a stance on it. But that examination will also try to follow Bloesch's caveat, and treat Barth with the respect he deserves. The attempt will particularly focus on his doctrine of sin, in order to discover his position on this doctrine. But there are other issues which must be examined first, without which none of Barth's doctrines can be assessed. These are his theological presuppositions, his doctrine of revelation, and his doctrine of Scripture. A brief word will, therefore, be said on these topics, followed by a discussion on Barth's exegesis of cardinal passages in Romans, and the place given to sin in the *Church Dogmatics*.

Barth's philosophical and theological presuppositions

Dr. Harold Whitney has demonstrated both in *The New Infallibility* and *The New Heresy* that Barthian theology is forged on a quite recognisable anvil, that of dialectical and existential thought. Whitney begins his survey of this mode of thinking with the Nature/Grace distinction of Thomistic thought, which itself was built on a faulty view of the Fall of man. Aquinas' theory that sin affected the will alone, while the intellect remained free, bifurcated man's field of knowledge into 'lower' and 'upper'. To the former belonged all that surrounds us in the world, and which is therefore capable of scientific analysis and investigation, while to the latter was relegated the whole religious category. The former was rational, the latter irrational.

It was Immanuel Kant who introduced these distinctions into philosophy. On the one hand, he wished to affirm the priority of experience, while on the other he stressed that our experiences are subject to radical interpretation by our thinking. This was to turn the whole field of philosophical reflection upside down. The most basic philosophical concept is defined in these terms: A is not non-A. Kant, however, by distinguishing between the phenomenal realm of our experience and the noumenal realm of our thought-processes was able to question even this fundamental philosophical postulate. 'A' might be understood or interpreted as 'non-A'. The subjective interpretation of the thinker is as valid as the experience itself, even if in real terms it issues in something quite different from it.

Dr. Whitney is correct to assert and maintain that Kantian dialectic was nothing more than a personal autonomy on the part of man. In *The New Infallibility* he presents a conclusive thesis to show that in every academic discipline, from science to philosophy to history, the Kantian distinctions are not only maintained but ruthlessly pursued to their logical conclusion. Especially telling is his analysis, for example, of current historiography, espousing as it does the dictum made famous by Collingwood, that the quest for historical accuracy and verifiability requires the historian to 'get inside' the event. The events of history, according to Collingwood, 'are not spectacles to be watched, but experiences to be lived through mentally'.[7] This type of 'Kantianism' has had monumental consequences for the study of the Scriptures, and, consequently, for the whole theological discipline.

This 'new infallibility', or, as Francis Schaeffer prefers to call it, 'the new humanism',[8] found a bed-fellow in existentialism, a philosophical system which covers every discipline. Of its leading lights it has been said that they are 'bound together by the refusal to belong to any school of thought',[9] emphasising the priority of experience, that is, of the subjective. The bridge between this form of thinking and Christian theology was erected by Martin Heidegger, an avowed atheist who denied the validity of revelation and its authority over any area of life and ethics. Søren Kierkegaard, the Danish scholar, struggled with the presuppositions of subjectivism. For Kierkegaard, there is no objective truth. Human existence is all-important, but even of this man must talk by means of paradox if he is to talk at all. Dr. Whitney sums him up thus: 'In his passion to expose aspects of Hegelianism, he fell a prey to the Hegelian methodology of synthesis, and became an exponent of the very thing he sought to expose.'[10]

Barth's theology imbibed the presuppositions of existentialism – that existence is above revelation – and the use of dialectic, with a place given especially to the paradoxical, the irrational and the absurd. Barth, it must be said, rejected existential categories as in themselves adequate for interpretation. In his Commentary on Romans 7:11, for example, he dismisses together the 'relentlessness of Calvin' and the 'dialectical audacity of Kierkegaard'.[11] Nevertheless, it is still true that 'Barth found his point of departure in Plato and Kierkegaard'.[12] Or, as Dr. Whitney puts it,

> 'For both Barth and Kierkegaard it is the human subject that projects the ideal of the absolute subject, so that, by it, a field of endless advance may be opened up to the autonomous consciousness of man.'[13]

Francis Schaeffer is particularly ruthless in his assertion that Barthianism is nothing other than the theologising of Kant, Hegel and Heidegger. Perhaps, however, Carl Henry is more accurate when he describes dialectical theology as 'inspired by Søren Kierkegaard and popularized by Karl Barth'.[14]

Barth's Doctrine of Revelation

In his work *Frontiers in Modern Theology*,[15] Carl Henry demonstrated that the basic issue in modern theology is the status and authority of revelation. He has highlighted this area in particular in order to demonstrate the dissatisfaction of theological students with Barth, Brunner and Bultmann, and the need for a viable alternative. Henry cites Pannenberg as the key figure in a revolt away from Barthian subjectivism to a more objectified view of revelation; striking particularly at 'dialectical theology's disjunction of revelation and reason, and at its consequent refusal to relate Christianity to the realm of objective knowledge'.[16]

In order to assess this view of Barth's theology, it will be necessary to uncover some of Barth's own statements regarding the presuppositions of his thought. Commenting on Romans 6:19, Barth expresses the principle on which he understands revelation to have been given. He says: 'Grace determines to see and hear and touch. It presses to Revelation and to sight.'[17] This quotation highlights that (a) Barth wishes to assert the priority of God over man, and (b) he reduces revelation to pure act.[18] By using such terminology as the word *grace*, that is, the language of the Bible, Barth is straining to assert the priority of God; while the use of such terminology as 'determines' and 'presses', shows that even his categories of God are thoroughly existential. In order for God to reveal Himself, He must *become*, He must act. All is subjective and, consequently, illusory.

It is axiomatic for Barth that in revealing Himself, God remains hidden. While he asserts that 'In the Gospel, in the Message of Salvation of Jesus Christ, this Hidden, Living God has revealed Himself, as He is',[19] he also maintains that 'In Jesus, God becomes veritably a secret: He is made known as the Unknown.'[20] This kind of ambiguous language demonstrates just how existential and subjective Barth is,[21] and also impresses upon the reader of Barth the reductionist trends of his thinking.

It is axiomatic also that all revelation centres upon Jesus Christ. In commenting on Romans 3:22 Barth says that if he is to discover any revelation at all, 'it must be revealed by the Father of Jesus, and by Him only'. In some sense, therefore, Barth allows a trinitarian distinction which makes the Father the Revealer and Christ the Revelation. But he will not allow any such revelation outside of the 'Christ-Event'. Thus he goes on to say (while commenting on the same text): 'The revelation which is in Jesus...must be the most complete veiling of His incomprehensibility.' It follows that the revelation, which is characterised by its keeping God a secret, is made in Christ, and in Him alone. It is thoroughly Christomonistic. The upshot of this is, of course, that God's self-unveiling (which is actually a self-veiling), takes place only over the duration of the life of Christ. So '[for Barth]...there is no revelation of God except through Christ, that is, over the period 1 to 30 AD'.[22] This axiom of Barthian thought will be demonstrated more thoroughly when we come to see how the doctrine of sin is presented in the Dogmatics.

Thirdly, it is axiomatic for Barth that Revelation possesses no objective authority. This will be important for our discussion of Barth's view of Scripture. Any authority which God's revelation may have is grounded for Barth, not in the revelation itself, but in our subjective faith in it. There is certainly no objective revelation in history, for Barth's contention is that 'The historian...sees history when he writes it'.[23] As Carl Henry demonstrates, neo-Orthodoxy has bifurcated revelation into historical 'deed-events' and experiential, or subjective, 'meaning-revelations'. [24] Thus Barth, while willing to admit a revelation of God in the 'deed-event' of a historical Christ, wishes also to maintain the priority of subjectivism for participation in such revelation. So Barth (on Romans 3:22): 'Faith in Jesus is to feel and comprehend the unheard of 'love-less' love of God...to call upon God in His incomprehensibility and hiddenness.' He continues, with a phrase straight out of Kierkegaard, 'it is a leap into the void.' The upshot of the subjectivism which is so characteristic of Barth is that any authority which God's revelation may possess it possesses only for me in my leap of faith. And when I leap, it is into the infinitude of darkness which belongs to the hiddenness of God.

Barth's Doctrine of Scripture

The foregoing discussion of Barth's view of divine revelation – the revelation on which the Christian religion is based – yields the following conclusion: 'faith and revelation [in Barth] are correlated in virtual independence of Scripture.... This subjectivisation of the idea of revelation is fatal to any faith in the authority of the infallible Bible.'[25] If Dr. Whitney is correct in his assessment of Barth at this point, and our conclusion is that he is, then it will have serious consequences for all that remains of Barth's theology. His doctrine of sin, with which we are more immediately concerned, in common with all his other doctrines, will be forged on the anvil of a purely subjective 'leap' of faith. Having removed objectification, Barth is left only with the purest form of subjectivism in his formulation of theological truth. The hazards of such a criterion are legion, especially when we remember that 'Christianity...is based upon and constituted by certain factual and doctrinal elements'.[26] This being so, it will be necessary to comment on Barth's doctrine of Scripture before looking at his formulation of the doctrine of sin.

Barth is difficult to follow on the relationship that obtains between the Word of God and Scripture. Following the analogy of the Trinity, he defines the Word of God in terms of its being proclaimed, written and revealed.[27] We are dealing here specifically with the second of these propositions – that the Bible is (in some sense at least) the written Word of God.

Barth, while commenting on Romans 9:6, defines the Word of God as 'The Theme of the Church'. It is clear, however, that he is unwilling, whatever place the Bible has for the practice and beliefs of the church, to identify the Word of God with the Bible. In one place Barth says: 'God's Word is never 'available' for anyone. God's Word is God's Spirit, who blows where He will.'[28] That is, there is no objective criterion to which reference can be made at all times, and by which doctrines can be assessed.

The relationship that obtains between the Word of God and Scripture is rather that the Bible is a 'witness' to the Word. So Barth, on Romans 3:31: 'we enable the Law, the Bible, Religion veritably to speak. We permit them to bear witness to their proper meaning.' The parables, he says while commenting on 3:21, speak concerning this theme (of the Word of God) – they bear witness to it. Carl Henry sees Barth's position here as symptomatic of his dialectical methodology. He says that

> 'the dialectical character of revelation, as Barth defined it, precluded an identification of this Word with Scripture...the crisis-theologians demeaned Scripture to "witness" to the Word, rather than recognising it as the Word written.'[29]

As he pursues his thesis that Barth has substituted the infallibility of the ontological self for the infallibility of God, Dr. Whitney concludes with Henry that the notion of Scripture as a witness to the Word of God has taken the place of an inscripturated, objective, written record of what God has done.[30]

This point has been well made by Fred Klooster in an article entitled 'Karl Barth, Evangelicals and Revelation', which appeared in the *Reformed Theological Journal* for November 1987. Klooster tries to be fair to evangelical scholars who have shown a renewed appreciation of Barth and his theology, but he has to take some of them, and especially Bernard Ramm, to task for coming short in their assessment. In particular, he chides Ramm for failing to reckon with what Klooster himself considers to be an all-important principle of interpretation for Barth, summed up in the following quotation:

> 'The Bible...becomes God's word in this event, and in the statement that *the Bible is God's Word* the little word 'is' refers to its being in this becoming.'[31]

Klooster's own comment on this statement is that 'when Barth says that the Bible *is* God's Word, *is* refers to its *being* in this *event* of its *becoming revelation*'.[32]

Klooster's point is that Barth's understanding of the relationship which obtains between Word and Scripture is thoroughly existential; the categories in which Barth is willing to underscore a loose connection between the two are hedged by his philosophical belief in matter obtaining validity in the act of becoming. There is, consequently, an ambivalence in his attitude to the Bible which is not only at variance with the Reformed position, but which is, on its own merits, quite staggering. The Scripture which may contain the Word of God at one moment may not contain it at another; similarly, the Bible authenticates itself as the Word of God only on a personal, subjective and momentary level.

Thus Barth is willing to allow the Bible some kind of place in the formulation of theological doctrine, but the place assigned to it is momentary and subjective. Barth makes it clear that he will not allow the Bible to be regarded as the Word of God, infallibly and inerrantly; he will, however, tolerate the notion that the Bible may contain, or at least become, the Word of God on certain occasions and to certain people. It is in his view not always so; but given the correct criteria and the correct approach, it may become authoritative in a person's experience when it bears witness (to him only and at that time only) to the Word. Thus a passage of Scripture may be both the Word of God and not the Word of God at the same time. Similarly, a passage which was the Word of God to me yesterday may not be so tomorrow, or ever again. So Craig makes the following comment concerning Barth and Brunner and the Dialectical theology that is their contribution to theological scholarship:

'According to these men the Word of God is in the Bible but in it only potentially... the Bible becomes to us the Word of God only as God speaks to us directly from it... [the Word of God] always consists of a direct address to the individual soul. God is always the subject, never the object of the address.'[33]

The implications of such an address are immediately apparent. Barth has been hailed as an evangelical scholar who called men back to the Bible. Yet with his 'semi-high' view of Scripture he applies to it the destructive techniques of a new criticism. He has succeeded in fusing reverent language about Scripture and the wholesale destruction of Scriptural authority. Craig, in a reference to the rise of the neo-orthodox theologians (or neo-supernaturalists, as he prefers to call them), sums it up thus:

'they, as a class, still hold that modern science has rendered untenable the view of nature generally held before the rise of the empirico-scientific world view, and that literary and historical criticism has made it impossible to identify the words of the Bible with the Word of God.'[34]

Thus any assessment of Karl Barth's theology must struggle both with the fact that Barth does allow the Bible to become the Word of God in some sense, and that he also validates negative attitudes of critical scholars to the Bible. This makes it extremely difficult to evaluate any of Barth's teaching. On the one hand, any aspect of his theology can be authenticated by the subjective witness of the Bible to the 'Something Else' behind Scripture; on the other, however, the right is reserved to question the authority of the Bible since modern criticism has removed it from its high standing. We despair of finding any objective or authentic revelation which might measure our doctrines for us. Dr. Whitney is quite correct to state that '[Scripture's] objectivity is the presupposition of any use to be made of it by a believing soul;'[35] this indispensable criterion for the theological study of Scripture is, however, the one thing Barth will not allow.

The foregoing has served to give a broad background to the theological presuppositions of Karl Barth. These presuppositions are firmly rooted in existential and dialectical thought; and find their denouement in an ambiguous view of the Bible not merely as containing the Word of God, but in part bearing the potential so to become. It is on this canvas that we now attempt to trace Barth's hamartology, his doctrine of sin.

The Doctrine of Sin in the *Commentary on the Romans*

The first edition of Barth's *The Epistle to the Romans* [36] appeared in 1919, eight years after he had accepted his first pastorate. It was a product both of his disillusionment with the support given by German intellectuals (including theologians) to the war policy of the Kaiser, and of his own developing interest in the hermeneutical task of recovering the 'Spirit' of the Bible. The oft-quoted jibe that his work was like 'a bombshell on the playground of the theologians' reflects the heated interest which followed its publication. That heat also generated major revisions in successive editions of the work.

When the Commentary was translated into English (from the sixth edition, 1933), Barth prefaced the English version with a plea to his readers to judge his work in the light of circumstances which prevailed at the time. His words are these:

> 'When...I look back at the book, it seems to have been written by another man to meet a situation belonging to a past epoch.... Those who now read it...ought not to bind the Professor at Bonn too tightly to the Pastor of Safenwil.' [37]

In assessing the main points of Barth's theology in *The New Heresy*, Dr. Whitney professes it to be his aim to respect Barth's wish to be judged by the contents of the *Church Dogmatics* rather than by the Commentary. Nonetheless, as Barth himself points out in the preface just referred to, the Commentary was indeed the beginning of a development; we turn to it now for that reason.

It will be helpful, first of all, to listen to some of the definitions proposed by Barth for the meaning of sin. These come out at various points throughout the Commentary. For example, while discussing Romans 1:23, Barth defines sin as 'a revolt against God', in which 'we assist at the birth of the 'No-God', at the making of idols'. Again, on 3:23, with its statement of universal guilt and condemnation, Barth says that 'Genuine fellowship [between men] is grounded upon a negative: it is grounded upon what men lack. Precisely when we recognise that we are sinners do we perceive that we are brothers.' When discussing Paul's use of Psalm 32:1 in Romans 4:6-8, Barth says that 'The Psalmist desires to be silent... concerning the iniquity of his heart – that is, concerning the unavoidable idolatry of all human worship'. He goes on to spell this out even further in his comment on

6:2 that 'As an event, sin is that interchanging of God and man, that exalting of men to divinity or depressing of God to humanity.'

It will appear quite obvious that such definitions as Barth gives of sin throughout the Commentary at various points, accord with the Reformed doctrine. It is precisely the case that sin is idolatry, the exaltation of man above God, and the brazen denial by man of the authority and the sovereignty of the Creator. And, in a very original turn of phrase, Barth reminds us that to sin against the God is to worship the No-God we have set up in His place. It is, according to Barth, not enough merely to define sin in terms of pure negation, as if it consisted only in the denial of the rights of the Creator over the created order of which man is a part. There is also the idolatrous substitution which sin effects, by which God is de-throned and the kingdom is given to another.

It is probably in commenting on 5:12 that Barth gives his clearest and most far-reaching definition of the meaning of sin. It is worth taking a moment to review this important passage in the Commentary. Sin, says Barth, is 'that by which man as we know him is defined'. All our definitions regarding man are subject to the important point of the sinfulness of mankind. That is because, he continues, 'Sin is power – sovereign power.... Sin is the sovereign power in the world as we know it.' All our categories, therefore, for a proper understanding both of man and his environment, require us to realise the sin-fact which attaches to the world in which we dwell. It is this fact that makes sin in particular 'an especial relationship of men to God.... Sin is a robbing of God: a robbery which becomes apparent... in our drunken blurring of the distance which separates us from God...[it] is the disturbing of the relationship with God which is defined by death.' There is, according to Barth, a three-fold corollary of all of this. First, sin is 'an assumption of independence in which God is forgotten'. Man in an environment of sin, having disturbed the relationship that obtained between himself and God, has forgotten his God. Second, there is what Barth calls 'an invisible significance' which attaches to sin, defined biblically as 'unrighteousness and ungodliness'. And third, which will have important consequences for Barth's doctrine of reconciliation, 'restoration is outside our competence'.

These quotations are extremely important for our understanding of Barth's hamartology, and they undergird some of the points made above. Sin is predicated by Barth of three subjects – of man, of his

environment, and of his relationship with God. There is death in its
wake, and it has the immediate effect of blurring the distinctiveness
of God as over against the world He has created. Sin diminishes God.
And inasmuch as it does so, it also gives birth to the most violent
expressions of unrighteousness and ungodliness. Particularly does
Barth throw all hope of deliverance from sin's nature and power away
from man onto God Himself.

So far so good. With such definitions Reformed thought is well
pleased. But there are other passages in which Barth speaks of sin
and its effects, and with which we shall now attempt to engage, which
are more problematic, and appear to strike at the heart of biblical
thought.

Barth, first, appears to regard sin as fundamental to human nature,
and a constitutive element of it. In dealing with Paul's teaching in
Romans 5:13-14, Barth makes the point that we must regard sin as
the presupposition which underlies every human activity and
engagement; sin is, he says, 'the characteristic mark of human nature
as such... it is the Fall which occurred with the emergence of human
life.' Barth is here struggling with the difficult concepts of the sinful
nature on the one hand, and the sinful acts committed by the person
on the other. But he leaves himself open to the charge of an inherent
Gnosticism. That ancient philosophy was built upon the premise that
all matter is evil; in expressing his own view regarding the sinful
nature of man, Barth almost suggests that man's human nature per se
is characteristically sinful, and that when man's human life emerges
there occurs also the Fall. He puts it otherwise when commenting on
Romans 7:7 – 'When eternity confronts human finite existence it
renders that finite existence sinful.' Given, therefore, that man is
confronted with eternity at every turn, he cannot escape the
consequence that it is his own very humanity that makes him a sinner.
The fact that he is a man at all makes him at variance with God.

There are two main difficulties with this idea. The first is that it
destroys the integrity of Jesus Christ, who Himself also has a human
nature. If Barth is correct in maintaining that human nature is sinful
by definition, then he cannot provide for the exempting of our Lord
from the general condemnation of the race. 'Which of you accuses
me of sin?' asks our Lord, and the pages of the Gospel narrative are
replete with the universal affirmation of His sinlessness. Yet it cannot
be so if human nature itself is characteristically sinful. On Barth's

definition, it becomes impossible to assert that our Lord took 'bone of our bone and flesh of our flesh' and remained sinless when He did so. His human nature must have been flawed.

In an article entitled 'Did Christ have a Fallen Human Nature?',[38] Professor Donald Macleod deals with this aspect of Barth's teaching. On the one hand, he respects Barth's professed belief both in the Virgin Birth of the Lord, and in the sinlessness of Christ. On the other, he shows how Barth requires the predication of our Lord of a fallen humanity, in order to give respect and credence to the view that Christ is in all things like us. Macleod quotes Barth's own words:

'the nature which God assumed in Christ is identical with our nature as we see it in the light of the Fall.... God's Son not only assumed our nature but He entered the concrete form of our nature, under which we stand before God as men damned and lost.'[39]

Macleod makes two points which are worth noting briefly. First, it is wrong for Barth to argue for total discontinuity between the human nature of Christ and ours. The very Virgin Birth which Barth defends is a reminder to us that there simply is not continuity here. Secondly, Macleod argues that if it is to be meaningful at all to say that the nature assumed by Christ is the same as our own, as we see it in the light of the Fall, then we would also have to apply all the definitions of sin which we have already noted to the Lord Himself, for it is only there that we can have any adequate or working knowledge of what it is that constitutes such a nature. And as Macleod argues, this kind of fallenness in one professing to be a Saviour and yet who in actual fact was inclined both to hate God and his neighbour, would be distinctly disadvantageous.

Macleod's article is a study in Christology, and it has the merit of pinpointing the ambivalence between a high Christology, such as Barth is generally credited with,[40] and the assertion of fallenness as a predicate of Christ's human nature. The relevance for our study has been to show how Barth, in attempting to highlight the all-pervasive power of sin in the lives of men, actually now defines their human nature itself as sinful, with the consequence that he is forced to do the same with the human nature of Christ. Here his Christology is clearly influenced by his hamartology.

The second consequence of Barth's definition is that it makes any concept of restoration or conversion very difficult to reckon with.

That Barth is willing to allow some kind of individual conversion is clear from the Commentary (in fact, what he says while commenting on 3:22 is that 'Faith is conversion'); what is not so clear, however, is the meaning of conversion or restoration. Commenting on *Romans 1:16 – the Gospel*, Barth says that the Gospel 'announces the transformation of our creatureliness into freedom'. The essence of conversion, therefore, he maintains, is an existential and ontological change, in which, for the individual, creatureliness would be replaced by freedom. The logic of Barth's argument would require the axiom that it is impossible both to be a creature and to be free simultaneously. In order to be converted we would require to become something other than human. The narrowing of the concept of sin, making it the fundamental predicate of our humanness, is open to serious challenge.

A second difficulty regarding Barth's hamartology concerns his understanding of the Fall of man. It is clear that he wishes to speak of some kind of Fall; but he leaves his readers in no doubt as to his dismissal of the account of the Fall as we have it in the book of Genesis. Throughout the Commentary, Barth has prepared us for his rejection of the historical account of the Fall by his reference at many points to the necessity of 'making' history in the very writing of it. This comes out clearly in the section 4:17b-25, which Barth entitles 'Concerning the value of History'. 'History,' he declares, 'is a synthetic work of art.' He argues that there can be no history until it is written; and this means that all objectivity must be surrendered. All is summed up in the meaning of Collingwood's phrase that the historian must 'get inside the event'. The great stress for Barth is upon the contemporaneousness of historical happenings. The Fall, Christ etc. – all past events – must become contemporaneous with modern man. This can only be done when a historian discovers the 'non-historical' meaning of history. Barth concludes that 'After this fashion the Genesis narrative is composed'.

In his book *The New 'Myth'-ology*, Dr. Whitney has demonstrated how Barth's type of thinking has become a hallmark of modern approaches to the Word of God. Modern man, he argues, requires a modern Gospel (pp. 66ff.). The presuppositions of modern man's self-assessment demur at the accent and form of the Christian message. Dr. Whitney compares such reductionist re-formulations of the Christian Gospel to 'streamlined models... recently come off the theological assembly lines', show-pieces with little power of locomotion. Among these he includes Barth's treatment of the Fall of man. It has become axiomatic in the reduction of the Gospel that 'Adam and Eve were not flesh and blood actors in the great drama of the garden. They are simply symbolical figures dramatizing the origin of human sin.'[41]

This is certainly the background to the thinking of Barth. 'Adam has no existence on the plane of history' is his declaration, while commenting on Romans 5:12. That is not to say, of course, that the Genesis account of the Fall is of no relevance. What relevance it has it assumes in the course of re-writing the account itself. Here we are back with Kantian distinctions between phenomenon and noumenon, between events-as-they-appear-to-be and events-as-they-actually-are, between the rational and the irrational, between *historie* and *geschichte*. It is this that forces upon Dr. Whitney the conclusion that 'Barth chooses Kant rather than Calvin'.[42] While Reformed thought has been content to accept and preach the biblical account, Barthian explanations of the Fall of men have assumed a non-literal and non-historical genre for the material of the opening chapters of Genesis, and consequently have concluded with non-biblical accounts of the origin of evil.

It will not be a work of supererogation to rehearse the principal difficulties with such a scheme as Barth proposes. First, Barth's scheme discredits the historical reliability of the Word of God. It is difficult to see how one can question the existence of a literal and historical Adam without running into almost insuperable difficulties. Of these, the two most serious are: (a) the integrity of the Saviour, who uses the Old Testament frequently and who never questions its historical accuracy (but takes it rather as a 'given' of revelation), and (b) the argumentation of Paul in Romans 5:12ff., where the closely reasoned argument for counter-imputation hinges on a personal parallelism between the first, historical Adam, and Christ, the last Adam. It is difficult to see how the arguments adduced by Paul can be sustained by reference to a non-historical and mythical Adam.

Second, if there is no historical Fall, then the existence of evil in the world reduces ontology to absurdity and despair. Either God created an evil world, and an evil man in it, or else man is endowed with an evil nature. As we have already seen, Barth seems at times to favour the latter of these propositions, but either of them is an unfortunate reflection on a supposedly benevolent Creator. The universe was either good at the point of origin or it was not. The biblical doctrine declares that the world's goodness was compromised with the entrance of sin as a historical fact and reality. Barth, however, will not allow this.

It is worth pointing out that secondary and critical sources which deal with the theology of Barth find difficulty with his view of the origin of evil. Bloesch freely admits this in his reassessment of Karl Barth. He says: 'In Barthian theology the source of evil lies in the chaos, the nothingness which God does not will but which thereby is given a temporal or provisional reality.'[43] Bloesch has to admit that there is more of Plato in Barth's views of evil and of sin than there is of the Bible. The resultant belief is, logically, that evil is more powerful than God (since God is limited – there appears to be no way by which He can create being without creating evil, albeit temporarily).

Third, because he has relegated the primitive Fall of Man to the area of non-literal history, Barth is able to drive a wedge between man's *fallenness* and man's *lostness*. It is possible for him to say that 'Men, though fallen, are not in [God's] sight lost' (on 5:15-16). This is what Bloesch calls 'Barth's unwarranted optimism'.[44] Although Berkouwer is undoubtedly correct to highlight that one of the main themes in Barth is that of the 'triumph of grace', nevertheless Barth's view of grace differs radically from that of inspired Scripture. Whereas the Bible portrays grace as indispensable for man in his lost and ruined condition, man in Barth's theology is not quite this impoverished. He has fallen, in some sense, undoubtedly; but he is not lost. He is 'basically good, even though he time and again falls into sin'.[45] Or, to put it otherwise, in the words of Dr. Whitney, 'God is not free to condemn man; man is not free to reject God.'[46] Barth's reluctance to concede a 'limitless' Fall (that is, the classic Calvinistic doctrine of total depravity), is shown by Whitney to be a logical corollary of the humanistic principle of determinism. Sin, on this kind of schema becomes an 'ontological impossibility'.[47]

Neo-orthodoxy, therefore, is reductionist by nature. Barth's treatment of the Fall of man, categorising it as he does in that world where things exist supra-historically but by no means actually, reduces sin to the existential plane, and man's sinfulness to a stage in his development. The most serious consequence of such a reduction is that Barth thereby reduces man's accountability to God. How can man be held responsible for something he did not actually do, for something which he could never do as long as it remains an ontological impossibility?

So much for Barth's treatment of the Fall in the Commentary. One other principal area of difficulty which confronts us here is Barth's treatment of what God has done in order to deliver man from his fallen condition. This brings us to treat of Barth's doctrine of reconciliation, with which we shall be more immediately concerned when we turn to the *Church Dogmatics*. It will be pertinent, however, to make one or two passing comments on the same doctrine as it appears in the Commentary.

Barth acknowledges that God has done something about the ruined condition of man. In commenting upon such a work as the Epistle to the Romans he could hardly do otherwise, for its primary contention is that the Gospel 'is the power of God unto salvation to every one that believeth' (1:16). Barth has some searching and thought-provoking things to say on this whole matter in his comments on this verse. He says that the Gospel is 'pregnant with our complete conversion'. Or again, 'we have... in the power of God, a look-out, a door, a hope.... The prisoner becomes a watchman.'

These are memorable lines. However, as Barth continues his analysis of the meaning of the Gospel and its relevance for fallen man, it becomes clear that his understanding of God's work of saving scarcely corresponds with the classic Reformed position. For one thing, Barth is obsessed with his concept of God as the 'Wholly Other' – one of his basic postulates is that the Gospel 'speaks of God as He is: it is concerned with Him Himself and with Him only' (on 1:16). It is difficult to escape the conclusion that such a Gospel presents an insurmountable barrier to man, requiring a 'leap of faith' in order to reach to the depths of divine self-disclosure (which, as we have already seen, is the disclosure of an eternally hidden God). Again, it is evident that Barth moves along Arminian lines when he talks of the power of God unto salvation as a 'free choice' which presents itself to man. We have already noted that, for Barth, the depravity of man is not co-extensive with his total humanness. Fallen he may be, but depraved he is not. It is not impossible for man, therefore, to make choice of the power of God unto salvation. Barth writes: 'There is no man who ought not to believe or who cannot believe' (on 1: 16). This is precisely the point at issue – while every sinner may come to Christ, no sinner *can* do so, apart from the sovereign work of the Spirit of God. Neo-orthodoxy has actually sown the seeds of a neo-Arminianism.

There are other difficulties connected with Barth's treatment of Christ's saving work. The most basic of these is his view of the subjective nature of the atoning work of Christ. In commenting on 3:25-26 Barth has some important insights into Christ as our propitiation. He examines the typology of the mercy-seat, the *hilasterion* [LXX] which covered the Ark of the Covenant. He does say that the life of Jesus 'is the place fitted by God for propitiation and fraught with eternity', just as the covering of the Ark with a layer of gold was the place where God was propitiated in the Old Testament. However, inasmuch as the mercy-seat was a covering, Barth sees it as another element in the *Deus Absconditus* – the hidden God – of revelation, so that even the atoning activity of our Lord is both covered and displayed in Jesus, both hidden and revealed. This is consistent Barthianism, in that it accords with Barth's whole approach to revelation; but it strikes a discordant note when he states that the Messiahship of Christ 'is a matter for faith only'. Here Barth's Crisis-theology comes into its own as 'the reality of the mercy of God and of our salvation' become the venture of what he calls 'the hazard of faith'.

Dr. Whitney in *The New Infallibility* shows the affinity that exists between Barth and Kierkegaard; and he demonstrates the thesis that a common naturalism, deriving from the self-appointed autonomy of man, underlies them both. For Kierkegaard, truth is always in the subject; there is no such thing as objective truth. Barth, argues Whitney, does the same. For him, 'a true approach to theology must be existential',[48] and on this basis we approach the atoning work of Christ. Christ is the ideal subject, and around the Christ-event all is centered. So Whitney: 'The whole relation between God and man is still, in Barth's latest theology, that of the act of reconciliation of all men in the Christ-event.'[49] The Incarnation – the whole drama of salvation – thus becomes subjective, that is, without any objective meaning; or, to put it otherwise, it becomes actualized, that is, a continuum.

The whole basis for this approach on the part of Barth is that there can be no direct revelation of God in history. The revelation of salvation must be viewed in this light; the Incarnation itself cannot be anything other than an ongoing process, with which every succeeding race of the fallen sons of Adam must become contemporaneous. Man must participate in God, in the divine subject. As far as our salvation from the ruins of sin is concerned, this is virtually to hold to a man-made and man-centered salvation. Barth's subjectivism belies all his disclaimers to the contrary. Despite himself, and his manifold attack on subjectivizing tendencies in other religious and philosophical systems, Barth has made the salvation of the individual entirely dependent upon the will of man. This is glaringly inconsistent with biblical evangelicalism. Says Bloesch:

> 'We hold that our salvation is both objective and subjective; its ground and center are at the cross of Calvary, but its realization and fulfillment lie in bearing the cross in a life of faith.'[50]

Barth's view of faith thus differs radically from that of Scripture – whereas the Bible holds faith as the sinner's trusting to the once-for-all (objective) work of Christ, Barth holds it out to be an acknowledgement of the Christ-event, but not ipso facto 'an event of salvation'.[51] Barth, indeed, takes the Reformers to task for not beginning with this view of the 'Christ-event', and maintains that consequently they did not have a true criterion of sin. In fact, Barth has so subjectivised the doctrine of salvation that sin in any biblical sense ceases to be a problem. It is not difficult to move from the idea of a non-historical, non-objective atonement to the notion of the salvation of all men. Whitney is, therefore, exactly correct to view this reductionism as the substitution of a new Gospel for the old, in which the orthodox doctrine of salvation is surrendered, and all that Barth can offer is at best the salvation of man by man.[52]

Another difficulty that attaches to Barth's doctrine of the saving work of Christ is his notion of what the cross of Christ has actually accomplished. In commenting on Paul's phrase in 5:1, 'we have peace with God', Barth discusses the nature of such a peace as the apostle holds out. Where is it to be found?, he asks. And how is it recognised? Quite apart from the fact that Barth wishes to relegate this also to a subjective plane of existence ('Peace is declared by faith.... By faith... their waiting is a waiting upon God alone; and this is to be at peace with him'), Barth further declares that 'In it no union of God and man is consummated, no dissolution of the line of death, no appropriation of the Fulness of God, or of His Salvation and final Redemption. The bitter conflict between flesh and spirit remains as intense as before; man remains man and God is still God.'

It is difficult to see how, on this line of reasoning, the cross of Christ has done any saving work at all. Barth wishes to maintain the wholly otherness of God even on the other side of the cross, as it were, so that the saving work of Christ has actually done very little, if anything, to redeem man from his fallen condition. It is categorically stated that whatever salvation is wrought in Christ, there is effected thereby no union of God and man, and no dissolution of the line of death. Sin remains what it was, unvanquished and unconquered. Consistent Barthianism requires belief in a salvation that is in fact no salvation at all. Dr. Whitney is, therefore, exactly correct when he maintains that the Christ of Karl Barth is in fact the idealisation of man,[53] which leads to a Gospel which is thoroughly reductionist and totally humanistic.

Barth also maintains that it is an obscuring of the message of the death of Christ to maintain a belief in the so-called *munus triplex*, the doctrine of Christ as Prophet, Priest and King. In commenting on 5:6 he states quite categorically that 'The doctrine of the munus triplex obscures and weakens the New Testament concentration upon the death of Christ'. Then, after listing some aspects of the life and ministry of the Lord, Barth concludes: 'none of these things exists in their own right. Everything shines in the light of His death, and is illuminated by it.' It must be conceded that there is a sense in which this is true; the cardinal doctrine of the Gospel is the death of Jesus Christ on the cross, and the whole sum and substance of the Gospel is contained in the theology of that death. But it is simply not possible to have any understanding of the significance of the atoning work of Christ without the facts that are stated about Him as actor, as well as His death as action, in the Word of God; the cross is of prophetic, sacerdotal and kingly significance, and without the *munus triplex*, questions relating both to the necessity and to the nature of the atonement become obscure. The offices of Christ are necessary to our understanding of the death which He died.

Unless, that is, one is consistently following through Barth's scheme of thought, insisting as it does upon the subjective nature of the atonement. On this view of things, it matters little what we say about Christ, or, indeed, what is believed concerning Him. In fact, given that objectivity may legitimately be sacrificed, we hardly need a cross at all. All that is required for the mystical salvation offered by Barth is a concentration on the death of Christ. Here, Barth seems to be at his most obscure, as he talks of the 'invisible atonement' which occurred in Christ. Of all of Barth's subjectivising tendencies, to talk of an invisible atonement must be the nadir. At this point, sinful man is offered only a phantom salvation; the drowning man is extended an invisible lifebelt.

We have already mentioned one of the definitions of sin offered by Barth in his Commentary in commenting on 6:2, where sin was defined as an interchanging of God and man, by which man is exalted and God humbled. While commenting on the same verse, Barth goes on to highlight the antithesis which exists in his thinking between sin and grace. These, he says, are incommensurable. Using an intriguing mathematical analogy, Barth says that sin and grace belong to different spaces, with no connection, no relationship between them: 'Sin is related to grace as possibility to impossibility.... He that has received grace neither knows nor wills sin.' We have already noted several difficulties with Barth's soteriology, especially in connection with the application of salvation, where Barth hardly seems to offer any positive comment on the new nature belonging to the Christian. Now, however, he wishes to assert the supremacy of grace to such an extent that he goes so far as to say of the man who has received the grace of God – 'He is not a sinner'.

It is difficult not to find some kind of inherent perfectionism in this kind of language. While Barth is undoubtedly correct to maintain the qualitative distinction between sin and grace, it is simply not true that they do not co-exist. The biblical teaching is quite clear: although the believer is a new creation in Christ, there is still conflict, still unbelief, still sin. But Barth makes it clear that his concern is not so much with biblical as with existential presuppositions. In the same passage he talks of grace as a 'superior existence', which questions the validity of our present existence and renders it non-existent. Grace is also defined as the 'invisible power of our eternal future existence'. Existence is the main theme of Barth's whole concept of the sin/grace dichotomy. Basic to his whole argumentation and reasoning are the existential presuppositions that underlie Neo-Orthodox thinking.

And axiomatic here again is the non-historical nature of these events which constitute the drama of salvation. It is not surprising that when he predicates invisibility of the atonement, or empties the work of Christ from the doctrines concerned with the Person of the Saviour, Barth should insist upon the non-historical nature of the saving work of Christ. In his section on 'The power of the Resurrection', commenting on Romans 6:8-11, Barth maintains that to insist on historical literalism is a threat to the very Gospel itself – 'if the Resurrection, be brought within the context of history, it must share in its obscurity and error and essential questionableness'. Barth accuses those of us who would insist on the essential historicity and factual objectivity of the accomplishment of redemption of 'seeking the living among the dead' and asks – 'Why do ye set the truth of God on the plane and in the space where historical factors...rise and fall, ebb and flow, are great and are little?'

Carl Henry sums the matter up thus:

> 'This bifurcation of divine revelation into a deed-revelation in history and a meaning-revelation in experience has propelled the problem of history to new prominence.'[54]

This is precisely the problem in the Neo-Orthodox schema – Barth wishes to make sense of the fact of Calvary, without placing any emphasis at all on Calvary as a fact. Its import rests not in its being a historical event, but an event that elicits the concentration of faith and brings salvation in through the back door of pure, unmitigated subjectivism. Or, to put it otherwise:

> 'Nothing that Barth says about sin...carries any weight whatever; it is mere words "full of sound and fury signifying nothing", because he represents it as an event which takes place not on earth, in history, but in Geschichte, in supra- or pre-history, and only then in symbolic personage.'[55]

This is true both of Barth's treatment of the Fall and of the salvation wrought in Christ. Whitney is not far wrong to label it 'pseudo-reconciliation for pseudo-sin'.[56]

These, then, are the salient themes of Barth's Commentary on Romans which affect our study of his doctrine of sin. They are light years away from the teaching of the Epistle itself, and stand as an indictment of a man reputed to be evangelical,[57] but in fact the pioneer theologian of a new way of thinking and believing. The *Church Dogmatics* may be representative of more mature reflection, yet the basic anti-orthodox flaws in Barth's hamartology which come to light in the Commentary are to be seen there also. It is to these that we now turn.

The Doctrine of Sin in the *CHURCH DOGMATICS*

Barth's magnum opus is his massive *Church Dogmatics*, a series which spans the years 1932-1967. There, the mature Barth has deposited the fruits of a lifetime's study both in the pastoral ministry and in the academic world. By any measure, these volumes represent a staggering amount of work and thought. Barth has interwoven dogmatics with exegesis and with a critique of historical theology that is so penetrating in its analysis and so detailed in its content that any adequate assessment of the work would itself require massive research and evaluation such as is outwith our scope and our space here. Some very useful work has already been done, notably by Van Til, Bromiley and Berkouwer, reference to whom will be made in this section of our study.

Much critical material that has focused on the Dogmatics has asked whether there is any kind of unifying method or approach used by Barth in his work. Van Til, in Bromiley's analysis, finds 'an ultimate Neo-Protestant presupposition'[58] in Barth's thought, while Berkouwer, in what Bromiley calls 'a more discerning study',[59] sees the 'overruling concept' of Barth 'in the idea of triumphant grace'.[60] Barth himself reacted unfavourably to both of these suggestions. In Van Til he detected, whether rightly or wrongly, a personal malice.[61] Berkouwer's analysis he found too abstract.[62] If there is any one theme dominating the Dogmatics it is Barth's unashamed Christomonism. 'The heart of the enterprise, both methodologically and substantively, is Christology.'[63] Every aspect of Barth's study in the Dogmatics, is related, in one way or another, to the Person and Work of Christ, to the Christ-Event. That is not to aver either the accuracy or the orthodoxy of Barth's Christology; it is simply to affirm what is the consensus of most of Barth's critics, namely that the Christ-Event has become the standard by which every other doctrine is measured, and from which every other doctrine is deduced.[64]

Along with the emphasis on the Christ-Event, we must also bear in mind the other methodological presuppositions which undergird the Dogmatics. For these, Reformed scholarship is indebted to Van Til's penetrating analysis of the Kantianism and the dialectic methodology apparent in Barth. Dr. Whitney, in Chapter IV of *The New Heresy*, in which he draws heavily on Van Til's studies, has also given an excellent discussion of these fundamental aspects of the theology of Barth. The thesis postulated by Van Til and underlined by Dr. Whitney is that 'Barth, by adopting Kant's dualism... adopted the dialectical or immanentistic view of reality'.[65] God remains Wholly Other, relegated to the sphere of reality where nothing is rational or reasonable, and everything is ultimately forever Unknown. In a memorable line, Dr. Whitney suggests that Barth 'sees Calvin's theology through the spectacles of Kant's religious dualism',[66] and tries, unsuccesfully, to amalgamate Reformed orthodoxy with Kantian dialectic. The result, according to Van Til and Whitney, is a natural theology such as Barth himself will not allow.

It is important to bear these two principles in mind in our study of the Dogmatics. On the one hand, it cannot be denied that Barth does seek to order his studies around the centrality of some kind of Christology. On the other hand, Barth steers a course through theology that is undergirded by Kantian dualism. Or to put it otherwise, the fundamental tenets of a humanistic and immanentistic philosophy undergird the christology which itself undergirds the Dogmatics. The result, for all of Barth's avowed return to Scriptural parameters, is that the Dogmatics is permeated with an approach to theology 'from below', rising out of man himself. This, as Dr. Whitney has cogently argued, is the 'new heresy' of theological modernism.

In this study of Barth's treatment of the biblical doctrine of sin, we shall deal specifically, though not exclusively, with Volume IV of the Dogmatics, entitled *The Doctrine of Reconciliation*. It is in the context of dealing with the reconciling aspect of the Christ-Event that Barth says most of what he has to say about sin. Further, most of what will be said concerning his hamartology will centre around sections 60-70 of Volume IV.

Barth's hamartology represents a consistent application of his Christological hermeneutic. As he comes to deal with the theology of sin, he makes it clear that his understanding of what sin is and what it has done is based upon what he discovers Christ to have been and to have done. Further, Barth's account of the various nuances and aspects of the sin question turns on the different aspects of the Christ-Event which appear to him most significant. These two facts undergird all that Barth says of sin in the Dogmatics; sin can be known only in relation to Christ, and its various differing aspects can be appreciated only in the differing concepts held forth in the Bible regarding the Person and Work of Christ.

It is important here to notice the basic structure of Barth's treatment of the doctrine of reconciliation. The reconciler is Emmanuel; Bromiley sees this as the most fundamental aspect of the whole doctrine in the Dogmatics. He writes: 'Reduced to its most simple form, reconciliation means Emmanuel, God with us.'[67] These last three words of the quotation form the basic nucleus around which Barth's doctrines are grouped, representing the reconciling God, reconciled man, and Jesus Christ, 'with' us, the reconciler. Barth goes on to maintain a three-fold form of this doctrine, following Calvin's doctrine of the munus triplex, despite his criticisms of the doctrine in the Commentary on Romans. Now he maintains that we look at the Reconciler, Jesus Christ, who is first Priest, or 'the Lord as Servant' (IV.14); second, he is King, or 'the Servant as Lord' (IV.15); and third He is Prophet, or 'the True Witness' (IV.16). It is in the light of this particular kind of Christology that Barth develops his hamartology.

It is consequently important to grasp the principle that for Barth the hermeneutical approach is not Christology per se, but a particular type of christology, which differs at many various points from classic Reformed thought. For example, Barth will not allow the Reformed doctrine of the two states of Christ, humiliation and exaltation, which follow one another in chronological sequence in the experience of our Lord. According to the Pauline Christology of Phillipians 2: 5ff, Jesus Christ takes the form of servant, and demonstrates his obedience unto death. Consequent upon His obedience God highly exalts Him. But Barth will not have this. In *The New Heresy*, Dr. Whitney argues that Barth rejects the customary arrangement of the two states of Christ on the argument that they contain 'a 'self-contained Christology',' which Barth rejects in his insistence on actualising the Incarnation, re-interpreting its historical factuality 'in a dynamic or activistic sense', converting it into 'an on-going process'.[68] Barth thus approaches the doctrine of salvation and, consequently the doctrine of sin, from the point of view of a particular Christological principle which results in a Christology from below, rather than one from above.

So insistent is Barth on this kind of approach that he firmly censures the Reformers for not remembering it in their own treatment of the sin question. His indictment of them, which comes right at the beginning of IV/1 section 60, is that their treatment of sin was too isolated, too divorced from the correct channels of interpretation. This Barth was anxious to avoid. His biographer puts it thus:

'...he did not want to present an isolated doctrine of sin, and certainly not
one which was presupposed by the doctrine of reconciliation. It was to be
directly incorporated into the doctrine of reconciliation and subordinated
to it...'[69]

Indeed, we can go further and affirm that even this is not the bottom
line. The doctrine of reconciliation itself was to be subordinated to
Christology as the underlying doctrine of the Dogmatics..

This Christological hermeneutic employed by Barth in his
treatment of sin is based upon the premise that the knowledge of sin
is enclosed within the knowledge of the One true God. The very fact
of man's sinnership closes to his mind's eye the knowledge of it.
'Access to the knowledge that he is a sinner is lacking to man because
he is a sinner.'[70] Indeed, he goes on, 'it is irrelevant and superfluous
to seek for a normative concept by which to measure sin.... It is indeed
a form of sin.'[71] The whole point is that sin has been revealed where
the knowledge of God is alone revealed – in the Christ-Event: 'the
man of sin and his existence and nature... are all set before us in Jesus
Christ.'[72] According to Barth, there are four points which follow from
this. First, 'The existence of Jesus Christ is the place where we have
to do with sin in its absolutely pure and developed and unequivocal
form;'[73] second, the revealer is Judge – Christ not only demonstrates
what sin is, but condemns it as He does so (this is Barth's theology of
crisis); third, in Christ, sin is revealed 'as the truth of all human being
and activity;'[74] and fourthly, and definitively, 'The knowledge of Jesus
Christ is finally the knowledge of the significance and the extent of
sin.'[75] Klooster sums all of this up in a simple phrase: 'In the light of
Jesus Christ... Barth draws conclusions as to the nature of sin.'[76]

Is this a valid approach? It certainly appears to be a laudable one,
as Barth struggles to maintain a method that is firmly grounded in
biblical exegesis. The difficulty is that, even although he begins here,
Barth is often led from his starting-point into very unscriptural waters.
Dr. Whitney suggests that the unscriptural nature of Barth's
Christological principle can be resolved into the thesis that 'Here a
philosophical principle takes precedence over the Word of God'[77] –
the principle of Kantian dialectic, which allows Barth to maintain
some scriptural truths and reject others. Hence Dr. Whitney's
conclusion, after 200 pages' reflection on the theology of Karl Barth:
'However honestly, however earnestly Barth seeks to present Christ,
it is not the Christ of Scripture he presents.'[78] It is Barth's insistence

that revelation is historically bound to the Christ-Event that necessitates his Christomonistic approach to the doctrine of sin.

The logical and practical upshot of all of this is that sin is seen only as a negation of all that Christ is and does. The word 'only' is important as a limiting concept; Barth cannot allow, for example, that the law of God is a measure of the nature and power of sin. Despite the insistence of Paul that 'by the law is the knowledge of sin' (Rom. 3:20), Barth will not allow the law such a function. Such power belongs to Christ alone. The only adequate understanding we can have of sin is to look at the life and work of Jesus Christ, the negation of which is the truth about sin. Klooster spells this out for us: 'Sin,' in Barth's thinking, 'involves man's doing the opposite of what Jesus Christ did...sin involves the parallel aspects of pride, sloth and falsehood, corresponding inversely to what Christ did.'[79]

We have already discussed some of the implications of Barth's doctrine of sin for the human nature of the Lord, and we saw how Barth ascribes to the Saviour a fallen human nature. However, he is insistent on the sinlessness of Jesus Christ: 'Christ was not a sinful man. He did nothing that Adam did.'[80] And this is precisely where we find the meaning of the revelation of sin in the Christ-Event. What Adam did, we do. What Adam did, Christ does not do. Christ does not do what we do. He does not sin. What he does not do is the revelation of sin.

It is interesting that Paul Van Buren, in his *The Secular Meaning of the Gospel* (first published 1963), followed exactly this line. Van Buren was an ardent admirer and pupil of Karl Barth. His work received critical acclaim from both liberals and evangelicals in the English-speaking world. Van Buren was attempting to give, as the title of his book suggested, an interpretation of the Gospel to secular, modern man, and in doing so was responsible for disseminating much of his famous teacher's doctrines. When he comes to deal with the doctrine of sin there are clear traces of Barthian influence, especially in his methodological approach. Says Van Buren:

'In the New Testament, man is seen in the light of the free man, Jesus of Nazareth, and compared to him, men are not free; they are bound by fear and anxiety, mistrust and self-concern. The word used to describe this condition, when measured by this standard, is "sin".'[81]

Van Buren goes on to demonstrate that this position does not accord with the traditional Christian doctrine; he continues:

'The logical structure of this teaching does not depend on the story of the "Fall", or even on a theory of "inherited guilt". The various traditional forms of the doctrine of "original sin" are not empirical observations about man; they are comparative statements of man's condition, measured by the historical standard of Jesus of Nazareth.'[82]

By this kind of reasoning, Barth might justifiably be charged with building his doctrine of sin on silence. If sin is what Christ does not do, and if there is no revelation of it apart from Jesus Christ, how can we ever hope to recover the true meaning of sin? How could we ever be dogmatic? The Christomonistic argument in fact becomes an argument from silence. It is all very well to say that the knowledge of Christ yields the knowledge of sin; but to maintain a jealously guarded conception of the sinlessness of Christ (which Van Buren also does, but which he is reluctant to concede except insofar as the writers of the Gospel narratives may have written the sinlessness of Christ into the Gospel account 'after Easter'[83]) means that all true and objective revelation as to the nature and power of sin is gone.

It is for this reason that Barth has to resort to another course. There is, he maintains, a true revelation of sin in the Person and work of Christ, because sin is the absolute negative of all that God does in Christ. Here we are back with Barth's famous usage of the 'Yes' of God confronting the 'No' of men. Every action on the part of Christ corresponds to God's 'Yes', of which its complete negation is the sin of man. Is Christ a servant? Then sin is pride. Is Christ the exalted Lord? Then sin is sloth and misery. Is Christ the true witness? Then sin is falsehood.[84] This is nothing more than revelation by counter-implication; Barth is constantly reading into a negative. All that he has to say about sin is characterised by the fact that he is reading his ideas into the perfection of Jesus Christ, and reversing them in order to recover a picture of what sin is. It is this type of negative reasoning that invalidates his approach to the doctrine of sin from the very start.

Barth, therefore, views sin in three general aspects. In considering the doctrine of Jesus Christ, the Lord as Servant, he sees sin, first of all, as pride. 'Sin,' he says, 'in its unity and totality is always pride.'[85] It is essentially pride that leads to, and issues in, disobedience to God. Now this has already become an unworkable concept, because Barth has denied the law a revelatory function. Dr. Whitney correctly charges Barth with one-sidedness, since for Barth grace alone is what reveals the nature of sin:

'He does not stress law – and it is law which awakens in man's heart that sense of guilt in the sight of God, which constitutes the need for satisfaction, if reconciliation is to be provided.'[86]

Yet even Barth himself has to resort to legal presuppositions; how can sin be disobedience in the light of grace only? There can be no disobedience apart from some kind of objective standard. Barth wishes to remove the objectivity of the standard God has given, while wishing at the same time to maintain the possibility of disobedience to it.

The way in which Barth does this is to argue from the servanthood of Jesus Christ. Of Christ it is true that 'He became a subject',[87] while man wants to rule 'On the little stool which he thinks is a throne'.[88] In order to assess the pride of man, it is necessary, Barth argues, to watch Christ at the nadir of His sufferings, where, when He cries out 'My God, My God, why hast Thou forsaken me?', He is utterly helpless. This stands in marked contrast to the situation of sinful man, because 'The history of every man is the history of his great and fantastic attempt to help himself;'[89] or to put it otherwise, 'to be without grace is to be without help.'[90] Man desires to be his own helper.

This, continues Barth, is the essence of the Fall of man. We have already seen in the Commentary that Barth dismisses the notion of a literal, historical Fall; this position is adopted again in the Dogmatics. Barth is specific on this point. History, he argues, in IV/1 section 60.3, is Adamic history, in which 'the little scene in the garden of Eden' is being constantly re-enacted: 'There never was a golden age', he declares in the same section of the work. 'There is no point in looking back to one. The first man was immediately the first sinner.' Adam, he goes on to maintain, was 'in a trivial form what we all are, a man of sin'. Moreover, Barth wishes to argue that this is a universal condition which obtains of all men everywhere. In this same section of the Dogmatics he wishes to counteract the claim of Roman Catholic theologians that man has a *donum superadditum*, a relic of goodness left over from the Fall, from which he has not been alienated by sin. Says Barth: 'We certainly cannot speak of any relic or core of goodness which persists in man in spite of his sin.... There is no territory which has been spared and where he does not sin.... At every point man is in the wrong and in arrears in relation to God.'[91]

It would appear that at this point Barth seems to be sounding forth the biblical note of the universalism of sin, but his thesis dies the death of the qualification to which he subjects it. He continues: 'But in another sense he is never apart, for in all these activities he continually stands and thinks and speaks and acts in the presence of God.... There is no sphere, however narrow and insignificant, no time however short, when the grace of God is not over him.'[92] Barth goes on to demonstrate what this means in practical terms. Man, he declares, 'has not forfeited his good nature and its dispositions and capacities by reason of his corruption.'[93] Man is still able to carry out worthwhile projects of artistic grandeur, and also of a charitable nature. But Barth runs into a difficulty; while on the one hand he wishes to maintain the notion of some kind of original sin which affects every man in every situation, he is in danger on the other hand of giving too much credit to sinful man and his abilities. While it is true that God by His grace does enable man to perform good works quite apart from any soteriological experience, nevertheless we must do justice to the biblical presentation which reminds us first that the very best a man can do is in bondage to the enthralment of sin; and second, that the goodness of God, according to Paul's reasoning in Romans 2:4, has as its design the repentance of the sinner.

The answer to man's sin is the pardon of God, as that is revealed particularly in the work of justification, in which God passes the sin of man by.[94] This, says Barth, is an 'act of divine power and defiance',[95] and issues in man learning true humility as the answer to his pride. It is singularly noteworthy at this point to realise that for Barth justification does not require the death of Jesus Christ. For all his alleged Christocentricism, mention of the work of Christ as the grounds of the justification of man is absent here. God requires merely to defy man. This is the real weakness of Barth's whole presentation; his discusion of sin as pride, which allows him to include in his presentation a form of goodness possessed by man in his sin-condition, also allows him to talk of a pardon which involves God merely in an act of overlooking sin. These are the foundations and the basis of Barth's universalism, and constitute what Whitney calls 'pseudo-reconciliation for pseudo-sin'.[96] It is enough for man to be humble.

The discussion of sin as pride takes up the larger part of Barth's treatment of the meaning and definition of sin. But he goes on to define sin, secondly, as sloth. Again, the ground for this definition is Christological; in the light of the Lordship of Jesus Christ the Servant, sin is seen as sloth. The exaltation of Jesus Christ, proclaimed through the Easter message of resurrection, is the exaltation of a king. Inasmuch as the One who is exalted was a servant, and in His servanthood was a real man, the exaltation of Christ shows the meaning of the true goal of manhood, to live in the freedom that Christ enjoys in His exalted glory. This is the basic reasoning behind Barth's definition,[97] and in the light of it, man's life is seen in terms of a shameful bondage from which man requires to be liberated by sanctification. Sin is thus seen as disobedience, of doing what God does not will. The cardinal form of sin is the rejection of the Saviour; Barth puts it thus: 'Sin in the form of sloth crystallises in the rejection of the man Jesus.'[98]

G.W. Bromiley sums up what Barth means when he defines sin as sloth. There is a total shaming on the part of man; man is a shameful creature in the presence of God. This is something that man cannot escape even if he does nothing that we would generally regard as extraordinarily bad; it means that we cannot detach ourselves from our sin as if it was some accident of nature, and that we cannot plead its inevitability. Man is responsible for his own sin. It becomes then both futile and foolish to refuse the gift of God, and it is apparent that man has been plummeted into an existence of factual and useless inactivity and inhumanity, dissipation and anxiety.[99] Or, as Berkouwer puts it: 'The sinful man persists in walking with his eyes closed, even in the light of full day.'[100] Against all this, the exalted and risen Lord sanctifies humanity, and, by integration into the community of the Church, frees man to obedience, worship and love.

Finally, Barth defines sin as falsehood. This is in contrast to Jesus Christ, who is the true witness. He gives light and He gives truth. Sin becomes 'untruth', and is characterised by seeking to evade the truth as it is identified with Jesus, as it is proclaimed in the word of the cross, and as it issues in the offer and extension of pardon to man. 'The falsehood of man results in his condemnation, his nailing to the lie.'[101] Or, to put it otherwise, 'In falsehood man takes his position against the method of redemption.'[102] The antidote to this kind of sin is not merely the acceptance of the truth, but the new life of bearing witness to the truth, in the community of the Church, of fulfilling one's vocation, and of living in hope. It is the witness to this hope that issues in the denouement of the *Church Dogmatics*, as Barth comes to deal finally with some aspects of eschatology which form the basis of the hope discovered by and witnessed to by the Church.

It remains now to analyse Barth's definition of sin as pride, sloth and falsehood. Do his definitions do justice to the biblical doctrine of sin? Are his categories adequate to that end? This is the question posed by Berkouwer in the course of his analysis of the meaning of sin. He cites Vogel, who uses other terms in his definition of sin, and concludes that both Barth and Vogel 'desire to honor the concreteness and seriousness of sin and to do so in the light that is only available in Jesus Christ'.[103] However, Berkouwer issues the caveat that perhaps in our definitions we ought not to steer clear of biblical usage. Berkouwer warns of the danger of obscuring the depths of sin – the 'manifoldness' of sin – by adhering too rigidly to any one set of propositions or definitions. Within the boundaries, therefore, of his Christological approach, Berkouwer thinks Barth has indeed highlighted the serious nature of man's sin; but he does appear to be less than happy about Barth's reluctance to go beyond his own definitions. At the same time it is stated that 'Barth does not regard these terms as fully exhaustive'.[104]

Others, however, have been more scathing in their criticism. Klooster, for example, charges Barth in the following terms: 'Although Barth does speak of the seriousness of man's sin and also recognizes the universality of sin, he has not really acknowledged the true nature of sin and its actual entrance into the world...'[105] He continues: '[Barth] does not really regard sin seriously enough. He does not view sin basically as guilt in the sight of God which demands satisfaction if reconciliation is to be provided. And because sin is not recognised in its basic relation to God's law, the whole direction of reconciliation is manward.'[106] Klooster's main contention is that Barth falls short at the most important point of defining what sin actually is. He can offer no concrete or objective standard by which sin may be measured, for he has bound himself to his Christological presuppositions to the extent that his definitions require his particular Christology at all points. We have already pointed out the methodological weakness in this subjectivising approach. Barth has made sin to hang on what he conceives Christ not to have been – a man of pride, sloth or falsehood. This is only to take the road into subjectivism.

The result is that Barth makes an almost wholesale dismissal of the biblical data. It is singularly interesting that the Bible never employs Barth's methodology. The Word of God bears out the testimony of the Shorter Catechism, that 'Sin is any want of conformity unto, or transgression of the law of God'.[107] Sin requires God-given law, and can only be defined within the parameters of such revelation.

Barth cuts himself off from such objectivity, and in doing so, cannot make an adequate assessment of the nature of sin.

Evaluation

In order to conclude this chapter on Barth's treatment of sin, it will be useful, by way of summary, to highlight the main areas of contention, and to make some kind of evaluation of Barth's doctrine.

In his chapter on Karl Barth in *Creative Minds in Contemporary Theology*, Bromiley emphasizes the difficulties attached to making any kind of fair assessment of Barth's theology. His caveats are (a) that the Dogmatics covers so wide a field that evaluation runs the risk of becoming 'facile and misleading generalization'; (b) that Barth's unique approach makes evaluation difficult (since there is little to compare him with); and (c) that Barth is seeking to attempt a modern evaluation and presentation of the Gospel.[108] These caveats must be borne in mind if an objective assessment is to be made. It seems to me, however, that the following points have been demonstrated in our study of Barth's doctrine of sin.

First, Barth's doctrine of sin is *methodologically suspect*. We have examined his treatment of the doctrine both in his major exegetical work and in his magnum opus. It is clear that in both of these areas – in the disciplines of exegesis and systematic theology – Barth has become the slave of his own presuppositions. His treatment of the Fall of man and of Adam demonstrated that he has imbibed the higher critical methods of discarding as mythical and irrelevant the historical passages of the Bible. This means that large portions of biblical testimony as to the nature and seriousness of sin may be discarded. John Murray levels this criticism against Barth in a review of Barth's *Christ and Adam*.[109] Barth repeatedly denies the historicity of Adam (as we have seen him do also in the Commentary), and declares that Adam's sin is only typically ours. Murray asserts that 'if we adopt this construction of Romans 5:12-19 we must abandon exegesis'.[110] Similarly, in the Dogmatics we have seen that Barth employs a Christological model which governs his whole thinking. Sin is seen in the light of his particular Christology. This method, as we have observed, both limits and obscures the true nature of sin and sinfulness.

Second, Barth's hamartology is *pure subjectivism*. It cannot be otherwise when Scripture is treated as Barth treats it. There are no standards, no measures of orthodoxy left, and theology becomes a species of anthropology. This is what it has become in Barth. Whitney declares:

> '[Barth] is merciless in his treatment of Subjectivism in theological systems.... Yet Subjectivism is the very thing Reformed thinkers level as a charge against his own theology. How could it be otherwise when he adopts human experience instead of Divine declaration as his criterion of Scripture interpretation?'[111]

Third, Barth's doctrine of sin opens the way for an *unashamed universalism*. Bromiley, in his evaluation, concedes this point.[112] So also does A.E. McGrath, in a study on Justification; although he allows that 'Barth insists on man's utter inability to justify himself,'[113] he has to concede that in Barth's thinking 'Man cannot accept or reject whatever God has elected for him.... Whether all men know it or not, they are saved.'[114] Bromiley does try to excuse Barth by reminding us that he is not an express universalist, but this is not adequate. Barth's categories of expression cannot lead in any other direction. We have seen and demonstrated that his doctrine of sin does not leave man impoverished; it may lead him into undesirable modes of living and self-expression, but man in Barth's presentation is essentially just before God. He may be sinful, but he is not lost. It is simply not adequate for Barth to lessen the impact of sin in this way; nor is it satisfactory for Bromiley to regard this major defect merely as a shadow on an otherwise excellent doctrine of reconciliation.

Finally, Barth's attempts to present a doctrine of sin for the modern world has resulted in wholesale *re-orientation of the doctrines of the Word of God*. This has meant a lessening of the seriousness of sin; sin has become a philosophical postulate and has ceased to be the violation of divine law. This has been the most serious legacy of Barthianism to subsequent theological reflection: instead of using the world's language to convince men that sin is as serious as ever it was, Barth has opened the way for a reductionist hamartology. 'Reprobation is no more than an idle threat hanging over the sinner's head. The reprobate are elect in Christ. Nothing anyone does will ultimately make any difference to his final end.'[115] If this is true, and we believe that our study of Barth's treatment of sin has demonstrated that this proposition is a valid summary of Barth's position, then it is at variance with the clear teachings of the Word of God. It is at this point that Neo-Orthodoxy shows itself for what it is.

NOTES

1. Webster, J., 'Karl Barth' in *New Dictionary of Theology*, p. 76.

2. Schrotenboer, P.G., 'Review of Karl Barth: Church Dogmatics Volume 1 – The Doctrine of the Word of God' in *Westminster Theological Journal* 19.2 (May 1957) p. 185.

3. Whitney, H.J., *The New Heresy* (hereafter T.N.H.), p. 11.

4. Webster, J., 'The Legacy of Barth and Bultmann', in *Evangel* 1.1 (Jan 1983), p. 11.

5. Bloesch, D.G., *The Evangelical Renaissance*, London, 1974, p. 80.

6. Bloesch, op. cit., pp. 80-81.

7. Quoted in Whitney, H.J., *The New Infallibility* (hereafter T.N.I.), p. 49.

8. Schaeffer, F., *The Church before the Watching World*, London, 1972, p. 20.

9. Cook, E.D., 'Existentialism', in *New Dictionary of Theology*, p. 243.

10. Whitney, T.N.I. p. 147.

11. Barth, K., *The Epistle to the Romans*, 6th ed., Oxford, 1968, p. 252.

12. Schaeffer, op. cit., p. 33 (quoting Nygreen).

13. Whitney, T.N.I., p. 183.

14. Henry, C., *Frontiers in Modern Theology*, 1968, p. 10, f/note 1.

15. Of this book Prof. Nigel Lee said that along with Dr. Whitney's *The New 'Myth'ology* it represented one of the best books published in America in the 1960s in contemporary theology.

16. Henry, op. cit., p. 40. This is the conclusion to which Dr. Whitney also is led in his comparison of Barth and Bultmann in *The New Infallibility*. On p. 222 he declares that ' 'The non-objectivity of divine revelation' constitutes the core round which the dialectical and existential theologians of our time, despite their differing emphases, crystallize their theologies.'

17. Barth, op. cit., p. 222.

18. Whitney, T.N.I., p. 152.

19. Comm. on Romans 9:1, ad.loc.

20. Comm. on Romans 3:22, ad.loc.

21. cf. also Whitney's Introduction to Karl Barth in T.N.H., p. 14, where he quotes it as Barth's intention 'to make the incomprehensible way of God to man comprehensible as the incomprehensible'; and also the ensuing discussion which demonstrates the kinship between this and Tillich.

22. Whitney T.N.I., p. 155.

23. Barth on Romans 4:23.

24. Henry, op. cit., p. 49.

25. Whitney T.N.I., p. 151.

26. Craig, S.G., *Christianity Rightly So Called*, 1947, p. 113.

27. Whitney, T.N.H., Introduction, pp. 14ff.

28. Barth, *God Here and Now*, quoted in Bloesch, op. cit., p. 82.

29. Henry, op. cit., p. 66, f/note 2.

30. Whitney, T.N.I., p. 163.

31. Barth in *Church Dogmatics* 1/1, quoted by Klooster, 'Karl Barth, Evangelicals and Revelation', *Reformed Theological Journal*, Vol. 3, November 1987, p. 38. One of the virtues of Klooster's article is to demonstrate that Barth is by no means an outdated issue.

32. Klooster, op. cit., p. 38.

33. Craig, op. cit., pp. 203-4.

34. Craig, op. cit., p. 22.

35. Whitney, T.N.H., p. 29.

36. Hereafter referred to as the 'Commentary'.

37. Barth, K., *The Epistle to the Romans*, 6th ed., English translation, Oxford, 1968, p. vi.

38. In *The Monthly Record of the Free Church of Scotland*, March 1984. See also Chapter 9 of his *Person of Christ*, IVP, (1998).

39. art.cit., pp. 51-2.

40. As, for example, in the SCM *New Dictionary of Theology*, p. 165, where we read: 'For Barth there is a return to the high classical Christology...'

41. Whitney, *The New 'Myth'ology* (hereafter T.N.M.), 1969, p. 70.

42. Whitney, T.N.I., p. 174 (paragraph heading).

43. Bloesch, op. cit., p. 88.

44. Bloesch, op. cit., p. 89.

45. Idem.

46. Whitney T.N.I., p. 160.

47. The phrase is used in Whitney T.N.I., p. 157, quoting Van Til.

48. Whitney, T.N.I., p. 182.

49. Whitney, T.N.I., p. 184. This quotation also demonstrates that, for all of Barth's objections to his being judged overmuch on the Commentary when he ought to be judged on the Dogmatics, the same principle of interpretation is followed through from the earlier to the later works.

50. Bloesch, op. cit., p. 85.

51. The phrase is used by Bloesch, op. cit., p. 85.

52. cf. Whitney, T.N.M., pp. 70-1.

53. Whitney, T.N.M., pp. 72-3.

54. Henry, op. cit., p. 49.

55. Whitney, T.N.H., p. 174.

56. Idem.

57. The question of whether or not Barth is to be regarded as an evangelical has divided many scholars. On the one hand, men like Professor Tom Torrance are in no doubt but that he is to be so regarded. In his article 'The Legacy of Karl Barth' in *Scottish Journal of Theology*, 39.3, p. 290, he states: '...in our day Karl Barth has had to battle contra mundum for the evangelical substance of the Christian faith'; and again (p. 292), 'Karl Barth's theology is at once evangelical and catholic'. According to Wallis, in his biography of

The Warhorse, Dr. Whitney was greatly encouraged by a statement of Prof. Torrance to the general Assembly of the Church of Scotland in 1984, calling for a 'fresh strategy for Evangelism', and the refashioning of church structures 'on evangelical grounds' (*The Warhorse*, 1986, p. 120). Wallis also notes that Torrance asked Dr. Whitney for copies of his 'Can Scotland do it again?' to distribute at this time. A rather different view has been published by the Banner of Truth Trust. In *Knowing the Times*, a collection of addresses delivered between 1942 and 1977 by the late D. Martyn Lloyd-Jones, and published in 1989, a lecture entitled 'What is an evangelical?', hitherto unpublished, is included. The following personal reminiscence is preserved: 'There was a great old professor in Scotland, Donald Maclean.... I will never forget meeting Professor Donald Maclean. He was one of the first men who ever mentioned the name of Karl Barth to me, and he spoke of him in the most lyrical terms, giving me the impression that Karl Barth was one of the greatest evangelicals who had ever lived. Why did Maclean do this? Well, because of Barth's onslaughts on the old liberalism.... Because Barth was so wonderful a critic of the old liberalism he was regarded as a true evangelical, *something that he, of course, never was*' (italics added).

58. Bromiley, G.W., 'Karl Barth' in Hughes (ed.) *Creative Minds in Contemporary Theology*, (1966), p. 51.

59. Idem.

60. Idem.

61. cf. Bromiley further: 'Van Til's study is so strained that Barth has apparently seen in it almost a willful caricature' (ibid., p. 52). cf. also the reference made by Van Til's biographer, William White, on pp. 146-7 of *Defender of the Faith*: 'Some readers of Christianity and Barthianism, including Barth himself, misunderstood the thrust of the Westminster professor's analysis and concluded that the author was engaged in a personal attack on Karl Barth. Nothing could be further from the truth.' White goes on to recount a reminiscence of William Jones, a friend of Van Til, to whom Barth said on one occasion of his famous protagonist at Westminster – 'Ach, he hates me.' According to White, Barth was actually moved to discover that far from hating him, Van Til often prayed for him (ibid., p. 147).

62. Bromiley's own theory is that 'Berkouwer's criticism... runs contrary to the plain attempts of Barth to find his basis and center, not in an abstraction like the triumph of grace, but in the person of Jesus Christ' (ibid., p. 52). Busch, Barth's biographer, records how Barth, in reacting to Berkouwer's thesis, claimed that he would have preferred the title 'The freedom of Jesus Christ...' rather than 'The Triumph of Grace...' (*Karl Barth: His Life from letters and autobiographical texts*, 1976, p. 381).

63. So Webster in *New Dictionary of Theology*, p. 78.

.64. Bromiley does not wish to bind himself to the use of any hermeneutical key for interpreting Barth; his complaint vis-a-vis the charge of Christomonism is that 'it falls rather wide of the mark in view of the ultimate trinitarianism of the Dogmatics' (ibid., p. 52). However, as far as the doctrine of sin is concerned, Barth does make use of extensive Christomonism.

65. Whitney, T.N.H., p. 93.

66. Whitney, T.N.H., pp. 95-6.

67. Bromiley, G.W., *An Introduction to the Theology of Karl Barth*, Eerdmans, 1979, p. 175. cf. also the statement by Whitney in T.N.H., p. 179 – 'for [Barth] reconciliation is christology and christology is reconciliation.'

68. Whitney, T.N.H., pp. 154-5.

69. Busch, op. cit., p. 378.

70. IV/1 (1961), 60-61.

71. Idem.

72. Idem.

73. Idem.

74. Idem.

75. Idem.

76. Klooster, F.H., *The Significance of Barth's Theology*, BBH, 1961, p. 79. cf. also Berkouwer, G.C., *The Triumph of Grace in the Theology of Karl Barth*, Eerdmans, 1956, p. 141: 'In the light of reconciliation, sin is exposed.'

77. Whitney, T.N.H., p. 201,

78. Whitney, T.N.H., p. 202.

79. Klooster, op. cit., p. 72.

80. Quoted by D. Macleod, art.cit., p. 51.

81. Van Buren, P., *The Secular Meaning of the Gospel*, (1965), p. 179. Van Buren is a useful measure of the influence of Karl Barth; in him we see the practical outworking of Barthianism – like other Neo-Orthodox theologians he was deeply indebted to Barth '[whose] radical transcendence was the starting-point of their practical emphases' (Whitney, T.N.H., p. 368).

82. Van Buren, op. cit., p. 179.

83. Van Buren, op. cit., p. 163.

84. cf. Dr. Whitney in T.N.H., p. 173: 'Barth describes sin in the light of his christological presuppositions as pride, sloth and falsehood.'

85. IV/1 (1961) section 60.2.

86. Whitney, T.N.H., p. 172.

87. IV/1 (1961) section 60.2.

88. Idem.

89. Idem.

90. Idem.

91. Idem.

92. Idem.

93. Idem.

94. IV/1 (1961) section 61.3.

95. Idem.

96. Whitney, T.N.H., p. 174.

97. In this section of the Dogmatics (pp. 65ff), Barth, of course, discusses much more than this. He discusses, for example, the whole question of the nature of the union which obtains between the deity and the humanity of Christ, and also the question of the Holy Spirit's bearing witness to the exalted Lord.

98. IV/2 (1958) 65.1.

99. Bromiley, *Introduction*, op. cit.

100. Berkouwer, G.C., *Studies in Dogmatics: SIN*, (1971), pp. 278-9.

101. Bromiley, art.cit., p. 49.

102. Berkouwer, Sin, op. cit., p. 279.

103. Ibid., p. 282.

104. Ibid., p. 278.

105. Klooster, op. cit., p. 85.

106. Ibid., p. 106

107. Westminster Shorter Catechism, Question 14

108. Bromiley, art.cit., pp. 50-51.

109. This review may be found in Volume 3 of the *Collected Writings of John Murray* (1982), pp. 316-321.

110. Ibid., p. 318.

111. Whitney, T.N.I., p. 185.

112. cf. Bromiley, art.cit., p. 54, where he calls it 'one outstanding weakness which may be the defect of a quality but which does in fact cast its shadow over the whole understanding of reconciliation'.

113. McGrath, A.E., 'Justification: Barth, Trent and Kung', *Scottish Journal of Theology*, 34.6 (1981), p. 523.

114. Idem. The frustrating thing about McGrath's study is that it concludes 'that Barth's teaching on these matters stands in the Reformed tradition, and is essentially that of Calvin' (p. 527)!!

115. Whitney, T.N.H., p. 491.

Chapter 10

The Doctrine of Sin in the Theology
of Rudolf Bultmann

BIOGRAPHICAL DETAILS

1884	Born Germany
	Studied at Tubingen, Berlin, Marburg
1921	Became Professor of New Testament at Marburg
1976	Died

Major Publications
History of the Synoptic Tradition (1921), *Jesus and the Word* (1926), *Primitive Christic~ity* (1949), *Theology of the New Testament,* 2 vols. (1952, 1955), *History and Eschatology* (1957). Published Commentaries on *John* (1941), *John's Epistles* (1967) and *2 Corinthians* (1976).

In his *Frontiers of Modern Theology* (1968), in which he seeks to give an evangelical critique of theological trends in the twentieth century, Carl Henry opens with these words: 'After ruling German theology for more than a decade, Rudolf Bultmann is no longer its king. Former students have usurped his throne and are scrambling for the spoils of conquest.'[1] He continues: 'The differences among the disciples of Bultmann signal an impending breakup of the total Bultmannian empire.... In his retirement, Bultmann has become but a symbolic ruler of the theological kingdom.'[2]

Henry's thesis is a reminder to us that in any attempt to judge the Neo-orthodox position, the thinking of Rudolf Bultmann cannot be ignored. If it is true that he was once king of the theological world, his theology deserves to be articulated; if his throne has been usurped, his theological position requires evaluation and appraisal.

Rudolf Bultmann (1884-1976) was born into an Evangelical Lutheran tradition, and was educated under some of the foremost exponents of the Higher Critical movement in Germany: Müller,

Gunkel, Harnack, Weiss (listed among those professors to whom Bultmann recorded his debt[3]). His own contribution to theological scholarship was made chiefly at Marburg, where he succeeded Heitmüller as Professor of New Testament and Early Christian History. From 1922-28 Martin Heidegger taught at Marburg with Bultmann, and Bultmann drew heavily on his philosophical emphases. Knudsen summarises Bultmann's contribution to New Testament studies thus: 'Bultmann,' he says, 'has been one of the foremost representatives in Germany of the scientific, radical criticism of the Bible.'[4] Ridderbos' evaluation is much the same, although he reminds us of the radical nature of Bultmann's thought when he says that 'Bultmann belongs to the radical-critical wing of German Biblical criticism. And yet he has given this criticism new ways, new paths and new perspectives.'[5]

This means in part that the reductionist influences which shaped Barth's thinking (see previous chapter) were also influential in moulding Bultmann's thought. The influences of the eighteenth-century Enlightenment, with their emphasis upon the self-ability of man, were to find their way into the realm of Biblical criticism, stripping the Bible of much of its content in order to discover the meaning of the kerygma, the gospel proclamation of the early church. This was what Dr. Whitney correctly labelled 'The Tyranny of "The New Infallibility"'[6]; after evaluating the quest and the conclusions of Neo-orthodoxy he comes to the conclusion that

> 'The words of the New Testament, traditionally regarded as the Word of God, are to be treated of little importance.... It is the historian himself, working with the tools of his own inner subjective standards of judgment, who decides, independently of objective Gospel facts presented in the New Testament, what actually constitutes the Gospel or the kerygma.'[7]

We have already seen how this principle is embedded in Barthian thought; in turning now to examine the Bultmannian hamartology, we discover the same principles undergirding Bultmann's theological position.

It may seem premature at this stage to make any kind of comparison between Barth and Bultmann, and this is an issue to which reference will later be made. However, it seems pertinent at this juncture to note that although similarities abound between Barth and Bultmann, and especially in connection with their fundamental presuppositions, there were also radical differences between them. Dr. Whitney devotes a chapter to this theme in *The New Infallibility*. He examines the views of Barth and Bultmann concerning God's revelation, and shows how this affects the view of Scripture which they embrace and preach. Barth, Whitney maintains, operates 'on the existential principle that experience is the final infallible criterion for both revelation and life'.[8] Bultmann, he argues, is not consistent; he wishes to argue for the subjectivity of the Gospel writers, but for the objectivity of the kerygma itself. This view we will examine in the following paragraphs. It is sufficient for our purposes here to note that Barth and Bultmann, in Whitney's estimate, follow the modern existentialists, like Kierkegaard and Heidegger, and that consequently 'the non-objectivity of divine revelation' becomes 'the core round which the dialectical and existential theologians of our time, despite their differing emphases, crystallise their theologies.'[9]

In a recently published edition of selected writings of Rudolf Bultmann, Professor Roger Johnson has noted what he calls the 'fragility' of the alliance between Barth and Bultmann. Despite the fact that they appeared to be waging war on the same front, they could not hold a united and sustained attack on the liberal position that had proved so unsatisfactory. In general, Johnson concludes that Bultmann was in 'agreement with Barth's critique of other positions and disagreement with his affirmations'.[10] Ridderbos also demonstrates how, although Barth and Bultmann began very close to each other, that is, with similar aims and presuppositions, within thirty years Barth was consciously attacking Bultmann's position. He records how Barth himself felt 'a certain homesickness' for the 1920s 'when he and Bultmann, with their supporters... formed a united front'.[11]

All this serves to remind us that it is not sufficient simply to place Bultmann along with Barth under a banner of 'Neo-orthodoxy', as if they were exponents of the same doctrinal position. It will become clear, as we proceed, that many similarities can be detected between the two; on the other hand the passages quoted above serve to remind us that Bultmann must be heard in his own right, and that his position was at times not favourable to some of the emphases in Barth.

If we are to understand Bultmann's hamartology aright, we must first study some of his philosophical and theological presuppositions, to discover how Bultmann approaches the Word of God. In order to do so, we must look at two main themes in his writings: the nature of Christianity and the demythologisation of the Word of God.

The Nature of Christianity

Bultmann's fundamental tenet is the syncretistic nature of primitive Christianity. Despite Whitney's excellent critique of Bultmann's aberrant views of Scripture – or, perhaps, *because* this is his main theme – he does not appear to me to have laid sufficient emphasis on this aspect of Bultmann's thought. The whole of Bultmann's reductionist demythologising programme is undergirded by a particular view of primitive Christianity, which, while it did not originate with Bultmann, was nevertheless so articulated by him that he can rightly be hailed its modern exponent.

This view of New Testament Christianity has two main features. The first of these is what could be called the *dispensableness of Jesus Christ*. In the view of Bultmann, Jesus Christ is not necessary to Christianity. To be more accurate, what is dispensable is any knowledge of the historical Jesus of the synoptic Gospels. But even this modification does not detract from the altogether radical nature of Bultmann's thought. Dr. Whitney does make this point in *The New Heresy*, where he maintains that Bultmann requires only the bare existence of Christ for his theological method; in Bultmann's view 'The Gospels...are concerned with the faith and the Church's preaching about Jesus; they are not concerned with Jesus'.[12] This latter statement is all-important, and is borne out in Bultmann's own writings. Despite his affirmation that 'No sane person can doubt that Jesus stands as founder behind the historical movement whose first distinct stage is represented by the older Palestinian community', Bultmann goes on to say: 'But how far that community preserved an objectively true picture of him and his message is another question.'[13] What matters to Bultmann is not whether or not historical accuracy has been preserved in the Synoptic tradition, but the fact that Jesus is given a place in the kerygma of the early church. So Bultmann in *The Message of Jesus* can declare: 'Christian faith did not exist until there was a Christian kerygma, i.e., a kerygma proclaiming Jesus Christ...to be God's eschatalogical act of salvation. He was first so proclaimed in the kerygma of the earliest Church, not in the message of the historical Jesus.'[14]

Although Barth, like Bultmann, did not hold that it was possible to recover the exact historical details of the life of our Lord, nevertheless his view of revelation demanded him to concede that it was in the life of Jesus Christ that God made His self-revelation.

Bultmann has gone further than this, in shifting the emphasis away from the earthly life of Jesus altogether. What mattered now was what the early church said about Christ, whether in fact it was historically verifiable or not. Carl Henry identified Käsemann's 1954 work *Das Problem des historischen Jesus*, in which the case was made for the necessary inclusion of the historical Jesus in any treatment of primitive Christianity, as the work which sounded the death-knell for Bultmannianism, and which impressed upon the disciples of Bultmann the need 'to insist...that some knowledge of the historical Jesus is indispensable.'[15] Until that point, it had been held as an axiom of Bultmann's thinking that historical details concerning the life of Jesus of Nazareth were only incidental to the nature of Christianity; what was of supreme importance was the proclamation of the early church.

The second feature of Bultmann's view of Christianity in its primitive form is its essentially syncretistic nature. This, of course, follows from the first point above; if Bultmann was not willing to concede the indispensableness of the historical Jesus as the *terminus a quo* for the study of Christian faith and doctrine, he had to supply the terminus himself. This he did by professing to find in Christianity a strange mixture of various elements from other religions and ideologies. In adopting this position, Bultmann was following in large measure the findings of the so-called History-of-Religions School, or *Religionsgechichtliche Schule*, in their attempt 'to understand the religious developments of the OT and NT and the early church by relating them to the context of other religious movements'.[16] At the turn of the twentieth century, the leading figures of this way of thought, and those to whom Bultmann himself expressed his own gratitude, were Heitmüller, Bousset and Reitzenstein.[17] Their studies of those elements common to early Christianity and various modes of thought contemporaneous with it yielded the conclusion that the Christian faith was actually a syncretism of those various strands of thought, and that the deposit of the early kerygma was in large measure only the collocation of extraneous religious matter.

It was in his 1949 work *Primitive Christianity in its Contemporary Setting* that Bultmann gave vent to his fullest and most mature reflections on this theme. There he identifies four quite distinct strands of thought which were to be gathered together into the phenomenon known as Christianity: Jewish apocalyptic writings, Hellenistic and Oriental star-worship, or astrology, the Mystery Religions, and

Gnosticism. Bultmann's conclusion, following Gunkel, is that 'Hellenistic Christianity is no unitary phenomenon, but, taken by and large, a remarkable product of syncretism...full of tendencies and contradictions, some of which were to be condemned later by orthodox Christianity as heretical.'[18] Ridderbos is, therefore, exactly right when he says that, for Bultmann, the formation of the Christian faith 'is determined in many ways by the religious concepts everywhere present in the Hellenistic world in which the young church arose'.[19] Indeed, continues Ridderbos, 'His entire work is determined by this radical-critical view with respect to both the content and the form of the New Testament proclamation.'[20]

It will not surprise us, therefore, to discover that Bultmann's doctrine of sin, with which we are more immediately concerned, will not be one with the orthodox doctrine. Orthodox Christianity presupposes the objective unity of the Bible as the criterion for truth; Bultmann, however, having robbed Christianity both of its continuity with the religion of the Old Testament, and also through destroying its own uniqueness as the religion of Him who says 'I am the Truth', has cut the cord of the authority of Scripture, and sails into completely subjective waters in his formulation of doctrine. The legacy of the History-of-Religions School has been a wholesale reduction of orthodoxy, and it is as apparent in Bultmann as it is in Barth.

Rudolf Bultmann and Demythologising

If Christianity is the product of a primitive religious syncretism, and if the Gospels bear witness to the faith and proclamation of the early church, the question remains as to what we are to do with the writings of the New Testament if we are to recover from them the doctrines and teachings of the first believers. It is important here to identify Bultmann's understanding of the nature of the New Testament. We have already seen how early Christianity in Bultmann's view imbibed many features of contemporaneous religion and philosophy, and deposited this material into the kerygma, the proclamation of the church. This is the New Testament which has come to us today, a New Testament written for the most part in mythological language which modern man can no longer understand or interpret. For this reason the myths must be excised, in order that we will understand intelligibly the nature of the Gospel. It is in this programme of demythologising that Bultmann's reductionism is most apparent, since clearly most of the doctrines of orthodox Christianity for Bultmann fall under this rubric. Dr. Whitney draws our attention to the fact that Bultmann describes the message of the New Testament with great accuracy and in orthodox terms 'until we remember that he is describing the mythical character of the New Testament cosmology... and furthermore that the origins of the various New Testament themes are easily traceable in the contemporary mythology of Jewish Apocalyptic and in the redemption myths of Gnosticism.'[21] It is in order to excise this extraneous matter from the New Testament kerygma that demythologising is necessary.

What is a myth? How does Bultmann define the term? The 1958 volume *Jesus Christ and Mythology* tackles this question specifically. There, Bultmann defines the central core of Jesus' teaching as the concept of the Kingdom of God, a kingdom which both Jesus and the disciples expected to see coming in their lifetime. This, maintains Bultmann, remained unfulfilled. The reason was the mythological nature of the kingdom concept, a concept which could claim no credibility in a modern, scientific world-view. It is the 'fact' that science has long since disproved the New Testament cosmology that leads Bultmann to maintain the necessary task of removing the myth element in which this cosmology is largely written. He is worth quoting at length on this point. He says:

> 'The whole conception of the world which is presupposed in the preaching of Jesus as in the New Testament generally is mythological.... This conception of the world we call mythological because it is different from the conception of the world which has been formed and developed by science since its inception in ancient Greece and which has been accepted by all modern men...modern science does not believe that the course of nature can be interrupted or, so to speak, perforated, by supernatural powers.'[22]

Whitney draws the logical conclusion from this, that since the world-view of Scripture is mythological, it is, therefore, 'unacceptable to modern man with his scientific orientation'.[23]

The corollary of this is to maintain that the Scriptural world-view is only an exercise of self-understanding on the part of the writers. 'Mythology,' continues Bultmann, 'expresses a certain understanding of human existence.... It may be said that myths give to the transcendent reality an immanent, this-worldly objectivity.'[24] It is this 'as if' quality that is the key to identifying myth, where the scientific world-view is spoken of as if it were something else. God's transendence is spoken of as if He was domiciled in Heaven. The transendence of evil is spoken of as if Hell was a real place. The overwhelming individuality of all evil actions is spoken of as if there were such a person as Satan. And so on.

Consequently, the only legitimate approach to the teaching of the New Testament is to de-mythologise, to expose the myths and to seek understanding of that which they symbolise. This hermeneutical method, according to Bultmann, is concerned with one fundamental question, the question, 'How is man's existence understood in the Bible?' The study of the Bible becomes then of the same order as the study of any historical document – 'by understanding history I can gain an understanding of the possibilities of human life'; but more than other historical documents, 'in the Bible a certain possibility of existence is shown to me... the Bible becomes for me a word addressed personally to me, which not only informs me about existence in general, but gives me real existence.'[24] The demythologising of Scripture is the necessary prerequisite to discovering the meaning and aim of the Bible – to speak authoritatively on the possibility of authentic existence for me. 'Here,' rightly concludes Knudsen, 'Bultmann is completely in line with existentialism'[25], or as Whitney puts it: 'Bultmann's theology is subordinated, not only to a secularized scientific world view, but also to a philosophy: Existentialism.' He continues: 'Bultmann's existentialist interpretation of redemptive history is based on his conviction that the entire revelation of God is resolved in the truth concerning human existence.'[26]

In order to meet our own objective, to state what is Bultmann's doctrine of sin, we must bear all these things in mind. We will have to ask whether sin is a mythological concept in Bultmann's thought – that is, is its function to shed light on man's existence? – and, if it is used mythologically, of what is it a symbol? To what in the scientific world view does the Scriptural doctrine of sin correspond? That is the task of any reader of Bultmann. And, as with Barth, we shall look both at Bultmann's major exegetical work, his commentary on John's Gospel, and then at the hamartology of his other writings. We will then be in a position to make a positive evaluation of his teaching.

The Doctrine of Sin in the *Commentary on John*

Bultmann's *Commentary on John's Gospel* (referred to hereinafter as the Commentary) was originally published in 1964 under the title *Das Evangelium des Johannes*. The English translation edition was published in 1971 under the editorship of Paul Beasley-Murray, who also translated the greater part of the volume. It has to be said that the Commentary is, therefore, a comparatively late work with which to begin, but its purpose for us will be served when we remember that Bultmann has deposited in it the fruits of his life's work in the study of the theology of the New Testament. As we read through the Commentary, we detect some of the emphases which we have already noted above; for example, one of Bultmann's hermeneutical axioms is that John was only an 'ecclesiastical redactor', collating and preserving various piecemeal strands of the New Testament kerygma. Consequently, Carson can say of him that he 'seeks to delineate sources right down to the half-verse', and that his work 'limits Johannine theology to that of the "evangelist".'[27] Ridderbos, in a discussion of Bultmann's treatment of the prologue to John, highlights for us what we have already seen of Bultmann's existentialist approach. He says, paraphrasing Bultmann: 'The question who Christ is must be answered from what He does to me. And what He does to me is to call me out of my illusory existence in the world to freedom.'[28] Thus the theological presuppositions which we identified earlier as being axiomatic in the theology of Bultmann undergird this, his most important exegetical work.

In particular, it must be said, Bultmann relegates much of the Gospel of John to the realm of the mythological. He declares that the Prologue, judged by its subject-matter, is clearly in the form of myth;[29] the Logos 'is spoken of as a person, in the language of mythology'.[30] Again, the statement in John 3: 35 that 'the Father loveth the Son' is a 'mythological statement'.[31] Similarly, in John 5:17ff., John is declared by Bultmann as taking as the basis of the narrative 'the mythological statement of the unity of the Father and the Son'.[32] Neither does the prayer of Christ in John 17 escape Bultmann's critical gaze: 'The language,' he says, 'is mythological: the Son's desire is to be raised again out of his earthly existence into the heavenly glory, which once he had in his pre-existence:– It accords fully with the thought-form of the Gnostic myth.'[33] The examples could be multiplied. The great characteristic of Bultmann's Commentary is that, as Carson reminds us, Bultmann does not rest until he has found a source for almost every syllable; and usually the source is to be found in the mythological cosmologies of pagan and Gnostic thought.

That this is so ought to set warning bells ringing in our minds as we proceed with our inquiry. The matter could not be put more succinctly than it is expressed by Dr. Whitney in the conclusion to his *The New Heresy*, where he says that 'Neo-Orthodox exponents simply do not believe the Bible in its plain grammatical sense'.[34] Bultmann is to the fore in this characteristically Neo-Orthodox methodology. His approach to the Word of God is saturated with his 'as-if' method of reasoning, which seeks to ask why the Bible speaks of this present world as if another cosmology obtained. Every statement in the Bible is consequently reducible to mere description concerning the world in which we live. It is with this modus operandi that questions concerning the nature of sin are broached.

In order to assess Bultmann's doctrine of sin, in terms of its meaning and of how God deals with it, it will be necessary to pay close attention to the discussions on this subject that appear before us in the Commentary. One of the first of these is dealt with by Bultmann as he examines the night interview between Jesus and Nicodemus. This passage, according to Bultmann, is one element in John's presentation of Jesus as the Revealer of God, encountering the world. It is this encounter that leads to *krisis*, to the need for judgment and response.

It is worth making the point that this response-orientation is axiomatic as far as Bultmann's understanding of the New Testament is concerned. The whole aim and purpose of preaching is, in his view, to enable man to make a decision that will authenticate his existence in the world. So Ridderbos:

> 'According to Bultmann, these moments of decision contain the existential significance of that which the New Testament describes in mythological form as the highest point of God's actions.'[35]

Indeed, Whitney goes so far as to say that 'The whole of Bultmann's theology is dominated by the image of encounter – and by this image alone'.[36] Moreover, this being so, it follows that the crisis-theology of Bultmann is the hallmark of his reductionist exegesis and interpretation of the New Testament. Knudsen has adequately demonstrated[37] that the mythological and non-historical elements in the New Testament are 'existentialist-inspired', and are designed to offer man a true and positive identity.

This, therefore, is the background to Bultmann's exegesis of John 3, and the dialogue between Christ and Nicodemus. Within the course of this dialogue, Christ talks of the condemnation of those who do not believe on the Son of God, a condemnation which, He declares, takes effect in this world in that men love darkness rather than light. Bultmann interprets this to mean that 'in the decision of faith or unbelief it becomes apparent what man really is and what he always was'.[38] The encounter of men with the light demands an existentialist response. 'Before the encounter with the Revealer the life of all men lies in darkness and sin.'[39] But Bultmann immediately goes on to make the startling statement: 'Yet this sin is not sin.... But for this enounter there would be no sin in the definitive sense of the word...'[40] It is only if the encounter leads to faith that sin is destroyed.

The whole passage demonstrates the unreasonableness of Bultmann's approach. On the one hand, he wishes to maintain that it is only by a positive decision on the basis of such an encounter that sin may be overcome; on the other, he wishes to maintain that without the encounter sin does not exist. In *The New Heresy*, Dr. Whitney discusses Bultmann's 'encounter theology'. He follows H.P. Owen's view that Bultmann does not do justice to the idea of divine immanence in his discussion of the relationship between God and man, and that consequently his procedure is self-contradictory. He wishes both to maintain that God wishes to speak to man and that He does not. The dialectical methodology of Bultmann is, concludes Whitney, 'no substitute for the doctrine of the Incarnation'.[41]

These difficulties confront us when Bultmann talks of sin in the light of John 3. It is, according to Bultmann, man's decision which authenticates him: 'the mission of Jesus is the eschatalogical event in which judgment is made on all man's past...in it God's love restores to man the freedom which he has lost, the freedom to take possession of his own authenticity'.[42] By this statement, Bultmann sums up what he believes to be the meaning of the dialogue between our Lord and Nicodemus.

Bultmann uses similar language in his exegesis of John 8:30-40, where Jesus offers freedom to his Jewish audience, if they continue in His word as His disciples. 'Whoseoever commits sin,' He concludes in verse 34, 'is the servant of sin.' Bultmann defines this bondservice to sin as man's having 'lost himself.'[43] The freedom offered by Christ is, according to Bultmann, an 'eschatalogical gift', defined as 'freedom from the world, and... at the same time freedom from the past, and so the freedom of man from himself.'[44] On the other hand, the Jews, enslaved as they are to their father, the devil, are robbed of life; so Bultmann concludes that 'their murderous purpose is but the behaviour that corresponds to their self-understanding'.

As far as Bultmann's undersanding of the nature and effects of sin is concerned, this kind of language presents us with several problems. The first of these is the subjectivity of Bultmann's approach. Sin is defined totally in terms of man's own existence, and whether that existence is, as Bultmann says, 'authentic'. For Bultmann, the whole purpose and content of revelation is to give man an understanding of his own existence, so that 'he is able to understand himself.'[45] The meaning of sin, therefore, has to be defined in this sense, as that which casts light on the being and the nature of man. Sin is that which leaves man in bondage. But, as Knudsen reminds us, what Bultmann means by this is simply that '[man's] sinful existence is a veiling of his true selfhood'.[46]

It is difficult to see what Bultmann means by all this. What is it that authenticates man? What is man's true selfhood? The biblical position, and one that has been reflected in orthodox theology, is that man knows true selfhood only by obedience to God. Disobedience opens the door to alienation, frustration and disappointment. In this sense it may indeed be true to talk of sin as that which veils the true selfhood of man. However, Bultmann employs his definitions without any reference to the law of God. God is not in his thoughts at all, except as an expression of man's self-awareness and self-understanding.

At least one evangelical theologian has maintained that this is a mistaken view of Bultmann. In an article to which reference has already been made, and in which he discusses and compares the theology of Barth and Bultmann, Dr. John Webster of Durham says that 'criticism along these lines should not make us unappreciative of the deeper theological motives behind Bultmann's existential reading of the New Testament...'[47] He concedes that much of Bultmann's language and usage is ambiguous and open to misunderstanding; Webster's caveat is expressed in the following quotation:

'it is clear that [Bultmann's] concern is not to offer a reduced, man-centered account of the Christian faith. Much more is he searching for ways in which that faith might be seen to be a matter of the most pressing concern for human existence. It is not so much that his theology is anthropocentric as that it seeks to spell out how the theocentric character of Christian faith might be made meaningful for the life of man in the world.'[48]

Part of the difficulty with Webster's approach is that it does not go far enough. Even allowing for the possibility that Webster's evaluation is a fair one, the charges of anthropocentrism and subjectivism against the writings of Bultmann can be demonstrated quite clearly from the Commentary. When Bultmann talks of sin, he does so in the context of man's existence. It is his existence in the world that is threatened by sin. If this is an attempt to contextualise the biblical orientation of sin in its God-ward character as that which offends God, then the attempt fails. It is precisely the manward orientation of Bultmann's doctrine of sin that is the primary difficulty with his writings. So Whitney can assert: 'there is no inevitable relationship to God indicated or implied. Sin is a private matter of personal disintegration.'[49]

A second major problem with Bultmann's reductionist view of sin is that it casts the possibility of deliverance onto man himself. Salvation is not at all of the sovereign mercy and grace of God. To be sure, Bultmann does hold to the view that salvation, if it is enjoyed at all, is enjoyed exclusively by virtue of Jesus Christ, but only as the Revealer, before whom man is faced with the necessity of a critical decision. In answer, therefore, to the age old inquiry, 'What must I do to be saved?', Bultmann's answer is not, 'Believe on the Lord Jesus Christ', but 'Make your existential decision before the Revealing God'.

It is difficult to find in the Commentary a straightforward definition of the biblical doctrine of salvation.[50] It does have to be said that Bultmann's language is often characterised by an almost orthodox flavour; for example, in commenting on John 4:24 he does say that 'There can be no true relationship between man and God unless it first be grounded in God's dealing with man. Any attempt by man to establish such a relationship remains within the sphere of human works from which God is unattainable.' Bultmann here seems to be building a foundation of the same order of the biblical teaching of salvation by grace without works. However, the edifice which he builds is not one with the Bible's doctrine of salvation. It is clear that for Bultmann, such salvation as lies within man's reach is defined not by Christ's atoning death, but by His work as Revealer. This is clearly stated in his comment on John 12:47, which is worth quoting in full: 'the promise which Jesus makes brings man at the same time face to face with a decision. The revelation must be judgment if it is also to be grace.... If he rejects the word of revelation he brings judgment on himself.'

One glaring omission in this quotation is any reference to the actual words of Jesus, as recorded by John – 'I did not come to judge the world but to save the world.' Here, it is the express purpose of Jesus Christ to offer salvation to the world. Yet Bultmann does not deal with the concept of saving; instead he insists on the need to interpret the teaching of Jesus Christ in terms solely of man's crisis-response to the Revealer, Jesus. Again, Jesus' words in John 10:9 ('whoever enters through me will be saved') is dismissed by Bultmann as one of 'The Evangelist's glosses', which is 'formally disruptive', and which merely expands Jesus' own salvation motifs.[51] And when John records definitively that 'this man really is the saviour of the world' (John 4:42), all that Bultmann offers by way of comment is 'not only that the title [*soter tou kosmou*] announces the universal significance of the Revealer, but the fact that this is expressed by an eschatalogical title'.[52] And in a footnote to these words, Bultmann adds that the title 'is taken from Hellenistic eschatology'.

It is clear, therefore, that what Bultmann offers is a much-reduced view of the biblical notion of salvation. Despite his insistence that salvation is of the order of grace, he has in reality made it very man-orientated. This reduction both parallels, and is a necessary consequence of, the reduced view of sin which his exegetical efforts produce. As a result, he is unable to offer much hope either for sin or for the sinner.

The Doctrine of Sin in the *Theology of the New Testament*

Having looked at the doctrine of sin as Bultmann presents it in his major exegetical work, we turn now to view the theological formulation of the doctrine within the context of his *Theology of the New Testament*.[53] This work appeared in two volumes, the British editions being published first in 1952 and 1955. The *Theology* is in four parts, dealing with the following subjects: Part I: Presuppositions and Motifs of New Testament Theology; Part II: The Theology of Paul; Part III: The Theology of John; and Part IV: The Development toward the Ancient Church. The First Part of the *Theology* lays the foundation for Bultmann's reduction of the New Testament, and his syncretistic view of the Christian religion. It is with the Second Part that we will be most immediately concerned in our evaluation of Bultmann's presentation of the doctrine of sin.

Bultmann classifies sin under the chapter heading 'Man Prior to the Revelation of Faith'. This draws the lines of demarcation within which Bultmann discusses and views the whole concept of sin. Sin is oriented towards the revelation God has made, and is to be defined anthropologically. These principles, as we have already seen, are axiomatic to Bultmann's whole theology, and in particular to that branch of it which we are now assessing.

In his discussion of the nature of man, Bultmann begins with the assertion that '[Paul] sees man always in his relation to God'.[54] In order to define man, Bultmann goes on to examine some of the various concepts employed in the Pauline corpus, in particular the word *soma* (body), and then more briefly the words *psyche* (soul), *pneuma* (spirit), *zoe* (life) and *nous* (mind). The treatment of the Pauline concept of *soma* draws heavily on Heidegger, and concludes that *soma* is used by Paul not in a merely physical sense, but is used pronominally, referring to man in the totality of his being. The particular definition Bultmann offers is this: 'The characterization of man as soma implies... that man is a being who has a relationship to himself, and that this relationship can be either an appropriate or a perverted one; that he can be at one with himself or at odds...because he is soma does the possibility exist for him to be good or evil – to have a relationship for or against God.'[55]

Bultmann is here combining man's relationship with God and man's relationship with himself as being commensurate the one with the other. His position, it must be said, embraces a profound truth – namely, that man's relationship with God is determinative of his whole moral, intellectual and spiritual integrity; at the same time, however, Bultmann talks of these two relationships almost interchangeably. It is striking to notice in particular that having begun with the assertion that true humanness is defined in terms of man's relationship to God, his general conclusion (which he takes as the basis of his discussion of the question of sin) is that 'man, according to Paul, is a being who has a relationship to himself, is placed at his own disposal, and is responsible for his own existence'.[56]

It is important to grasp what Bultmann is doing here. It is not merely that man's relationship to God and his relationship to himself are discussed in parallelism; it is that the former of these is defined almost exclusively in terms of the latter. Man's relationship to God is his relationship to himself. In the thinking of Bultmann, this axiom rules supreme. Man is to God what he is to himself. Nothing more and nothing less. This is nothing other than the wholesale reduction of the Bible in its entirety. This is Bultmannianism.

The Bultmannian hamartology applies this axiom with ruthless logic: '...the alternative,' says Bultmann, 'to lay hold of one's true existence or to miss it is synonymous with the alternative to acknowledge God as the Creator or to deny him.'[57] The anthropological and existential parameters of this type of reasoning are everywhere apparent. Sin is to miss one's true existence; salvation is to have it. The possibility of salvation is centered in the freedom of man, and his ability to make a reasonable acknowledgement of the Creator-hood of God. This is a subtle shift away from the orthodox doctrine of sin and salvation, where the alternative is between estrangement from God (and self-frustration) and reconciliation to God through the death of Christ (and self-fulfilment). In Bultmann, the ultimate sin is not the refusal of this salvation or the rejection of the salvation offered, but is, by his own definition, 'the false assumption of receiving life not as the gift of the Creator but procuring it by one's own power, of living from one's self rather than from God'.[58]

Bultmann's discussion of the meaning of sin then centres around Paul's use of the word *sarx*, the fleshly existence. His general conclusion is that when Paul talks of living 'according to the flesh', he is talking of 'an existence or an attitude not as natural-human but as sinful'.[59] The meaning of sin in this context is, according to Bultmann, 'the pursuit of the merely human, the transitory'.[60] This can mean either giving oneself over to worldly pursuits and pleasures, or busying oneself in zealous moral and religious activity. Wherever there is 'a life of self-reliant pursuit of one's own ends,'[61] there is sin.

The personification of sin in several Pauline passages (especially Romans 6 and 7) is not 'realistic mythology', according to Bultmann, but 'figurative, rhetorical language'.[62] Sin becomes a power to which man has fallen victim. The result is an inner disintegration and dividedness, whereby man's true self has been destroyed. This, according to Bultmann, constitutes for us 'the essence of human existence under sin'.

At the same time, however, Bultmann will not allow that the doctrine of sin is treated of by Paul in a way that is completely non-mythological. In fact, in his discussion of the universality of sin, and particularly in his treatment of original sin and Paul's argumentation in Romans 5:12ff., Bultmann concludes that 'Here...Paul is unquestionably under the influence of the Gnostic myth'.[63] The universality of sin is deduced not from a mythical notion of original sin, but only from the fact that every refusal to acknowledge God in the existential situation is of the same nature as the proto-sin of apostasy.

It must be stressed, however, that despite his affirmations to the contrary, Bultmann does not in fact succeed in demonstrating the universality of sin. He can only go so far as to say that 'everyone exists in a world in which each looks out for himself...sin is always already here'.[64] The possibility still remains that man may, from the very beginning, escape the general condemnation of the race by living an authentic life. In no way does it follow by absolute and necessary consequence that the presence of (this kind of) sin in the world establishes the universality of sin.

When Bultmann comes in the *Theology* to deal with what he calls 'the salvation occurence', as that is presented by Paul, it is clear that he regards much of Paul's teaching as mythology, in need of radical de-mythologising. According to Bultmann, Paul interprets Christ's death 'in the categories of the Gnostic myth'.[65] Further, that the death and resurrection of Christ are 'cosmic occurences, not incidents that took place once upon a time in the past'.[66] There is a subtle attack here upon the historical reliability of the Gospels; whatever the death and resurrection of Christ were, they were at the very least historical incidents which took place upon the plane of space-time history. That the incidents themselves were of cosmic significance cannot be denied; but they cannot be of any significance unless their historicity is granted. Bultmann brings this into question, and is consequently able to read what he likes into the New Testament. In particular, he is able to correct the Apostle Paul's distorted view of the death of Jesus Christ!

The practical consequence of this is expressed by Bultmann in the following quotation: 'Belief in the resurrection and the faith that Christ himself, yes God Himself, speaks in the proclaimed word...are identical.'[67] This is radical Bultmannianism, the de-mythologising of the whole New Testament schema of salvation. The death and resurrection of our Lord, held forth in the Bible as the sine qua non of personal salvation, has been identified with (and consequently reduced to) the crisis-encounter of the kind which dominates Bultmann's thinking. Whitney is exactly correct to conclude that 'In so arguing Bultmann cuts the very heart out of the Christian proclamation'.[68]

Before coming to make a critical assessment of the doctrine of sin as portrayed in the Theology, a brief word may be said on two themes from the Second Volume (Parts III and IV), dealing with sin in the theology of John and in the theology of the early church. Much of what is contained in Bultmann's treatment of the former of these topics has already been noted in our discussion of the Commentary on John, above. One or two comments will, however, be relevant.

Three things are axiomatic for Bultmann in his approach to the theology of John. First, Bultmann maintains that there is a divergence between the thinking of John and that of the apostle Paul. While there are elements common to both, Bultmann's thesis is that 'the relation of John to Paul cannot be understood on a linear scheme of development from the theology of the earliest Church; the two lie in quite different directions'.[69] There is, according to Bultmann, a radical divergence within the thought of the New Testament itself, a divergence which has its practical expression in the differing emphases of John and Paul.

Again, Bultmann views John as having been under the (extensive) influence of Gnostic mythology in his writings.[70] This, he argues, is characteristic both of John and Paul, especially in their respective christologies; but Bultmann suggests that John uses less language borrowed from Judaistic thought, and more directly Gnostic terminology, particularly in his use of dualistic concepts, such as the antitheses of truth/falsehood and light/darkness.[71]

Thirdly, Bultmann approaches the theology of John with a particular view of John's attitude to Jesus Christ as 'the Revealer whom God has sent'.[72] Almost everything is subordinated to this basic principle; the last meal of Jesus and his disciples, for example, becomes neither Passover nor Lord's Supper, but merely the point of departure for the Revealer's farewell speeches to the disciples. Bultmann sees in John a Christ whose every action is designed to bring man to the necessity of critical response.

This view of Christ as the Revealer is the foundation of Bultmann's treatment of sin in the theology of John. It has to be said, however, that Bultmann offers no comprehensive treatment of John's doctrine of sin anywhere in the Theology. Where it is dealt with, however, it is clear that Bultmann sees this particular Johannine Christology as foundational to the apostle's doctrine of sin. So Bultmann declares: 'Since man never exists by his own power, but can only commit himself to a power that controls him, reality or unreality, God or Nothing...the encounter with the Revealer calls into question whether this existence-from-Nothing is existence at all.'[73] The existential categories within which man's being and nature are discussed by Bultmann are everywhere apparent. So also is the primacy afforded to man's crisis-response: 'the decision in response to the Revealer's word...does not take place out of man's still unquestioned existence.... On the contrary, here he is asked just this: whether or not he wills to remain what he was – i.e. to remain in his old existence or not.'[74] This leads to about the only clear statement of a specifically Johannine hamartology: 'in sin it comes to light that man in his essence is a sinner, that he is determined by unreality, Nothing.'[75]

This, therefore, is Bultmann's conclusion as to the nature of man's sin – his existence is governed by unreality. Coming face to face with Christ the Revealer, 'there opens up to [man] the possibility of being otherwise than he was'.[76] Sin has rejected this offer; man has chosen to maintain his unauthentic, his unreal existence, even in the face of a new possibility of being something other than what he was. Both sin and salvation are discussed existentially.

Bultmann declares also that 'the thought of Jesus' death as an atonement for sin has no place in John'.[77] This declaration is made even although Bultmann gives the lie to it. By his own admission, although he dismisses the references in 1 John to 'expiation for our sins' as 'redactional glosses',[78] 1 John 1:7 embraces the view that Christ's death is an atoning sacrifice. Bultmann dismisses this also by suspecting some kind of redactional interference. How easily he does so! He holds forth his theories as to the mythological character of the Bible, and dismisses as editorial mis-handling those passages which belie his theories. On the word of another authority, 'We must never assume that which is incapable of proof,'[79] yet Bultmann is willing to present a theology which has cut the umbilical cord of biblical authority. Dr. Whitney's conclusion is once again substantiated: 'Bultmann's faith...is irrational;...its sole authority is Bultmann himself.'[80]

In our study of the *Theology*, it will be necesary, for the sake of completeness, to allude briefly to Part IV, in which Bultmann deals with 'The Development of Church Order and Doctrine'. As far as the doctrine of sin is concerned, Bultmann argues that the true biblical doctrine 'gets lost in moralistic-legalistic thinking – especially under the influence of the synagogal tradition'.[81] This, suggests Bultmann, shows that the developing church has lost sight of 'the radical fallen-ness of man outside of Christ';[82] in surveying most of the early Fathers on the subject, Bultmann draws the conclusion that 'practically never is sin mentioned as a power that dominates man'.[83] One practical upshot of this was that early church discipline centered for the most part around distinguishing lighter sins from more serious ones. But Bultmann argues that 'To distinguish between light and grave sins imperils from the outset the radical understanding of sin, as it had been conceived by Jesus, Paul and John'.[84] Thus in Bultmann's view, the correct (de-mythologised) biblical view of sin is radically departed from in the early church.

This conclusion, of course, ought not to surprise us. Bultmann has so altered the plain, straightfoward meaning of the text of the New Testament that he makes it read something other than and contrary to the original intention of its authors. When the early Christian church preaches the Gospel, therefore, in obedience to the commission of Christ, it is little wonder that Bultmann charges it with having departed from the earliest kerygma. Thus, Bultmann's conclusions as to the theology of the early church are seen to be consistent with his own subjective criteria; only because of his wholesale alteration of the Christian faith can he accuse the primitive Christian church of such a radical departure from the truth.

The Doctrine of Sin in Bultmann's other writings

There are three other writings to which reference ought to be made at this point for the sake of completeness. A brief word will be said regarding the doctrine of sin as Bultmann deals with it in these works. It will be useful to survey them in chronological order.

The first of these is Bultmann's 1924 essay and lecture, 'Liberal Theology and the Latest Theological Movement'. The lecture, delivered at Marburg University, was essentially a critique of the older liberalism.[85] In it, many of Bultmann's later emphases are made with clarity and lucidity; he attacks a wrong emphasis on God as 'Wholly

Other', and also expresses his syncretistic view of Christianity by
defining it as 'a phenomenon of this world, subject to the laws of
social psychology'.[86] Part of Bultmann's critique of classical liberalism
is that it failed to give meaningful and adequate definitions either of
God or of man. His doctrine of sin forms part of his own alternative
anthropology.

Man, for Bultmann, is always under the 'question mark' of God's
judgment.[87] Man's fundamental sin, according to Bultmann, 'is his
will to justify himself as man'.[88] Faith is the insight of certain men
who are aware of this fundamental sin. Man is in despair because he
is trying to flee from God; the knowledge of sin is extremely personal:
'The sight of God's judgment and God's grace together belongs to
the nature of faith.'[89]

What is one to make of this? First, it is apparent that Bultmann is
using the language of orthodoxy and filling it with an unorthodox
meaning. On the face of it, many of his expressions are able to stand
the test of Scripture, until they are analysed for what they are. It then
becomes clear that the meaning of man, and consequently the meaning
and effects of his sin, are conceived of in purely existential categories.

Again, one has to note the sheer inaccessibility of Bultmann's
Gospel. His is a Gospel for scholars, not for sinners. The Bible is clear in
its definitions and condemnation of sin. Bultmann, on the other hand,
places a massive reinterpretation of the Gospel teaching before men
as their condition for salvation. What, for example, is the meaning of
man's willingness to justify himself as man? Is it man's manhood,
his humanness, that makes him a sinner? By what criterion or standard
does Bultmann arrive at this definition of sin? His existential categories
place the need of man and the provision of God beyond the reach of
any who are not prepared, first, to cross this philosophical Rubicon.

A third point to be made here is that Bultmann vacates both the
doctrine of sin and the doctrine of salvation of any reference to Jesus
Christ. Bultmann is in scathing form when he pens the following:
'How widely the pictures of Jesus presented by liberal theologians
differ from one another! How uncertain is all knowledge of 'the
historical Jesus'! Is he really within the scope of our knowledge?
Here research ends with a large question mark – and here it ought to
end.'[90] The truth both of man's sinfulness and his salvation are divorced
from the Person, teaching and work of Jesus Christ. The new
infallibility is indeed the subjective standard. Once Jesus Christ is

lost in a fog of historical uncertainty and unreliability, anything goes. And with Bultmann, everything does go.

The second work to which reference will be made here is another of Bultmann's lectures, entitled 'The Crisis of Faith', delivered at Marburg in 1931. Part of it deals with a recurring theme in his writings – namely the conflict between the Christian faith and modern culture and the modern world-view. 'Crisis' is also a recurring word, and one which firmly anchors Bultmann's thought in his existential philosophy.

Bultmann deals with sin in the section on 'Christian Faith in God'. 'The Word of the New Testament, the Word of the Christ-Event', declares the possibility to man of his exercising faith in God, by promising him the forgiveness of his sins. It is at this point that Bultmann offers the following definition of sin: 'Here we are not to think of sin as immorality,[91] but as the human claim to seek to exist in one's own right, to be one's own master, and to take one's life into one's own hands, superbia, wishing to be like God.'[92] This desire, says Bultmann, is lovelessness.[93] This leads to selfish living and abandoned, wilful, self-assertion. The result is the staining of the person: '[Man] is guilty and impure because so much callousness and ingratitude, falsehood and meanness, thoughtless spoiling of joys of others, and selfish neglect of the other person, so much coolness towards others and insistence on his own rights...cling to him unforgiven, and make him impure.'[94]

It is clear once again that Bultmann's categories are here thoroughly existential. Sin has been reduced to a level of importance as between man and man; the fundamental biblical teaching of the radical effects of sin at the level of human-divine encounter are almost completely ignored. The above quotation does highlight a new element in Bultmannian thought; that is, the communal aspects of the sin question. Sin is no longer conceived of in purely personal categories, but embraces a much wider constituency.

It is clear also that at this level, the forgiveness of sin also is communal in its deepest aspects. Thus Bultmann on sin: 'only the goodness and purity of the other person can free me from it.'[95] Here, Bultmann has completely severed himself from any doctrine of salvation by monergistic, divine grace. Sin is communal; freedom and salvation from it are also communal. Sin, in the sense of personal impurity, is to wrong my neighbour. Only he can set me free from the resultant defilement. Again, Whitney's conclusion is exactly correct:

'here, misery as the expression of sin, has only a man-centered, indeed, an ego-centric significance, being caused by discomfort through man sinning against himself. It has no necessary, God-orientated significance – not being conceived of as primarily sin against God.'[96] This also demonstrates the reality of Ridderbos' general conclusion when he argues that 'All theology and Christology can according to [Bultmann] be expressed in the categories of anthropology,'[97] and that 'Bultmann's interpretation of God's redemptive work is not orientated to the New Testament but to a modern secular philosophy'.[98]

The third, and final, work to which reference will be made here is to Bultmann's important and controversial work *Jesus Christ and Mythology*. In a lecture delivered in Frankfurt in 1941, Bultmann presented his new and radical proposals on demythologising. These were revised and presented in America, resulting in the publication of *Jesus Christ and Mythology* in 1958. Although some discussion of Bultmann's demythologising programme has already been entered into, it is necessary at this point to see where sin is dealt with in such a schema as Bultmann proposes.

It was in *Jesus Christ and Mythology* that Bultmann gave expression to his theory regarding the world-view of the New Testament; he states that 'The whole conception of the world which is presupposed in the preaching of Jesus as in the New Testament generally is mythological...'[99] Moreover, he argues that 'These mythological conceptions of heaven and hell are no longer acceptable for modern men...'[100] It is against the background of this kind of thinking about the teaching of the Bible that Bultmann engages in his quest for a de-mythologised doctrine of sin, that is, one which conforms to the scientific view of man and his environment.

Bultmann challenges modern man, faced as he is with an infallible science to keep him right, with forgetting 'that his plans and under-takings should be guided not by his own desires for happiness and security...but rather by obedient response to the challenge of goodness, truth and love.... There is no real, definitive security, and it is precisely this illusion to which men are prone to succumb in their yearning for security...'[101] In other words, man's sin is to become so wrapped up in the illusory world around him that he becomes selfish and alienated. The Word of God alone calls man back to genuine freedom.

Such freedom, Bultmann argues, is thoroughly existential. By his own admission, it has little to do with man's relationship to God, and everything to do with his relationship to himself. This might be illustrated by his reference to the apostolic phrase to be 'freed from sin'. This, says Bultmann, is not a dogmatic statement but an existential one.[102] It is this that characterises Bultmann's whole approach to the question of the meaning of man's sin, which is to be regarded existentially, rather than dogmatically. And this is the fundamental error in the whole presentation of his theology, summed up by Van Til when he says that 'with all his best effort, Bultmann did not really escape from a measure of control in his thinking by an existential methodology'.[103]

Summary and Conclusion

In this chapter, an attempt has been made to state Bultmann's doctrine of sin, and to view it within the context of his whole theological approach and method. An attempt has been made to assess his hamartology as it appears in his major works, including his *Commentary on John*, his *Theology of the New Testament*, and some of his lesser, but equally important writings. It remains now simply to summarise some of the conclusions reached, and make a general assessment of his doctrine of sin.[104]

First, it is clear that for Bultmann *the Bible requires massive and extensive re-interpretation*. Its world-view and working concepts are not valid for modern man, come of age in the maturity of scientific discovery. Before Christian doctrine can be stated theologically, the whole of the Word of God requires to be re-assessed. One thing which Bultmann will not allow, in common with other Neo-Orthodox theologians, is a literal interpretation of the Bible as infallible, inerrant and authoritative. So Whitney: 'The Neo-Orthodox Word of God is not...God's word written. It is never identified with the words of Scripture.'[105] Indeed, what the Bible says about man and his sin hardly matters to Bultmann at all. His whole approach requires a destructive and reductionist attitude towards the Word of God.

Second, Bultmann's doctrine of sin *requires a substitute for the Word of God, which he finds in the conclusions of existentialist philosophy*, with its emphasis on the centrality of man and of existence. Theological statements about man are irrelevant; what matters is how such statements affect man's existence in the world, both at an individual and communal level.

Third, *what the Bible does say about man and sin hardly matters* to Bultmann at all. Although he may, in common with other Neo-Orthodox theologians, use the vocabulary of the New Testament, it is clear that they are only pegs on which a totally alien theology is hung. Ridderbos is worth quoting at length on this point: 'Naturally Bultmann knows very well that sin occupies a central place in the New Testament.... In conformity with his analysis of existentialism, Bultmann sees human misery in being involved in this world of relativity; only when man is free with respect to the latter does he reach his authentic 'self'.... But this is something different to what the New Testament calls 'repentance'.'[106] He continues: 'From this it is established that Bultmann's interpretation of the New Testament cannot do justice to the character of sin, as guilt with respect to God. It can only conceive of it as a power whose function is to bind us to the relative, the visible, and so on.'[107] Ridderbos' analysis is exactly correct. Bultmann simply cannot, on an existential view of the Bible, do justice fully to the biblical doctrine of sin.

Fourthly, Bultmann's doctrine succeeds only in *reducing man's accountability to God*. Having reduced sin to a purely existentialist level, he has established it firmly as a matter of personality. God is not in his thoughts at all. The meaning of sin having been reduced, Bultmann has only succeeded in removing guilt from man. Whereas the Bible clearly presents man as a sinner accountable at last to the God against whom sin has been directed in an attitude of rebellion, Bultmann reduces the concern over such accountability by robbing sin of its guilt aspect.

Fifthly, and finally, the reductionist nature of Bultmann's hamartology is seen in *the Christless salvation which he offers*. Victory over sin and deliverance from it are both within the power of man. As we have seen, the kerygma, according to Bultmann's analysis, can dispense with the historical Jesus either in His Person or work. And as far as the sinner is concerned, salvation can dispense with Jesus also. To be sure, Bultmann does maintain a salvation through Jesus; but what he means is an encounter of faith made through the proclamation of the Word. In the words of Knudsen, Bultmann has 'dissolved the once-for-all event of Jesus into a recurring, paradoxical contemporaneity of Jesus Christ in the preaching of the Church'.[108] And, at last, this is nothing other than a salvation by works.

The foregoing study in the hamartology of Rudolf Bultmann has demonstrated the radicalness of the cleavage between his thinking and the conclusions of Reformed Orthodoxy. Bultmann's work has been to demolish the biblical structures of salvation by Jesus Christ through faith in His once-for-all and completed atonement. In the following chapter, the theology of Emil Brunner will be assessed and evaluated, and his doctrine of sin will be studied. The foregoing study of Bultmann has found Whitney's conclusion to be accurate:

> 'Bultmann cuts back the whole drama of God's activity in creation, redemption judgment, to the actual encounter of God with individual man. He has no room in his system for God's activity with the whole world, for faith in God's all-embracing plan of Salvation, for the whole universe which He created, sustains and rules, and which in Christ He operates to save and transform.'[109]

There is, as Moises Silva puts it, 'a fairly direct line from the Kantian dichotomy to the recent claim that biblical interpretation can have no objective significance at all',[110] and while this Bultmannian approach to revelation sits well on modern ears, it undercuts every attempt to understand the truth of what the Bible says about sin, salvation and Jesus Christ.

NOTES

1. Henry, C., *Frontiers in Modern Theology*, Moody Press: Chicago, 1968, p. 9.
2. *Ibid.*, pp. 11-12. cf. also his comment in Henry, C.F. (ed.) *Jesus of Nazareth, Saviour and Lord*, 1966, p. 6, where he says that 'Today the search is under way for an alternative to Bultmann'.
3. See Knudsen's 'Rudolf Bultmann' in Hughes, P. E., *Creative Minds in Contemporary Theology*, Eerdmanns: Michigan, 1966, p. 132.
4. Knudsen, art.cit., p. 133.
5. Ridderbos, H., *Bultmann*, Presbyterian and Reformed: New Jersey, 1960, p. 10.
6. Whitney, H.J., *The New Infallibility* (hereafter T.N.I.), p. 116.
7. Ibid., pp. 116-7.
8. Ibid., p. 216. See also chapter 9.
9. Ibid., p. 222.
10. Johnson, R.A. (ed.), *Rudolf Bultmann: Interpreting Faith for the Modern Era*, Collins: London, 1987, p. 15.
11. Ridderbos, op. cit., pp. 15-16.
12. Whitney, T.N.H., p. 272.
13. From Bultmann: *Jesus and the Word*, R. Johnson (ed.), op. cit., p. 97.
14. From Bultmann: *The Message of Jesus*, Ibid., p. 103. cf. also Ladd's

summary where he says: '...the Christ who is proclaimed in the kerygma is purely a mythological construction and had no existence in history, for mythology by definition is nonhistorical.... The kerygma is the expression of the meaning Christ had for the early Christians, formulated in mythological terms' (*A Theology of the New Testament*, Lutterworth Press: Cambridge, 1987, p. 22).

15. Henry, op. cit., p. 15. cf. also his comments to the same effect in Henry (ed.), op. cit., p. 7.

16. Yamauchi, E.M., article 'History-of-Religions School', in *New Dictionary of Theology*, IVP. : Leicester, 1988, p. 308.

17. So Yamauchi, art.cit., p. 309: 'The views of such scholars as Reitzenstein and Bousset had a great impact upon Rudolf Bultmann.' cf. also Johnson (ed.), op. cit., p. 158: 'Bultmann was particularly involved with the work of those scholars who came to a new understanding of Christianity by comparing its teachings with those of other religious movements from the first two centuries of the Common Era. In particular, Bultmann acknowledged his indebtedness to the writings of Wilhelm Heitmuller, Richard Reitzenstein and Wilhelm Bousset.'

18. Johnson (ed.), op. cit., p. 185.

19. Ridderbos, op. cit., p. 13.

20. Ibid., p. 14.

21. Whitney, T.N.H., p. 286. cf., for example, Bultmann's treatment of the Prologue of John's Gospel, the source of which he purports to belong 'to the sphere of a relatively early oriental Gnosticism, which has been developed under the influence of the OT faith in the Creator-God' (Commentary, p. 30).

22. Johnson (ed.), op. cit., p. 291.

23. Whitney, T.N.H., p. 260.

24. Johnson (ed.), op. .cit., p. 293.

25. Knudsen, art.cit., p. 138.

26. Whitney, T.N.I., p. 198. Bultmann's existentialism and his demythologising programme have been the subject of much study, and to devote much time to them here would side-track us from our main area of study. The following points, however, are worth noting. Clark alleges in Henry (ed.), op. cit., p. 216, that Bultmann does not approach historical problems as a professional historian. They are to him, he says, 'a side issue blocking his path'. This is a serious point, but is borne out, we believe, in Bultmann's own writings. Again, Küberle, writing in the same volume, p. 65, demonstrates the difference between the cosmic representations of mythology and the 'precise data as to time and place' which confront us in the Gospel. Perhaps, however, it is James Dunn (writing in I. Howard Marshall, (ed.), *New Testament Interpretation* p. 296) that is nearer the mark by suggesting that Bultmann's problem is not with the language of mythology per se, 'but the problem of any language which objectifies God'.

27. Carson, D.A., 'Selected recent studies of the fourth gospel' in *Themelios* 14.2 (Jan/Feb 1989) p. 58.

28. Ridderbos, H.N., 'The Word became Flesh: Reflections on the distinctive characteristics of the Gospel of John', in *Through Christ's Word*, Presbyterian and Reformed: USA, 1985, p. 6.

29. Commentary, p. 14.

30. Ibid., p. 19.

31. Ibid., ad. loc., p. 165.

32. Ibid., ad. loc., p. 282.

33. Ibid., p. 496. cf. also Carl Henry's point in Henry (ed.), op. cit., p. 15, where, by reference to the Dead Sea Scrolls, the evidence of which Bultmann's a prioris force him to ignore, he shows that Bultmann is swimming against the stream of New Testament scholarship.

34. Whitney, T.N.H., p. 538.

35. Ridderbos, op. cit., p. 41.

36. Whitney, T.N.H., p. 319.

37. art.cit., p. 140.

38. Commentary p. 159.

39. Idem.

40. Idem.

41. Whitney, T.N.H., p. 323.

42. Commentary, pp. 159-60.

43. Ibid., p. 438.

44. Ibid., p. 439.

45. Whitney, T.N.H., p. 311, quoting Barth. It is this point that demonstrates the difference between Reformed and Neo-orthodox/Bultmannian thought. For the former, revelation is in order to the understanding of God, for the latter in order to the understanding of man.

46. Knudsen, art.cit., p. 146.

47. Webster, J., 'The Legacy of Barth and Bultmann', in *Evangel*, 1:1 (January 1983), p. 10.

48. Idem.

49. Whitney, T.N.H., p. 299.

50. Interestingly, in the 1971 Basil Blackwell edition of the Commentary, the word 'salvation' is not listed in the index of theological motifs at all.

51. See Commentary ad. loc., p. 377.

52. Commentary, p. 201.

53. Hereafter referred to as *Theology*. Particular volumes will be designated *Theology I* or *Theology II*.

54. *Theology I*, p. 191.

55. Ibid., pp. 198-9.

56. Ibid., p. 227.

57. Ibid., p. 232.

58. Idem.

59. Ibid., p. 237.

60. Ibid., p. 238.

61. Ibid., p. 241.

62. Ibid., p. 245.

63. Ibid., p. 251.

64. Ibid., p. 253.

65. Ibid., p. 298.

66. Ibid., p. 299.·

67. Ibid., p. 305.

68. Whitney, T.N.I., p. 201. Dr. Whitney is here dealing specifically with Bultmann's rejection of 'Paul's appeal to the reality of the resurrection'.

69. *Theology II*, p. 6.

70. cf. the following quotations from the Introduction to the Commentary: 'John is directly dependent on Gnostic traditions' (p. 9). This Bultmann seems to modify, but with little actual difference of thought, by saying that John 'uses the language current in Gnostic circles to give expression to the Christian understanding of faith' (Idem.).

71. See *Theology II* p. 6; cf. also such statements as the note on John 3: 6 — 'this form is characteristic of Gnostic (dualistic) revelation literature in general' (Commentary, p. 140 n.2).

72. *Theology II*, p. 6.

73. Ibid., p. 23. This quotation is taken from the section on 'Johannine determinism'.

74. Ibid., pp. 24-5

75. Ibid., p. 25.

76. Idem.

77. Ibid., p. 54.

78. Idem. Even here Rudolf Bultmann says that this is only a probable conclusion.

79. George Henry Lewes in *The Physiology of Common Life*, ch. 13.

80. Whitney, T.N.I., p. 208.

81. *Theology II*, p. 207.

82. Idem.

83. Idem.

84. Ibid., p. 236.

85. Interestingly, Barth was present to hear it. Johnson (ed.), op. cit., p. 65, points out that it was in criticism of other positions, rather than in their own, that Barth and Bultmann were in agreement.

86. Johnson (ed.), op. cit., p. 68.

87. Ibid., p. 69.

88. Ibid., pp. 69-70.

89. Ibid., p. 77.

90. Ibid., p. 67.

91. Bultmann uses a similar formula throughout his writings in defining sin. What he does not make clear is whether sin is ever to be conceived of in such terms.

92. Johnson (ed.), op. cit., p. 249.

93. Ibid., p. 250.

94. Idem.

95. Idem.

96. Whitney, T.N.H., p. 300.

97. Ridderbos, op. cit., p. 38.

98. Ibid., p. 43.

99. Johnson (ed.), op. cit., p. 291.

100. Ibid., p. 294.

101. Ibid., p. 302.

102. Ibid., p. 323.

103. Van Til, C., *The Later Heidegger and Theology*, Philadelphia, 1964, p. 14.

104. These conclusions show a marked consistency with Clark's three-fold assessment in Henry (ed.), op. cit., p. 223, where he says that Bultmann's New Testament criticism is 'arbitrary', his notion of historiography confused, and his existentialism unintelligible.

105. Whitney, T.N.H., p. 462.

106. Ridderbos, op. cit., p. 44.

107. Idem.

108. Knudsen, art.cit., p. 149. cf. also the phrase on page 155: 'all of the powers that Bultmann takes from Jesus Christ he gives to the primitive church.'

109. Whitney, T.N.I., p. 200.

110. Moises Silva writing in M. Silva (ed), *Foundations of Contemporary Interpretation*, 1997, p. 86.

Chapter 11

The Doctrine of Sin in
the Theology of Emil Brunner

BIOGRAPHICAL DETAILS

1889	Born in Switzerland
	Educated in Zurich, Berlin and New York
	Brief spell as pastor prior to taking up Zurich professorate
1924	Became Professor of Theology at Zurich
1955	Teacher in Japan for two years
1966	Died

Major Publications
The Mediator (1934), *The Divine Imperative* (1937), *Man in Revolt* (1939), *Justice and the Social Order* (1945), *Dogmatics*, in 3 volumes (1949, 1952, 1962)

In the Lent Term 1940 edition of the periodical *Inter Varsity*, a review of Brunner's *Man in Revolt: A Christian Anthropology* appeared. The reviewer was the then pastor of Westminster Chapel, London, Dr. D. Martyn Lloyd-Jones. In his review, Lloyd-Jones gave expression to the ambivalence which characterises almost every evangelical assessment of the renowned Swiss theologian, Emil Brunner, who is our third representative of modern Neo-Orthodoxy.

On the one hand, Lloyd-Jones speaks of Brunner in glowing terms. In a passing comment on two earlier works, Brunner's *The Mediator* and *The Divine Imperative*, he states that 'these two books have done more to promote a return to evangelical preaching of the gospel in this country than any other agency'.[1] And of reading *Man in Revolt* itself, Lloyd-Jones says that it was 'a valuable and enjoyable intellectual exercise that should lead to spiritual results also, as one is forced to re-examine and to reconsider the fundamentals of the faith'.[2]

On the other hand, a warning note is sounded. Lloyd-Jones' caveat is worth quoting in full:

> 'While reading this volume I found myself repeating to myself as I had done when reading all the previous translations of Brunner's works, "Oh! the pity of it, the pity of it." Why? Because this man, who, in general, is so right, and who so effectively displays the utter superficiality and total inadequacy of the liberal and idealistic view of man that has held sway for so many years, nevertheless still clings to certain of the presuppositions that were really responsible for these false views.'[3]

This thesis leads Lloyd-Jones to call Brunner 'a soul struggling towards the light'.[4]

There is no doubt that Brunner finds his niche within the Neo-Orthodox movement which has been occupying our thoughts in these chapters. Many of the distinctive characteristics of this movement in theology over the past sixty or so years are to be found in Brunner also. We shall see as we proceed that Brunner operates with the same presuppositions as Barth and Bultmann, although in some areas his conclusions are vastly different to theirs. Most writers on modern theology link Brunner's name with that of Barth as the two representatives of what is known as Neo-Orthodoxy. At the same time, however, it is lamentable that so little work has been done on Brunner, while Barthian studies have occasioned no end of research. For example, the Blackwell 1989 publication, *The Modern Theologians: An Introduction to Christian Theology in the Twentieth Century* (edited by D.F. Ford in two volumes) has no chapter at all on the thought of Emil Brunner, despite the fact that in the same volume R.W. Jenson, writing on Barth, calls Brunner one of the 'leaders of the 'dialectical theologians' [who] went on to become great names in their own rights'.[5]

Brunner's influence on modern theological reflection was largely commensurate with his professorship of systematic and practical theology in Zurich from 1924 to 1955. However, unlike Barth and Bultmann, he also coupled with his academic work an interest in missiology and ecumenism. Indeed, the last two years of his teaching career were spent ministering in Japan. In many ways, therefore, there is a personal and practical touch in Brunner which is lost in Barth. This may lie behind the popularity which has attended the publication of some of his works, even although they do not approximate the ability of Barth. This may also go some way to explaining the warm commendation offered by Lloyd-Jones above. Another reviewer, commenting on Brunner's *The Great Invitation and Other Sermons*,[6] preached in Zurich before Brunner left for Japan, identifies in his thought a 'warm, evangelistic fervor as he invites men to Christ;...a welcome emphasis on sin, divine grace and the centrality of Jesus Christ; [and]...a belief in the supernatural.'[7]

It was this personal and practical approach which led Brunner to identify as the basis of the Christian faith a revelation based upon 'a person-to-person encounter'.[8] Dr. Whitney is correct to emphasise, in *The New Infallibility*, (pp. 225ff.), that this emphasis in Brunner reflects the influence of Kierkegaard. This influence is explicitly acknowledged by Brunner himself in his writings. Kierkegaard's main emphasis, as we have already noted, is that truth is always subjective, paradoxical and existential. On this basis, Brunner postulates that the Christian faith is also based upon such an existentialism, whereby truth is known in the encounter between God and man (a theme which forms the title of one of Brunner's works), in a moment of personal decision. Moreover, this, says Whitney, is an act of self-validation, by which 'Truth is encounter, and encounter is truth'.[9] Schrotenboer sums him up thus: 'He took issue with the advocates of impersonal dogmas in order to engage man in the existential encounter of personal truth. He will perhaps be remembered most for the impact he gave to theology by his stress upon dialecticism and personal correspondence.'[10]

At the very outset, therefore, and engaged as we are in the attempt to formulate Brunner's doctrine of sin, it has to be acknowledged that, like Barth and Bultmann, Brunner has removed from the discussion any notion of the authority of the Bible. Brunner resists every attempt to objectivise truth, and especially the traditional position of authority claimed for the Bible. In fact, Dr. Whitney goes as far as to say of him that 'Brunner's whole view of Scripture emasculates the words of Scripture to such an extent that their meaning is almost without value'.[11] Or, as Murray puts it otherwise: 'Brunner's view of incompatibility and contradiction in the word of Scripture compels him to adopt a dialectic which has its affinities not with the biblical revelation but with the de-mythologization which, he himself contends, demolishes the total structure of the Christian faith.'[12]

Dr. Whitney demonstrates in *The New Heresy* that Brunner, in common with Barth and Bultmann, serves himself heir of all the subjectivising tendencies of Kantian dialectic. The distinction between the phenomena of reality (things-as-they-appear-to-the-senses) and the *noumena* (things-as-they-are-in-themselves) is also apparent in Brunner's theology. The distinction also between *historie*, plain history, and *geschichte*, supra history, also undergirds his theological reflection. Brunner's doctrine of sin is coloured at every point by these presuppositions. To these now we briefly allude.

Brunner on Revelation

In his *Revelation and Reason*, Brunner shows that he regards revelation as absolutely necessary both for our knowledge of God and our salvation by Him. Indeed, his definitions show that revelation and salvation are, in his view, interrelated in such a way that one is impossible without the other. He says: 'the history of revelation is the history of salvation, and the history of salvation is the history of revelation;'[13] and, moreover, ' 'divine revelation' always [means] the whole of the divine activity for the salvation of the world.'[14]

Brunner wishes to assert the priority of revelation over reason in order to undergird the notion of God as Pure Subject. The transcendence of God is, as we have seen, an important linchpin of Neo-Orthodox dogmatics, and Brunner also wishes to lay much emphasis upon it. Since 'God's essence...defies human conceptualization',[15] it logically follows that 'All Christian doctrine...points to an entity outside itself.'[16] This is the witness of revelation, which points to God, the Absolute Subject.

Central to the whole of this witness as revealed in the New Testament is the semi-historical Event of Jesus Christ. 'God has revealed Himself in the once-for-all event of the Incarnation and the person of Jesus Christ.'[17] There is a Christological principle here which is not as thoroughgoing as that of Barth, but which is nevertheless decisive for Brunner's understanding of revelation.

Dr. Whitney evaluates Brunner's Christocentrism in this context, and highlights the truth concerning it. Far from Brunner accepting the biblical idea of Christ Jesus as the [objective] Truth about God (cf. John 14:6), Dr. Whitney is insistent that for Brunner 'Jesus Christ is only revelation when He is recognized by someone as the Christ – He is only Redeemer when He redeems. He is what He does.'[18] This actualisation of revelation has two corollaries. First it makes God dependent on man – 'God cannot reveal Himself unless man grasps the revelation, and the choice to grasp the revelation is ultimately man's choice.'[19] This is to assert both the sovereignty and infallibility of man, and is consistent with Dr. Whitney's whole thesis of a new infallibility governing Neo-Orthodoxy. Secondly, Brunner's notion of revelation also requires complete participation by man in the act of revelation. A personal encounter is required, and this not with the Jesus of history [historie], but with the Christ of supra-history [geschichte], who is for Brunner 'hidden behind the veils of history and of human life'.[20] This is the Christ-Event, a symbol of man's ability to re-write the whole of Scripture.

Brunner on the Authority of Scripture
Brunner is willing to concede a relation of some kind as existing between God's self-revelation and the words of Scripture. The doctrine of the Church is the Church's reflection on God and His being and nature, and Scripture is the norm of this doctrine. '[Scripture's] witness,' he says, 'is normative for us'.[21] However, for Brunner, Scripture's authority is not commensurate with the text of the Bible. For example, when the Bible speaks of the world, it is clear, according to Brunner, that demythologisation is necessary, in order to have a world-view compatible with modern science. In Whitney's words, 'Theology...has to acknowledge the primacy of Science.'[22] At the same time, Dr. Whitney demonstrates that in some areas, for example in his doctrine of the Atonement, Brunner has had to accept the biblical doctrine as it stands, without alteration. The result, therefore, of Brunner's whole approach is a Bible from which the Church is at liberty to pick and choose what is authoritative and what is not.

As far as the Doctrine of Sin is concerned, it is clear that in Brunner's view the testimony of the Bible is unsuitable as a criterion for the formulation of a Christian hamartology. Its authority is undermined by Brunner, in common with other Neo-Orthodox theologians, with his emphasis on the subjectivity of truth, and the need to supplement, or even replace, the Bible, with the authority of personal experience.

This point is made with great clarity by Gordon H. Clark in his *Religion, Reason and Revelation* (pp. 84-87), where he discusses Brunner's contribution to the whole debate on faith and reason. Clark cites Brunner as an example of the irrational emphasis in post-Hegelian Christianity. His value for our purposes is apparent in that Clark takes Brunner's hamartology as the basis of his discussion. Brunner, he argues, recognises the power of sin in human life, and says that it is more apparent in theology than in physics, 'but he adds that mathematics and logic are so far removed from the religious center of life that in them there is no error at all.'[23] Clark's discussion demonstrates that this is an essentially irrational argument, and is in reality a confusion between the subjective and the objective. Objective mathematics and objective theology are, he argues, both alike free from error; subjective maths and subjective theology are both open to human error.

What Brunner has done, according to Clark, is to subjectivise truth, so that propositions become 'merely pointers to a so-called but poorly defined personal truth'.[24] Such pointers, Brunner argues, to be effective require neither to be true nor false. Clark brings this to its logical conclusion that 'Brunner's words point to a God who tells lies'.[25] Therefore despite the fact that Brunner can say that 'God has made known the secret of His will through...the Holy Scriptures',[26] Dr. Whitney's conclusions remain true, that for Brunner only Christ, and not Scripture, has unconditional authority.[27] Scripture can only point to Christ; it can claim no infallibility for itself. Above all, it cannot be authoritative. Hence Whitney's conclusion as to Neo-Orthodoxy's 'new infallibility' is once again verified: 'Brunner holds this view because of his dialectical principle of the incommensurability of personal truths of revelation and faith with the rational, scientific, impersonal truths of the world.'[28]

Hence the Bible cannot be the standard of orthodoxy as far as sin, or any other doctrine is concerned. In common with the Neo-Orthodox school of which he is part, Brunner will not concede the infallible authority of the Word of God, or at least will not identify that Word with the words of Scripture. 'Brunner's view of Scripture,' says Whitney, 'substitutes...subjective feeling for objective fact.'[29]

It has to be said that Brunner himself eschewed this approach to theology. In *The Divine-Human Encounter*, for example, he argued that the extremes of objectivism and subjectivism were alike 'a threat to the integrity of the Christian faith'.[30] At the same time, Brunner wishes to assert the primacy of the personal encounter in any meaningful act of revelation, thus invalidating the proposition. It becomes clear in Brunner that for him personal encounter means, if anything at all, the subjectivising of truth. Like Barth, Brunner becomes the exponent of the very liberalistic tendencies he professes to despise.

Schrotenboer discusses this thoroughly in his assessment of Brunner in *Creative Minds in Contemporary Theology*. The whole basis of Brunner's thought is, he argues, that 'Revelation is indirect'.[31] This is what really lies at the centre of Brunner's theology. Direct revelation, according to Brunner, is heathenism.[32] Among other things, this means that it cannot be static. The act of revelation becomes a continuum, and it finds its whole basis and meaning in personal encounter.

This means that Brunner can claim fallibility for the Word of God on account of the humanness of the biblical text: '[the Bible] is... a human word and therefore is afflicted with all the deficiency and incompleteness of all that is human.'[33] More serious still is the corollary of this wholesale reduction of the Word of God, by which man becomes 'absolutely indispensable in his role of recipient of God's revelation. He is one half of the encounter. Brunner stresses the I-Thou relation, for God's acts which comprise Brunner's concept of revelation are always personal acts.'[34]

And this, at last, is the major difficulty with Brunner and the Neo-Orthodoxy of which he is an exponent, that man becomes indispensable to revelation, as the judge and criterion of truth. This becomes immediately apparent in Brunner's thought, for he has no objective authority for his theological position. In the words of D.M. Macintyre, 'he can anchor to no certainty.'[35] The dearth of such authority will become even more apparent as we proceed.

The foregoing discussion of Brunner's view of revelation and its consequent, his view of biblical authority, has revealed one aspect of his thinking which must be borne in mind at all times. That is his willingness to profess one thing and practise another, a kind of theological double-mindedness. This point is emphasised by Prof. Donald Maclean in a review of Brunner's *Our Faith*, in which Brunner appears to ground all his thinking on the authority of the Word of God, to the point that he declares that 'the importance of the Bible is that God speaks to us through it',[36] and that we must be prepared to listen to Him. Maclean, however, notes that 'we know from Dr. Brunner's great work *The Mediator*, that while he clings to verbal inspiration as a serviceable theological term, he shows scant respect for its operating principle. Moreover... his acceptance of higher critical conclusions...[appears] to contradict the claim: "the Bible is all His voice".'[37] This seems to accord with Dr. Whitney's claim that for Brunner 'faith defies reason and evidence and is praiseworthy in proportion as it disregards both fact and logic',[38] for Brunner's position, as Maclean points out, is nothing if it is not illogical. At face value, Brunner appears to be so evangelical, but in practice he retreats into irrationalism, an irrationalism which 'plays such a decisive part in rendering the Neo-Orthodox view of Scripture both unscriptural and inconsistent'.[39]

It is with this caveat in mind that we turn to study in more detail the doctrine of sin espoused by Emil Brunner.

Brunner's starting point: the Imago Dei

Before entering into a detailed study of Brunner's hamartology, it is important to note that his point of departure is the concept of the divine image in man. It is to be noted that the Reformed Doctrine of sin is also closely linked with the concept of the divine image, and in this sense Brunner's insistence on it as a starting-point is not unusual. What is unusual is the length of discussion of it in his main treatment of sin in *Man in Revolt*.

In his assessment of Brunner's theology, Schrotenboer both evaluates and commends this order of the discussion of the sin question. He says that 'Man's likeness to God and man's sinfulness are the two basic determinations...of man as he now exists. Logically, the consideration of man as image bearer should be prior to the consideration of sin, for sin is impossible apart from the image.'[40] Similarly, in his Ph.D. thesis on 'Sin and Human Responsibility in the Theology of Emil Brunner', Dr. Malcolm Grant devotes the second chapter to a consideration of the *imago* both in biblical thought and in the thought of Brunner. Both of these writers are agreed that the whole concept of the image is foundational to Brunner's hamartology.

Brunner uses the terms 'formal' and 'material' when talking of the image of God in man, in common with other theologians. But Brunner especially emphasises that the image is primarily a relational concept, 'identical with man's responsibility'.[41] The image marks man off as standing in a specific relation to God: 'Brunner construes the image of God in an activistic, personalistic sense, so that man is always a theological being, always related to God.'[42] Nelson, after discussing several views of the divine image in vogue at one time or another, summarises Brunner's views in similar terms: 'Against these widespread ideas [of the image], Brunner has contended that the Imago Dei is simply man's personal relation of total responsibility to the holy, loving God. It is this which makes man human.'[43] Or, in Brunner's own words, '[man's] being is...responsible and responsive existence;...his distinctive element is the quality of decision.'[44] This is a thoroughgoing crisis-theology.

In Brunner's view, therefore, it is meaningless to talk of the loss of the image, either in part or in whole. Sin, in Brunner's thought, is 'the total perversion and disruption of [man's] being',[45] a personalistic and activistic destruction of man in opposition to the image of God in him. O'Donovan, who has recently re-examined the tension between Brunner and Barth in this whole area, makes the point that for Brunner the image cannot be destroyed by sin. This accords with Brunner's own assertion that 'Sin itself is a manifestation of the image of God in man; only he who has been created in the image of God can sin.'[46]

This is hardly satisfactory. Quite apart from the fact that Brunner orientates his discussion around the non-historicity of creation and the Fall, his understanding of and his emphasis on the image is problematic; the very fact that Barth engaged in debate over Brunner's view itself proves the point. Traditional Reformed and orthodox thinking has emphasised that sin requires the loss of at least part of what is understood as the image of God in which man was created. It is clear that for Brunner this is a non-starter; the image of God, he argues, is what sets man apart as responsible, and apart from this image man could not sin. There is, therefore, a tension between Brunner's thought and Reformed thinking in this area. Our subsequent discussion on the doctrine of sin will demonstrate that Brunner's emphasis on responsibility, while welcome as a valid scriptural principle, means that his discussion is flawed all along the line, from his own starting-point, the image of God in man, to the mythological categories in which he talks of the consummation of all things. We turn, therefore, to summarise and evaluate the doctrine of sin, first as it appears in Brunner's *Dogmatics*.

The Doctrine of sin in the *DOGMATICS*

It is in the Second Volume of his *Dogmatics*, entitled *The Christian Doctrine of Creation and Redemption* that Brunner gives full systematic expression to his understanding of sin. From the outset, Brunner makes it clear that for him sin is a thoroughly existential concept, denoting 'man's need of redemption...seen in the light of his divine destiny'.[47] It is not primarily something moral, but a category which sets man apart as in need of divine redemption and salvation.

The understanding of this category is the task of theology. In order to understand sin, says Brunner, two ground rules are necessary: (a) that it is in the light of the Christian revelation alone that sin can properly be understood;[48] and (b), that the authority for such a theology of sin as can be gained thereby rests on the New Testament, and not on the Old.[49] Especially does Brunner insist that we ignore the testimony of the opening chapters of Genesis for any understanding of sin. The primacy of science forbids this as a legitimate source of enquiry, since these chapters imply 'a view of time and space which has passed away'.[50]

Brunner has two particular reasons for rejecting the testimony of Genesis 3. First, he argues that 'the narrative contained in the 3rd chapter of Genesis has had very little influence upon the doctrine of Sin in the Bible – whether in the Old Testament or in the New'.[51] Secondly, he suggests that the reason why so many have been led into difficulties by starting with the traditional account of the primitive Fall of man is because they have failed to reckon 'with the multiple-narrative in Genesis'.[52]

Brunner therefore lays the foundation for his enquiry by insisting on the Fall as non-event. The Fall of Adam did not occur, according to Brunner, in space-time history. Part of the problem here, as Florovsky correctly states, is that

'The logic of Brunner's own argument seems to compel us to regard [the Fall] as event, as a link in the chain of events. Otherwise it would be just a symbol, a working hypothesis, indispensable for interpretative purposes, but unreal.'[53]

Dr. Grant argues that the conclusion of Brunner's whole thinking in this area is that 'each of us by our own actions is Adam',[54] as Brunner invests the account of the Fall with a didactic rather than with a historical sense.[55]

There is a real difficulty with Brunner's view here. Concerned as he is both to define sin in terms of act and to identify Adam's sin with that of each one of us, Brunner requires an activistic concept of fallenness. Indeed, he insists that 'The statements of the New Testament only apply to a fallen humanity'.[56] But by challenging the factual historicity of the Genesis narrative, Brunner has actually weakened his existentialist understanding of sin. He insists on the universal identity of all men with Adam, existentially and actually fallen, and yet he claims that the Fall of Adam did not actually take place. Despite the fact, therefore, that Brunner insists on regarding man as fallen, there is nothing, logically, to prevent us denying our own fallenness, just as he dismisses the Genesis record. To be sure, Brunner does logically apply his dismissal of the Fall of Adam by denying the possibility of localising sin in time and space, since sin is personal transaction between God and man. He says: 'We can no more localise personal transactions between God and man in the world of time and space than we can localise the spirit of man in the brain.'[57] But this is the whole point – Brunner wants to argue both that sin is existential/activistic and that it cannot be localised. The two theses are not, however, compatible.

Brunner defines sin first as rebellion, 'a turning away from the beginning'.[58] It is not primary, but the reversal of the primary element in man's existence as responsible to God. Sin is also apostasy, 'emancipation from God, giving up the attitude of dependence'.[59] Moreover, man's sin is so deep that it defies his understanding – it is 'deeper than his awareness of it'.[60] Brunner then argues that sin affects the whole man, as man in his rebellion creates for himself a new conception of life itself: 'we are here concerned with a decisive act, which determines the whole of existence. Sin then means the creation of a whole new conception of life.'[61]

Brunner is also at pains to stress the universality of sin. In the *Dogmatics* he puts it thus: 'Sin is not only something which affects us all in the same way, but it is something which affects us all as a whole.'[62] This emphasis is welcome, and seems to accord with the Reformed doctrine, except that immediately Brunner is at pains to prove that the doctrine of original sin does not necessarily follow from the fact of sin's universality. Brunner rightly recognises that this doctrine requires such a concept of the Fall in space-time history as he will not allow, and argues that it 'follows a method which is in no sense biblical'.[63] He then accuses the church of adhering too rigidly to an Augustinian interpretation of Romans 5:12, suggesting that its meaning is that 'each of us becomes a sinner by his own act',[64] and not, therefore, by the imputation of the sin of Adam to us.

There are two main difficulties with Brunner's interpretation of this all-important passage. First, it is difficult, if not impossible, to agree with him that 'there is really nothing in Romans 5 which describes the nature of sin'.[65] Paul's theme, he suggests, is that Christ has conquered death. It is true that in this passage the discussion of sin is parenthetical, and is incidental to the main theme of justification by faith. At the same time, however, it is simply not true that there is nothing in the passage to describe the nature of sin. Quite the opposite; by means of the parenthesis, Paul establishes the condemnation of all in the sin of Adam because sin is transferred to Adam's progeny. It brings death and judgment in its wake precisely because of the sin of the first man. The presuppositions of Neo-Orthodoxy, however, demand that Brunner follow the line that he has taken.

Secondly, if Brunner is correct in his treatment of this passage, then it is difficult to establish his foregoing thesis of the universality of sin. He wants to describe sin, as we have seen, in an activistic and existential sense. Sin, says Brunner, is total act, and issues in a new conception of life. It is this, he argues, that establishes the universality of sin. But on this definition he cannot accept the sinfulness of, say, a newborn child, who has committed no act of sin, and who is not, therefore, in this sense 'fallen'. Witness, for example, his definition of sin at a later point in the *Dogmatics* when he returns to Romans 5 and its interpretation: 'Sin,' he says, 'is responsible action.'[66] The law recognises that there are some categories of people of whom responsibility cannot be predicated – babies, handicapped people, etc. For a baby there is no conception of life governed by the act of sin; sin, therefore, cannot be held to be universal, since on Brunner's definition there has to be some exclusion clause, and some exceptions to the rule. If he holds to an activistic interpretation of sin in the teaching of Romans 5, then Brunner has to change his categories and forego the universalism of sin; if he accepts Romans 5, however, without the colouring of Neo-Orthodoxy, then his emphasis on the universality of sin is welcome.

In the *Dogmatics*, Brunner argues that we cannot enquire as to the meaning of the Fall by the ordinary methods of historiography. He

220 THE NEO-ORTHODOX VIEW OF SIN

says: 'We are aware of sin as our constitution.... But the question of When and How of the Fall is one which cannot be answered from the standpoint of human history.'[67] Or, to put it otherwise, 'Sin, like faith, lies beyond the empirical sphere in the sphere of man's relation to God.'[68] This, as Dr. Whitney argues, is the linch-pin of Neo-Orthodox thinking, operating as it does on the *a priori* that the Kantian distinction between phenomena and noumena is valid at every level of reality, dividing reality into the rational and the irrational. He argues correctly that Brunner follows Kierkegaard here, for whom 'Faith...is not rational; it is not an act of the mind, but a personal leap, venture or risk. It is a not-knowing. Faith is the decision to live in objective uncertainty and subjective certitude.'[69] Sin, the Fall, and faith belong to the irrational and unverifiable world of the noumena. The Fall of man into sin is, therefore, not capable of verification as an historical act. It is irrational. Sin is a 'necessary truth of reason',[70] but it cannot be verified or demonstrated by historical research. This is what Dr. Whitney calls an 'anti-historical view of history'.[71]

Brunner brings the discussion of sin in the *Dogmatics* to a conclusion by examining various theories of the Fall, and by looking critically at the whole question and problem of original sin and the demonic element in sin. On original sin, he says that the classical Augustinian doctrine combines the two-fold emphasis on sin as a dominant force in man's experience, and on the solidarity of all men in sin. Brunner wants to emphasise both of these also, but he does not wish to tie himself to the Augustinian interpretation of Romans 5 and the doctrine of original sin in its traditional form.

Grant believes that 'Brunner's accusation of a false exegesis is entirely credible'.[72] He agrees with Brunner that Augustine's rendering of *eph ho* in Romans 5:12 as 'in quo', i.e. that all mankind was 'in lumbis Adami' is not correct. The correct exegesis, he argues, is not 'in whom' but 'in that', meaning that we all sin, as Adam did, and are held accountable for our own sins, and not for his. But Grant also accuses Brunner of so over-emphasising this element of responsibility that his concern to do so 'is prohibitive of an adequate expression of the element of 'totality'...traditionally affirmed in the doctrine of Original Sin'.[73]

As a final point in this summary of the doctrine of sin as expressed in the *Dogmatics*, Brunner emphasises once again his belief that sin is to be regarded in an activistic sense. 'Sin is act, never state' for

Brunner.[74] It involves personal responsibility precisely because it is to be defined in terms of action on the part of man. It is not a naming word, but a doing word. Sin is verb, never noun. So Dr. Whitney on Brunner's hamartology: 'Sin does not become a quality or substance – it is act, a personal act of apostasy, of disobedience, of alienation from God.'[75]

There is a marked inconsistency in Brunner at this point. He has been saying consistently that sin is irrational and inexplicable, and that it is impossible to localise. This fact stems at least in part from the mythical approach to the early chapters of Genesis, and Brunner's insistence that the Fall is not to be interpreted at all literally. It is difficult to see how Brunner can hold to this while at the same time insisting on defining sin as 'responsible action'.[76] How can sin be an act if it cannot be localised? And how can responsibility be attached to it if it is historically unverifiable? An act, by its definition, needs to be performed, it needs to be done, on the plane of space-time history. It requires localisation. Again, responsibility for sin requires that the act performed be verified as actually having taken place. Brunner wishes to define sin as act, and as responsible action, but his insistence on the non-localisation of sin, as well as on the unverifiability of sin, leads him into irrationalism. And if he will grant the importance both of activism and of responsibility, there is then no justification for his denying the historicity of the Fall of Adam in Genesis 3.

And this, at last, is the lament we must raise for Neo-Orthodox thinking all along the line, that having severed itself from the sure authority of the Word of God, it has plunged itself into agnosticism, anti-propositionalism and even anti-rationalism. Everything, Brunner's doctrine of sin included, is moved over, in the words of Dr. Whitney, 'into an area where it cannot be subjected to rational scrutiny, and is therefore a completely personal thing beyond both the reach and the need of verification.'[77] This being so, it is difficult to see how man can be responsible for his sin. It is by reducing the guilt of man's sinnership that Neo-Orthodox theology has done most damage in its presentation of sin.

Man in Revolt

Man in Revolt is subtitled 'A Christian Anthropology', which alerts us to the fact that it is not a study of sin, but a study of man. Strictly speaking, we should have to say that it is a study of man in sin, for there is more to Christian Anthropology than the fact that man is in revolt. The combination, however, of title and sub-title does alert us to the fact that for Brunner the sin-question is fundamental to any anthropological discussion.

As we have noted, Brunner begins with a detailed study of man's constitution and being as created in the divine image. Man's nature – that which sets him apart from, say, the animal and plant kingdom – is 'the fact that he derives his being from God and is at all times dependent on him, that God calls him to responsibility and obedience, that he is made so that he can only truly live in community with his fellows'.[78] This, however, is not the truth concerning man's existence now – man is now 'in contradiction to his origin, to the divine intention in his life'.[79]

In *Man in Revolt*, as in the *Dogmatics*, Brunner takes as his starting-point the image of God in man. As we have noted, his study of the image in this work is extensive. The bearing of the image on the sin question is, according to Brunner, twofold; (a) 'only he who has been created in the image of God can sin, and in his sin he shows the 'supernatural'...which issues from the primal image of God.'[80] This point is further demonstrated by the observation that 'No animal is able to sin'.[81] It is precisely because man bears a divine image that he has the capacity to revolt against his Maker. And (b) sin has so destroyed the image of God that it can be defined now as 'the one great negative mystery of our existence'.[82] From these two basic premises, Brunner constructs his picture of man in revolt from God.

Brunner defines sin in different ways in *Man in Revolt*. In discussing the Genesis narrative – the 'Primal Sin' of man – Brunner says that it is 'the revolt of the creature against the Creator... it is a positive negation. Sin is defiance, arrogance, the desire to be equal with God...a deliberate severance from the hand of God.'[83] In essence, sin is a mistrust of God and a fear of committing our all to Him: 'it is not simply impudence, but anxiety about oneself; it is not merely rebellion, it is a kind of dizziness which attacks those who ought to step over the abyss leaning only on God.'[84]

It is clear that in all of this Brunner is thinking in activistic terms: 'To be a sinner means: to be engaged in rebellion against God. Sin never becomes a quality or even a substance. Sin is and remains an act.'[85] The Church, claims Brunner, has slipped into the notion of regarding sin as physical and inherited, no different to claiming, for example, that a child has the same colour of eyes as his father. Sin is never, however, a state, as having blue eyes might be regarded as state, claims Brunner; it is always an act. Brunner expands his thinking in this regard in a footnote on page 116 of *Man in Revolt*. He claims that the Old Testament and the teaching of Jesus 'always speak of sin (or more correctly of sins) in the sense of act, and scarcely ever in the sense of being'. Even the notion of original sin, he suggests, is to be so regarded, as 'a wholly personal act which determines the being of the person as a whole'.[86]

It has to be said at this point, however, that Brunner himself does use language which suggests that sin may be regarded as the state of man. He discusses the Creation narratives, which teach, he suggests, that 'we are bound together in a quite unique way, in that way which is called mutual responsibility'.[87] This, he argues, is our origin; and if this is so, then our opposition to our origin 'cannot be an experience, an act, of the individual as an individual...it is that state of 'being against God'.'[88] Brunner is here relating individual acts of sin to social and communal sin, but he does suggest that sin has its origins not in acts but in a state.

The real, objectified result of man's sin is that now there is guilt between God and the sinner. Paradise lost cannot be regained. Brunner has some marvellous prose, an almost preaching style in his writing at this point. Of man's guilt he says this: 'Man is able to destroy his life, but he cannot restore it again. He is able to blind his vision, but he cannot restore his sight. He is able to destroy his communion with God, but he cannot restore it. The way of return to Paradise is barred, the angels with flaming swords stand on guard at its gates; it is impossible to go back; between us and God there lies guilt, an obstacle which we cannot remove, something which cannot be set aside and cannot be got over. The avalanche has fallen and has blocked access to God.'[89] This knowledge is, according to Brunner, registered by a 'bad conscience', which 'preaches the angry God'.[90]

Man in Revolt emphasises the four main themes in Brunner's treatment of sin: the prerequisite of knowledge of the divine image, by which man is able to sin and against which he rebels; the definition of sin in terms of rebellion, mistrust and arrogance against God; the idea of sin as pure act, and the recurring guilt of man's apostasy. There are difficulties with Brunner's discussion with which we shall now attempt to engage.

First it is necessary to highlight a matter which has recurred in discussion of Barth and Bultmann as well as in the foregoing chapter on Brunner, namely, the treatment of the earliest chapters of the Bible as pure myth, incapable of acceptance as factual history. This, as we have seen, is characteristic of Neo-Orthodox thinking, and Brunner also approaches these passages in this light. He says: 'For most of our contemporaries Adam is a kind of legendary figure; it can no longer play any part in the thinking of the succeeding generations as a historical force.'[91] This is not to aver the falsehood of the teaching of the Adam and Eve story; myth, in the thought of Brunner, is not necessarily untrue. 'The Creation and the Fall' may both lie 'behind the historical visible reality',[92] but 'their pre-suppositions...are always present, and are already being expressed in the historical sphere'.[93]

It is clear that there is an element of demythologisation going on here, as many modern critics point out. Strict and literal historicity is abandoned as the events related in Genesis 1ff. are given a purely didactic significance. In Nelson's words, summarising Brunner, 'There is no need to take the story of Adam's Fall literally...every man is Adam'.[94] It must be remembered, however, that for Brunner such an approach to Genesis is not made on purely scientific grounds, but on what he regards as fundamentally religious ones. So Brunner:

'It is not for scientific reasons, in the main, that the historical form of the doctrine of the Fall is questionable, but for religious reasons; it has led to serious distortions of the faith, of the understanding of sin, and of man's responsibility in the sight of God.'[95]

This is an important point to bear in mind. Brunner acknowledges that scientific investigation itself yields the conclusion that Genesis 3 is not to be taken literally, and there is also a hint that form-critical investigation of the Scriptures points in the same direction.[96] However – and in this he is going beyond Bultmann – Brunner rejects the historicity of these early accounts because of a fundamentally religious reason, that is, that they have been misinterpreted in the Church down through the years.

It is important to grasp what Brunner is doing here. His plausible sounding thesis that the scriptural record may be mythical but not necessarily untrue means nothing other than that the Bible cannot mean what it says, and that in its place there must be substituted the consensus opinion of the Church down through the centuries. There must be a dichotomy between the Bible's *teaching* and the Bible's true *meaning*, and that further, the abandonment of the principle of biblical infallibility is made on the basis of a notion of the infallibility of the church, that is, of man. It is the necessity to pursue this line of reasoning that has led Neo-Orthodoxy down a road other than that mapped out by the teaching of our Lord and the holy apostles. [97]

Again, *Man in Revolt* shows an ambivalence between the nature of sin as act and the nature of sin as state. This has been discussed above in the preceding paragraphs. The whole discussion, however, does highlight a factor in Brunner's whole reasoning which Dr. Whitney emphasises, namely, Brunner's devaluation of law. In *The New Heresy*, Dr. Whitney assesses Brunner's emphasis on the freedom of God, and points out that Neo-Orthodoxy is at pains to defend God's freedom even at the expense of God's law. So Whitney: 'God stands over His law and displays His freedom in acquitting the sinner. When he chooses to do so, God can set aside His law.'[98]

The results of this devaluation of God's law are everywhere apparent in Neo-Orthodox thinking. The failure to identify either God's revelatory act or His salvific act with the giving of law, casts its dim shadow over definitions of sin. As law is devalued, so too is the sin which is the breach of it. In this way Brunner can oscillate between his twin premises of sin as state and sin as act. He has no final authority. For him, the divine image in some sense constitutes the divine standard. What he will not concede is that the same God who made man in His image also set the boundaries for the fulfilling of that image in wholesome personality. And to the extent that law is devalued, and devalued in Brunner into something impersonal, to this extent is the nature and gravity of sin diminished.

Thirdly, *Man in Revolt* is extremely unsatisfactory in its treatment of original sin. For this point we might rehearse the objections of Louis Berkhof. Berkhof is dealing with the place given to original sin in Crisis-theology, and illustrates his thesis by referring to Brunner. Brunner, says Berkhof, rejects the two traditional, orthodox, poles of the doctrine of original sin, (a) that the first sin of Adam was placed to the account of his descendants; and (b) that Adam's act resulted in a sinful state passed on to his posterity as the root of all actual sin. Berkhof is willing to admit that Brunner has some correct and proper emphases, as for example when he stresses the solidarity of men in sin and the hereditary transmission of the sinful condition. But he also recognises that, whereas the teaching of the apostle is that original sin is the explanation for solidarity, Brunner wishes to arrive at this destination by some other route.

Berkhof correctly identifies Brunner's rejection of the doctrine of original sin as being because 'the traditional view has an undesirable amount of determinism in it, and does not sufficiently safeguard the responsibility of man';[99] or, in Brunner's own words, the traditional doctrine 'destroys the unity between responsibility and necessity'.[100]

It is to this question that Malcolm Grant has addressed himself in his Ph.D thesis on 'Sin and Responsibility in Brunner's Theology'. He stresses continually that Brunner's insistence on human responsibility is a thoroughgoing motif in his theology. For this reason, Grant argues, Brunner rejects a literal account of the Fall.[101] The problem is put by Grant in these terms: 'To stress the freedom of sin whereby responsibility is predicated, without thereby weakening the contrary assertion of the inevitability of sin, is by no means a simple task.'[102]

Brunner's wholesale rejection, therefore, of the traditional Reformed doctrine of original sin is necessitated by his insistence on the responsibility of man in his sin. But it is a mistake to think that the Reformers in teaching this doctrine understood that it somehow mitigated man's responsibility before God; and to think, consequently, that Brunner has done us a favour by safeguarding this responsibility. Calvin, for example, speaks in these terms of the nature of imputation: 'by Adam's sin we are not condemned through imputation alone, as though we were punished only for the sin of another; but we suffer his punishment, because we also ourselves are guilty.'[103] And again, 'we are guilty through the offence of one man, in such a manner as not to be ourselves innocent.'[104] By these, and a host of other quotations, could we demonstrate that, despite the assertions of Brunner, the doctrine of original sin as originally taught safeguards the fact of responsibility. Brunner is not the sole defendant of the responsibility of man in sin; nor does he require to jettison the traditional doctrine in order to maintain it.

A fourth, and final, problem with Brunner's whole approach, is his approach to the end of sin and the final judgment. It is clear that he understands these things in mythical terms, as for example when he defines hell as 'that one would like to be free from God at last, and it is impossible'.[105] This is a point of criticism which Schrotenboer also picks up in his study of Brunner's anthropolgy. Man, in Brunner's thought, he argues, is considered empirically. This requires as its corollary a massive demythologisation programme for biblical reality. One offshoot of this is that 'There is no resurrection of the body... Brunner accepts man as he now is in the fallen state as normative for the understanding of man.'[106]

There are two serious consequences of this. The first is that it reduces the gravity of sin by removing any notion of final, eternal punishment. God cannot punish sin, because there is no localised hell. This casts grave doubts upon the morality and justice of God. This apart, it also reduces the need to concern ourselves with sin, because there is no impending doom, against which the Gospel is good news.

And secondly, this type of demythologising leaves us all in despair, for if there is no hell, there can be no Heaven. There can be no hope of final deliverance from sin and its consequences. The whole moral universe is in bondage to sin, and, as in the teaching of St. Paul, it groans and travails in pain; but unlike the apostolic hope of the New Testament, for Brunner there is no forthcoming or expected emancipation. This point is explored by Hebblethwaite in his work on *The Christian Hope*. In examining the teaching of Brunner in this whole area, Hebblethwaite concludes that Brunner's demythologising is not as radical as, for example, that of Bultmann, against whom Brunner argues that 'the New Testament hope for an eternal future is not inextricably bound to apocalyptic mythology'.[107] At the same time, Hebblethwaite realises that in Brunner's thought, 'the New Testament pictures of the Parousia are mythological. The final event is unimaginable.'[108] It is Brunner's unwillingness to concede the Bible's clear teaching on the literalness of the end consummation that is the hallmark of his theological reflection. Hebblethwaite's conclusion is that 'Brunner remains a dialectical theologian! As for the final consummation, this can only be expressed in symbols and myths, whose underlying truths can only be barely stated.'[109]

In other words, according to Brunner, we can have no final, certain hope that sin will be overcome. To be sure, we can talk symbolically, but when we have exhausted all our symbols, with what are we left? Certainly with no final assurance, such as is proffered in the Gospel. Brunner may, in common with Barth and Bultmann, make much use of biblical language and concepts, but for him they are of no value in offering assurance to a sin-sick world that its great disease will finally be eradicated by an all-pervasive Saviour.

Descent into Irrationality

Before bringing this chapter to a conclusion by summarising the salient features of Brunner's doctrine of sin, it will be useful to notice that, as with all Neo-Orthodox discussion, the eventual outcome is the jettisoning of reason. Brunner concedes as much by insisting that sin is irrational *and* that it is the overarching principle in our understanding of what man is. Man is sinner; man is, therefore, irrational.

The corollaries of this are striking. Brunner lays much store, for example, by science, and particularly scientifico-critical investigations of the Bible. These investigations have shown, argues Brunner in several places, that we do not need to accept the infallibility or inerrancy of the Word of God.[110] But such investigations have been carried out by sinful (irrational) men. It is difficult to see how Brunner can build so much on the supposed infallibility of scientific investigation, when he has so modified man's capacity for knowledge by his insistence on the all-pervasive power of the irrational in man's existence. This is precisely the conclusion of Schrotenboer, when he argues that if sin is irrational, and if all men sin, then 'If Brunner were to apply his personalistic principles with consistency and to all of reality, he would delete the world of its rational aspect'.[111]

Brunner's theology is thus illustrative of an important point emphasised by Whitney when he states that 'the New Theologians delight in symbols, play with paradox, evade verification, *revel in the irrational*, by-pass logic, excel at ambiguity'.[112] In *The New Infallibility* he applies these criteria directly to Emil Brunner. Following Clark's conclusions in *Religion, Reason and Revelation*, Whitney concludes that Brunner empties revelation of all conceptual content, and also 'accepts or rejects inferences by subjective preferences'.[113] *The New Heresy* works this out in greater detail, as Whitney shows that Brunner's theology leads to a divided field of knowledge and a finite God.[114] The facts – the phenomena – of the world and reality are, for Brunner, totally contingent, governed by internal laws. Brunner's philosophy, argues Whitney, is in common with that of Kant, and both alike, he argues, end 'in the cul-de-sac of modern irrationalism'.[115] There is the sharpest possible dichotomy between science and personality, which obviates any need for God, although His name is used by Brunner as a limiting concept.

In all that we have noted, therefore, concerning Brunner's doctrine of sin, it must be emphasised that in the end he is a slave to what

Whitney calls 'The Paralysis of Presupposition'.[116] The existential dualism of Kant and Kierkegaard are applied ruthlessly by Brunner to the whole theological field. Merely to dress up the conclusions to which he comes in orthodox language does not change the irrationalism of their content one iota. This is Reymond's great lament for Brunner, a lament which is not dissimilar to that of Lloyd-Jones with which this chapter began:

> 'Though a man of massive breadth of learning, a man of unquestionably great intellectual and literary achievement, Brunner is unable to overcome a very poorly defined and colourless Christ Event, about which, as soon as he says anything at all, he must speak in biblical terms, terms the truthfulness of which he is not at all sure.'[117]

Summary

It remains, therefore, at this point in our study, to emphasise the salient features of Brunner's doctrine of sin. First, it has to be noted that Brunner is a thorough-going crisis theologian, whose whole theology is based on *the importance of person-to-person encounter*. It is only on the level of such existential encounter that truth can be verified. Truth is, consequently, subjective; it is whatever man makes it to be. Sin has become, in Brunner's language, solely a matter of unauthentic existence; it is nothing more than a limiting and modifying concept. Man in sin is simply man failing to realise his full potential for living.

Yet, curiously, Brunner wishes to talk of the objectivity of the guilt of man's sin. Man is a responsible creature. Man is answerable and accountable. Sin cannot go unnoticed. But it is this very point, stressed so repeatedly by Brunner, that is at variance with his emphasis on person-to-person encounter in crisis. There is a glaring inconsistency in Brunner – one simply cannot hold both to the subjectivity of truth and the objectivity of guilt. Sin has to be more than act, it must be state and condition also. This alone gives sin objective reality as well as subjective reality. Man is not only a sinner in himself; he is a sinner before a holy God. His sin is culpable exactly for that reason. The whole foundation, however, of Brunner's hamartology, is that although truth is subjective, guilt may be, indeed requires to be, objective.

Secondly, and enough has been said on this point, so that it requires now merely to mention it – Brunner *jettisons the authority of the Word of God in his discussion of sin*. He makes it clear that existential philosophy makes a greater contribution to our understanding of the sin question than the Word of God. It is the substitution of the infallibility of man for the infallibility of God. God's Word is rejected as mythical and non-literal. By adopting this attitude Brunner, like Barth and Bultmann, has severed himself from the one sure foundation for the knowledge of all truth.

Thirdly, Brunner is at pains to stress *the important place of the image of God* in man in any discussion of man's sin. It is this factor that sets man apart from the animal kingdom and makes man a responsible and responsive animal.

Fourth, Brunner's key concept of sin is that *it is activistic*. It is nothing if it is not personal transaction. It is rebellion, arrogance etc. As such, Brunner uses biblical language in his formulations, but it is impossible for him to sever himself from his existential presuppositions, and so he constantly devalues both the reality and the gravity of sin into a meaningless concept of personal existence.

Fifthly, Brunner *rejects much that is emphasised in traditional Protestant orthodoxy*, especially the doctrine of original sin. He wishes to retain that part of the doctrine which emphasises the universality of sin, but it is clear that he construes the doctrine in such a way as to suggest that it moves the emphasis away from individual responsibility. This, as we have seen, is neither a true representation of the Reformers, nor is it a true representation of the Bible's own teaching.

Finally, Brunner's whole approach has led to the *devaluing of God's law in order to safeguard God's freedom*, as if the two were mutually exclusive. It is, however, by no means certain that they are; and Brunner only succeeds in devaluing the gravity of sin further by pursuing such a notion in his thinking. It is clear, therefore, that in his case, a defective theology (in the sense of theology proper) has led to a defective hamartology – wrong views of God cannot lead to right views of sin.

One theologian, writing in the mid-1960s, predicted the future for Brunner's theology in these terms:

'The dust raised by the demythologising controversy...will in time settle. When this happens, Emil Brunner's achievement will be more clearly seen in its continuing relevance and importance for the future.'[118]

After nearly three decades of reflection, however, it has to be said that this did not happen. Nelson, writing more recently, makes this very point when he aptly says that 'The adjective "Brunnerian" is seldom ever seen or heard'.[119] Contrast this with the ongoing influence of Barth, for example. The point is that Brunner's influence has been minimal, although his name is frequently coupled with that of Barth as the two champions of Neo-Orthodoxy. However, the inconsistencies of Brunner's thought, together with the irrationalism and inherent tensions of Neo-Orthodoxy, have meant that his opinions are now seldom hailed as authoritative.

NOTES

1. Lloyd-Jones, D.M., Review of E. Brunner, *Man in Revolt: A Christian Anthropology*, in *Inter-Varsity*, Lent Term, 1940, p. 29.

2. Ibid., p. 30. cf. also Murray's point in his review of Brunner's *Eternal Hope* (in *Westminster Theological Journal*, 17.2 May 1955, p. 170): 'At numerous points Brunner not only stimulates thought but contributes to our understanding of the significance, character and implications of the Christian message of hope.' Dr Noel Wallis, in his unpublished Th.D. thesis on 'The Theology of Karl Barth' (Central School of Religion, 1986), also refers in one place (p. 22) to 'the moderation of Brunner' (as over against the radicalism of Bultmannianism) in which 'some comfort' was found for conservative interpreters of the Word of God.

3. Lloyd-Jones, art. cit., p. 30.

4. Idem.

5. Jenson, R.W., in *The Modern Theologians: An Introduction to Christian Theology in the Twentieth Century*, 1989, p. 32.

6. Sanderson, J.W., in *Westminster Theological Journal*, 18.2, May 1956.

7. Ibid., p. 189.

8. C.A. Baxter, writing in the *New Dictionary of Theology*, 1988, p. 110.

9. Whitney, H., *The New Infallibility*, 1974 (hereafter referred to as T.N.I.), p. 228.

10. Schrotenboer, P., 'Emil Brunner', in Hughes, P. E. (ed.), *Creative Minds in Contemporary Theology*, Eerdmans, 1966, pp. 99-100.

11. Whitney, H., *The New Heresy*, 1974 (hereafter referred to as T.N.H.), p. 233. In his biography of Professor John Murray of Westminster (Vol. 3 of the *Collected Writings of John Murray*, (1982)), Iain H. Murray alludes to this by reference to the invitation by Princeton Seminary in 1937 to Brunner to become Professor of Systematic Theology there. The chair had, says Iain Murray, been made famous by such champions in the defence of Biblical infallibility as Alexander, Hodge and Warfield. The invitation was symptomatic of Princeton's spiritual decline, since 'Brunner did not believe in the infallibility

of the Bible, nor even in Scripture as a trustworthy record of history' (I.H. Murray, op. cit., p. 77).

12. Murray, J., art. cit., p. 175.

13. Quoted in T.N.H., p. 229.

14. Idem.

15. Brunner, quoted by Schrotenboer, art. cit., p. 104.

16. Schrotenboer, idem.

17. Idem. I call it 'semi' historical in order to register Brunner's qualification of the meaning of history, as we shall see in our discussion.

18. T.N.H., p. 230.

19. Idem. cf. also R.L. Reymond who says that 'God, according to Brunner's construction, needs man as much as man needs God in his salvation', *Introductory Studies in Contemporary Theology*, 1968, p. 106.

20. Ibid., p. 231.

21. Schrotenboer, art. cit., p. 106.

22. T.N.H., p. 236.

23. Clark, G.H., *Religion, Reason and Revelation*, (1961), p. 85.

24. Idem.

25. Ibid., p. 86. Clark argues that this is the basis of Neo-Orthodox epistemology – 'Instead of saying, Let God be true and every man a liar, they say, Let God be false, and every man will be a liar too. This type of philosophy is self-contradictory, self-destructive and intellectually stultifying.'

26. Brunner, E., *Our Faith*, 1949, p. 18.

27. See T.N.H., p. 209.

28. Idem.

29. Ibid., p. 233.

30. So J.R. Nelson in Marty, M.E., and Peerman, S.G. (eds.) *A Handbook of Christian Theologians*, (1984), p. 417.

31. Schrotenboer, art. cit., p. 105.

32. Idem.

33. Idem.

34. T.N.I., p. 232.

35. Macintyre, D.M., Review of E. Brunner *The Mediator*, in *Evangelical Quarterly* 6.4 (October 1934), p. 444.

36. *Our Faith*, op. cit., p. 20.

37. Maclean, D., Review of E. Brunner *Our Faith* and *God and Man*, in *Evangelical Quarterly* 9.2 (April 1937), p. 202 (quoting from Our Faith).

38. T.N.H., p. 475.

39. Ibid., p. 477.

40. Schrotenboer, P. .G., *A New Apologetics: An Analysis and Appraisal of the Eristic Theology of Emil Brunner*, 1955, p. 70.

41. So Schrotenboer, summarising Brunner in art. cit., p. 113.

42. Idem.

43. Nelson, art. cit., p. 420. cf. also Cairns, writing on 'Brunner's Conception of Man as Responsive, Responsible Being' in Kegley, C.W. (ed.), *The Theology of Emil Brunner*, Macmillan: New York, 1962, who stresses that the divine image in man stresses relationships rather than substances.

44. Brunner, E., *Man in Revolt*, p. 133.

45. O'Donovan, J.E., 'Man in the Image of God: The Disagreement between Barth and Brunner Reconsidered' in *Scottish Journal of Theology* 39.4 (1986), p. 437.

46. *Man in Revolt*, pp. 132-33; in an interesting and original use of words he describes sin as the copy wanting 'to be like the model itself' (p. 133).

47. Brunner, E., *Dogmatics Volume II: The Christian Doctrine of Creation and Redemption*, (1952), p. 89.

48. Idem.

49. cf. idem.: 'Here once more we take our stand on the theological principle that we must start from the witness of the New Testament, and not from that of the Old.'

50. Idem.

51. Ibid., p. 90.

52. Idem.

53. Florovsky, G., 'The Last Things – The Last Events' in Kegley (ed.), op. cit., p. 211.

54. Grant, M.C., 'Sin and Human Responsibility in the Theology of Emil Brunner', Unpublished Ph.D. thesis, University of Edinburgh, 1967, p. 215.

55. cf. Ibid., p. 215: 'The historical significance of Adam is dissolved into a didactic significance, whereby Adam is not the originator of sin, temporally considered, but rather an illustration of the power of sin, an element of the frailty, of the non-spiritual, of the sense element.'

56. *Dogmatics II*, p. 90.

57. From *The Christian Understanding of Man*, quoted in Schrotenboer, art. cit., p. 113.

58. *Dogmatics* II, p. 91.

59. Ibid., p. 93.

60. Idem.

61. Idem.

62. Ibid., p. 96.

63. Ibid., p. 98.

64. Ibid., p. 99.

65. Idem.

66. Ibid., p. 106.

67. Ibid., p. 100.

68. Ibid., p. 106.

69. T.N.I., p. 226.

70. To quote from Lessing's aphorism that 'Accidental historical truths can

never become proofs for necessary truths of reason' (quoted in T.N.I., p. 234).

71. T.N.I., p. 235.

72. Grant, op. cit., p. 215.

73. Ibid., p. 200.

74. Schrotenboer, art. cit., p. 113.

75. T.N.H., p. 214.

76. *Dogmatics II*, op. cit., p. 106.

77. T.N.I., p. 280.

78. Allen, E.L., *Creation and Grace: A Guide to the Thinking of Emil Brunner*, p. 9.

79. Ibid., p. 10. Allen has borrowed this phraseology from the title of the sixth chapter of *Man in Revolt* – 'The Contradiction: The Destruction of the Image of God.' Most of our comments on Brunner's hamartology in *Man in Revolt* will concentrate on this chapter.

80. *Man in Revolt*, pp. 132-33.

81. Ibid., p. 133.

82. Ibid., p. 132.

83. Ibid., p. 129.

84. Ibid., p. 132.

85. Ibid., p. 148.

86. Ibid., p. 117.

87. Ibid., p. 140.

88. Ibid., p. 141.

89. Ibid., p. 135.

90. Idem.

91. Ibid., p. 120.

92. Ibid., p. 142.

93. Idem.

94. Nelson, art. cit., p. 425. cf. Allen (p.13): 'Adam...is man himself at every stage in... history.'

95. *Man in Revolt*, p. 120. By 'historical form' Brunner means the church's traditional acceptance of the literalness of Genesis.

96. For example, in a footnote in *Man in Revolt*, p. 120, he says: 'The theme of the Bible is not the historical origin of sin, but the universal and irresistible power of sin as affecting man's being.'

97. cf. Schrotenboer's evaluation when he says that Brunner regards orthodox Protestantism as having made a 'paper Pope' out of the Bible (art. cit., p. 118).

98. T.N.H., p. 212.

99. Berkhof, L., *Systematic Theology*, 1959, p. 249.

100. *Man in Revolt*, p. 119.

101. Although as Grant says (p. 164): 'That it is necessary to abandon the story of Genesis III in its narrative form in order to secure the reality of each person's Fall is by no means the obvious conclusion.'

102. Grant, Ph.D. thesis, p. 198.

103. Calvin, Comm. on Romans 5:17.

104. Calvin, Comm. on Romans 5:19.

105. *Man in Revolt*, p. 163.

106. Schrotenboer, art. cit., p. 112.

107. Hebblethwaite, B. *The Christian Hope*, Eerdmans, 1985, p. 142.

108. Ibid., p. 143.

109. Idem.

110. cf. Schrotenboer, art. cit., p123, where he summarises Brunner's teaching in *Dogmatics* III thus: 'Thanks to the new research of Scripture we have learned that it is impossible to believe in an inerrant Scripture.'

111. Schrotenboer, op. cit., p. 72.

112. Whitney, H.J., *T.N.M.*, p. 90. My emphasis.

113. T.N.I., p. 230.

114. T.N.H., p. 243.

115. Ibid., p. 244.

116. T.N.M., p. 117.

117. Reymond, op. cit., p. 109.

118. D. Cairns, writing on 'The Theology of Emil Brunner', *The Expository Times*, 76.2 (1964), p. 58.

119. Nelson, art. cit., p. 485.

Section 4

The Relationship Between Neo-Orthodoxy and Reformed Thought

Chapter 12

The Theologies of the Reformation and the Neo-orthodox Theologians

BIOGRAPHICAL DETAILS

John H. Leith
Born South Carolina; Presbyterian Pastor in Auburn, Alabama; Lindale Georgia; and Nashville, Tennessee, before becoming a Professor with research interests in the Reformed tradition.

Cornelius Van Til
Born Holland 1895; teacher of philosophical apologetics at both Princeton and Westminster Seminary. Major publications dealing with Barth and modern thinkers; pioneered a 'presuppositional' approach to Christian apologetics.

In the foregoing chapters, the two themes which have occupied our attention have been the doctrine of sin as it is portrayed in biblical and in Reformed theology, and the doctrine of sin as it appears in the writings of three representatives of Neo-Orthodox thinking, Karl Barth, Emil Brunner and Rudolf Bultmann. In this final section, we shall make a critical evaluation of the trends in Neo-Orthodoxy, and the relationship between the Reformed, orthodox position, and the modern theologians we have been studying.

Many scholars, in making a critical evaluation of Neo-Orthodox theologians, are happy to use the term 'Reformed' of the Neo-Orthodox theologians. Professor Hugh Kerr of Princeton, for example, makes the following evaluation of Brunner:

'Brunner is a self-conscious Reformation and Reformed theologian. This is Protestant theology in the great tradition, not simply because it takes issue with much in Romanism, but because it accents the positive insights of the Reformation regarding Scripture as the Word of God, the centrality of Christ, the sovereignty of God, the sin of man, and justification by faith.... [Brunner] is deeply critical of the post-Reformation theology of the seventeenth and eighteenth centuries which formalized the theology of the Reformers and stereotyped their creative dynamic.... Brunner is, therefore, also a Reformed theologian in the sense that the church and its theology must always be in the process of reformation under the judgment of the Scriptures as the Word of God.'[1]

Brunner's *Dogmatics* is also listed by John Leith in an appendix in his work *Introduction to the Reformed Tradition*. The appendix lists 'Representative Reformed Systematic Theologies', and includes Calvin, Hodge, Dabney, Berkhof and Karl Barth.[2]

In this work by Professor Leith, Karl Barth is also described as being 'Reformed' throughout, as the following excerpts show: 'Karl Barth, the great Reformed theologian of the twentieth century...';[3] 'Preaching has also been the great theme of the two best-known Reformed theologians of the twentieth century, Emil Brunner and Karl Barth';[4] 'From the beginning in the sixteenth century to Karl Barth in the twentieth century, Reformed theologians have been in intention and in fact theologians of the Bible.'[5]

The claim that Barth and Brunner are 'Reformed', made so categorically by Kerr and Leith, has already been challenged in the respective chapters of this thesis. But further discussion regarding the relationship between the two traditions is necessary at this point. If, for example, Calvin and Barth belong to the same tradition, how can their hamartologies be so radically divergent? Is the claim of Whitney more accurate when he talks of a 'determinative difference between Barth and the Reformed tradition'[6]? Leith and Whitney cannot both be correct.

Areas of tension

There are clear areas of tension between Reformed and Neo-Orthodox thinking. In his discussion of Karl Barth's theology in *The New Heresy*, Whitney highlights six trends of Neo-Orthodox thought which are in direct tension with the Reformed position. The first concerns Scripture. Barth's view of Scripture is, according to Whitney, 'the source of most of [his] theological errors'.[7] By taking the position that the Bible contains mythical and symbolic language and imagery, Barth has cut himself off from its objective authority. Professor Leith's claim that 'Reformed theology has always been intensely biblical'[8] cannot be denied, but his attempt to show that Calvin and Barth belonged to the same tradition in this connection is not convincing. Calvin states that

> 'So long as your mind entertains any misgivings as to the certainty of the word, its authority will be weak and dubious, or rather it will have no authority at all. Nor is it sufficient to believe that God is true, and cannot lie or deceive, unless you feel firmly persuaded that every word which proceeds from him is sacred, inviolable truth' (*Inst.* III.2.6).

This, as Whitney points out, is where theology must begin: 'in making the Bible the starting-point of theology, we are assuming, on its own evidence, its infallibility and inerrancy.'[9] Barth, Brunner and Bultmann unite in a view of the Bible which requires massive re-interpretation of it, and concludes that on no account is it to be taken literally.

Secondly, Whitney lays emphasis on the view of history which Barth espouses. Although he argues against Bultmann's demytholo-gising programme, Barth still maintains Kantian distinctions between *historie* and *geshichte*, and applies them to biblical history: for example, to the Fall of Adam.

Thirdly, Whitney stresses that Barth rejects a Scriptural distinction between the Person and the Work of Jesus Christ. The Reformed theology maintains such a distinction. As we have seen, Barth uses the analogy of the Trinity to express his view of the Word of God as proclaimed, written and revealed. But the written word is witnessed to by the Bible, and these two cannot be identified with one another. In this way, Barth is able to make the Trinity itself a mythological concept and to integrate 'the Person and the Work, the two natures and the two estates of Jesus Christ'.[10]

This leads to the fourth area of tension which Whitney identifies: Barth's rejection of the states of Christ, especially his argument that the Christology of the Reformers has been 'arbitrarily constructed from Scripture and tradition'.[11] This, as we have seen, is what Barth means by the actualising of the Incarnation, converting it into something ongoing and recurring.

Fifth, for Barth, reconciliation with God occurs through the Incarnation, rather than through the atonement. In becoming man, God in Christ has become fully identified with man, so that man's salvation requires little or nothing beyond the incarnation itself. To talk of atonement or substitution is to use the language of revelation rather than the language of redemption. It is in the incarnation itself that the reconciliation is effected. Webster puts it thus: 'God's being is described [i.e. in Barth] as his being-in-act, that is to say, God is himself or becomes himself in the loving act of creating fellowship with man in Jesus Christ.'[12]

Finally, Whitney highlights the inevitable conclusion to which this thinking leads – to an unashamed universalism. He reminds us of the difficulties faced by any attempted evaluation of Barth's works: 'He will not affirm, nor yet will he deny, universalism. The thrust of his logic, however, is in favour of universalism, and the implications of his basic position cannot be denied.'[13] This leads, of course, out of what Bloesch called 'Barth's unwarranted optimisim',[14] an optimism which grew out of the emphasis on the 'powerlessness of the adversary of God and man' and also on the nature of man itself.[15] Man is, in Barth's language, basically good but occasionally bad. The fact of incarnation requires that men recognise that in Christ God has taken steps to reconcile all men.

In summarising the relationship between Barth and traditional Reformation theology, Whitney quotes from Fred Klooster who says that 'in spite of his very impressive effort at reconstructing the doctrine of reconciliation within a framework seemingly Reformed, Barth has discarded the most basic elements of the Reformed view.'[16] It is this caveat that must be applied to a work such as that of Dr. Leith's *Introduction to the Reformed Tradition*, where Brunner and Barth alike are hailed as modern exponents of the Reformed point of view. In assessing this position, we shall look at some of the reasons why Leith's work takes this view, and then turn to Van Til's role in the debate over Karl Barth and modern theology.

Dr. Leith's arguments

Leith's *Introduction to the Reformed Tradition* begins with a general overview of the history of the Reformed tradition and also of the main emphases of the Reformed theology. His basic premise is revealed in the following statement from the preface:

'The Reformed tradition cannot be precisely defined. Here it is broadly understood to be that pattern of Protestant Christianity which has its roots in the sixteenth-century Reformation in Switzerland and Strasbourg. The tradition is well established theologically by the authoritative achievements of Calvin's Institutes of the Christian Religion in the sixteenth century and Karl Barth's Church Dogmatics in the twentieth.'[17]

Leith's yardstick for measuring the continuity of Reformed thought is in terms of 'tradition'. This becomes for him more important than the Bible itself: 'The high place that Protestantism has always given the Bible obscures the importance of the living tradition even for the Bible itself.'[18] For this reason, the Bible has to be itself subject to the ongoing Reformed traditioning of Jesus Christ within the church. It is for this reason that Barth rates so highly in Leith's work, since he has rooted his theology in Church Dogmatics, that is, firmly within the living community which 'traditions' Jesus.

In his chapter on 'the ethos of the Reformed tradition', Leith identifies nine motifs in the Reformed way of being a Christian. These are the majesty and praise of God, the polemic against idolatry, the working out of divine purpose in history, the ethic of holy living, the mind in the service of God, preaching, church polity and pastoral care, discipline and simplicity. Leith sees Barth and Brunner as reflecting these motifs in their work, especially in their emphasis on preaching.

Leith's discussion of theology and its place in the Reformed tradition is significant for our current purposes. Leith sees theology as continuing dialogue, particularly within the context of Christian experience and community. He writes that 'no doctrine is fully understood until it is studied in actual experience'.[19] For all his confessed adherence to the teaching of the Scriptures, Leith's actual position is that biblical revelation requires the authentication of experience. This is pure existentialism in a religious guise. Leith is correct to identify Barth as belonging to this milieu of theological thought and method; he does actually wrestle, as Leith puts it, 'with the data of theology, especially the Bible and the history of doctrine, in such a way as to allow Christian faith to be expressed in the contemporary situation in a way that is true to the data from which it arises.'[20] Whitney, in the light of this, is correct to maintain that 'Barth is irrevocably committed to a foundational proposition: 'existence is more basic than revelation'. His use of the apparatus of dialecticism and existentialism, despite his valiant efforts to tear himself loose from this apparatus, has robbed his theology of Scriptural validity.'[21]

It is this thread that runs implicitly through the writings of Barth, despite his disclaimers to the contrary. And even although Leith says that Barth, in common with other Reformed theologians, is a theologian of the Bible, this must be qualified. For all that Scripture is given a high profile, it is clear that to Barth Scripture is not enough; Whitney is thus able to summarise the modern theology of Barth and others in these terms: 'Since there is no objective standard of verification available, the only criterion we have is psychological plausibility.'[22] This is to substitute human psychological plausibility for final truth, and to make man the measure of all things in the recurring theological dialogue.

Leith also lays stress on predestination and election as distinguishing Reformed theology. Predestination, he says,

> 'brings the Reformed understanding of God to focus upon the believer and the church.... Reformed theologians have always known that psychologically and historically the life of faith and the life of the church were the work of the people of God. Yet, they also insisted that the root of this life was not first in the decision of individuals or of the community but in the election of God.'[23]

Election is a radical motif in the thinking of Barth also. Whitney devotes a chapter of *The New Heresy* to this doctrine as Barth presents it. His general conclusion is that 'we are face to face with Barth's habit of taking Evangelical words and infusing a new meaning into them. It is palpably evident that here Barth is in conflict with Calvin, yet he is often quoted as being in harmony with Calvin.'[24] This can be borne out by a study of the *Church Dogmatics* which asserts that Christ is the elected man, in whom all have been elected. This is not the view of the traditional Reformed documents in the matter of divine predestination.

Leith goes on to discuss Barth in detail under the heading 'The new reformation theology, 1918-1955'. His contention is that while theologians of a previous era had stressed the continuity between God and the world, Barth stressed the discontinuity, reaffirming classical and traditional beliefs, but doing so as a theologian of his own age, of the twentieth century. So Leith:

> '[Barth] accepted the fact that the nineteenth century had happened. He did not deny the reality of the scientific revolution, of historical-critical study, or of the Industrial Revolution. He was neither a fundamentalist nor a liberal, and both alike were unhappy with him.'[25]

In a more detailed study of Barth as a representative theologian of the Reformed tradition, Leith suggests that the recurring motif in Barth is the fact of dogmatics as being an authentication on the part of the church of its own message and proclamation. He quotes Barth himself who says:

> 'I listen as unreservedly as possible to the witness of Scripture and as impartially as possible to that of the Church, and then consider and formulate what may be the result.'[26]

It is not without good reason, then, that Whitney declares that 'Barth's theology is a monument to Barth – it is not a monument to Scripture!'[27]

The parallel between Calvin and Barth which is so crucial to Leith's thesis is further made in a discussion of 'Liturgy and the reformed tradition'. Leith argues that both Calvin and Barth gave the whole subject of worship more place than any other representative theologian of the tradition. He concludes that 'Karl Barth has renewed the Reformed understanding of liturgy by his emphasis on the centrality of worship in the existence of the church and by his emphasis on the importance of theology over against aesthetic, social and psychological considerations in worship.'[28]

Van Til's position

Leith's study is an introduction to the Reformed tradition. Its basic thesis is that the Reformed tradition is, in fact, beyond definition. That two such contrasting theologians as John Calvin and Karl Barth can, in Leith's view, belong to this tradition is consonant at least with his thesis. But it is not the position taken by other Reformed scholars. Most notably, Cornelius Van Til, late professor of Apologetics at Westminster Theological Seminary, took quite a different stance with regard to the theology of Barth and other Neo-orthodox theologians.

Van Til's roots are in the Reformed movement in the Netherlands. His biographer says that part of the legacy left him by his parents was 'exposure to a rich heritage of Calvinistic theology'.[29] When emigration brought the family to America, Van Til found himself studying theology in the heyday of liberalistic teaching, which was splitting denominations across America. Under the influence of Geerhardus Vos and Gresham Machen, Van Til became a leading scholar and defender of Reformed dogmatics, devoting the greater part of his life to the testimony and work of Westminster Theological Seminary.

Van Til's defence of Calvinistic doctrine brought him into conflict with the theology of Barth, and much of his work was concerned with highlighting the flaws in Barth's position. A summary of his work *Christianity and Barthianism* (1962), his sterling contribution in this field, is appropriate here.

According to Van Til's biographer, *Christianity and Barthianism* represents 'Van Til's concentrated study of the Swiss scholar [Barth] for a period of forty years'.[30] Van Til's starting point, which he lays down in the Preface, is that 'for all its verbal similarity to historic Protestantism, Barth's theology is, in effect, a denial of it.'[31] He is also careful to make the point that it is in the light of the *Church Dogmatics*, rather than in the light of more popular works, that Barth's theological system is to be understood. Despite one's admiration for Barth, he says, 'One must look back to the Christian Dogmatics of 1927....in order to trace the development of Barth's thinking. But in the Church Dogmatics we have the ripe fruition of a long lifetime of arduous reflection and research.'[32]

In his analysis of Barthianism, Van Til points out that Barth set out to state his theology over against the 'consciousness-theology' of Schleiermacher, who has been called the father of modern theology. Schleiermacher begins with the fact of man's self-consiousness, and ends up with a theology in which religious language is pure psychology, where religious truths embody only personal projections. In Schleiermacher, 'the objective moment of religion dissolves into the subjective.'[33] Barth's expressed view is that he wishes to turn from this and return to the Reformers. But this is precisely the issue for Van Til: 'Did Barth really turn away from consciousness-theology? Did he really return to the principles of Reformation theology?'[34]

Van Til concedes that 'There is no doubt that Barth aims to set forth a Reformation theology. He rejects Romanism, he says, in terms of the Reformation principle. He seeks to build upon the theology of Luther and of Calvin.'[35] At the same time, there is a sense in which Barth's theology is designed to go far beyond the Reformation theology, so that while taking Calvin as his starting-point, Barth can drift into a sea of independence. Van Til is at pains to show that Barth's analysis of the Reformed doctrine of Scripture, and therefore his Christology, is quite different to that which actually appears in the writings of the Reformers themselves.

Barth's Christological principle centres upon Christ as electing God and elected man. This, says Van Til, is nowhere found in Calvin, who believed 'in an electing God back of the electing Christ'.[36] Barth criticises the Reformers for having a grossly defective Christology, and therefore a defective anthropology; beyond Calvin, Barth wishes to argue that 'Man exists inasmuch as and in so far as God is present in him as the Saviour of all men. Man can never escape the lordship of Christ over him.... Man is man because God's work takes place in him, because God's kingdom comes in him.... Man as man serves God in Christ.'[37] Van Til presses home the logic of this reasoning:

> 'How then can Calvin be expected to see that sin is an ontological impossibility? How could he see that sin and unbelief are defeated in advance (zum vornherein)? Having an arbitrarily electing God back of Christ, how could Calvin see the essence of all men is their election in Christ?'[38]

Barth's criticisms of Calvin and the Reformation theology show us that however much he begins with the thinking of the Reformers, or employs their language, he has, in fact, moved outwith the parameters of their thinking, and has re-written their theology. We have already noticed (in chapter 2) that the Reformers did not believe in the ontological impossibility of sin, and certainly did not conceive of such a doctrine arising out of a biblical Christology. It is, however, as Noel Wallis argues, out of such a doctrine of Christ that Barth builds his doctrine of sin:

> 'Here we have illustrated once again Barth's use of his Christological principle. Protesting that revelation in Jesus Christ leaves no room for abstract metaphysical speculation, he proceeds to speculate by grounding the 'ontological impossibility of sin' in Christology.'[39]

Van Til discusses Berkouwer's insistence that Barth's intention is not to minimalize sin or its consequences. Berkouwer argues that it is the condition of man's being 'appointed "beforehand" in "the history of victory which Jesus Christ has unfolded" '[40] that makes sin ontologically impossible; the grace which elects Jesus means that sin, however real Barth may try to paint it, is man grasping for what he cannot actually grasp since God has dealt with it. This is far removed from Calvin's insistence that 'Every sin should convince us of the general truth of the corruption of our nature'.[41] Van Til summarises thus:

> 'In the theology of the Reformation, there is a genuine 'transition from wrath to grace' in history.... Barth rejects this position in toto.... On the basis of Barth's theology, there is, says Berkouwer, no transition from

wrath to grace in history. No more basic criticism of Barth's theology can be made.'[42]

In the second section of his major critique of Barthianism, Van Til summarises the position of certain representative Reformed theologians vis-a-vis Barth. It will suffice for our purposes to focus on sub-section four of this Section Two of his work, where Van Til looks at the writings of Dr A. de Bondt and G.C. Berkouwer on the subject of sin. He shows how, in his theology entitled *The Dogma of the Church*, de Bondt assumes that Scripture, rather than church tradition, is the terminus a quo for information on the subject of sin. After surveying the relevant biblical data, de Bondt concludes that Barth's view of the image of God in man precludes any serious notion of sin: 'On Barth's basis, man has not lost the image of God for the reason that he never possessed it.'[43] But man was not created neutral – he was created good. This is what Barth lacks, and the deficiency is apparent throughout his theology.

Berkouwer is also summarised by Van Til in respect of the question of the *imago*. Van Til's point here is that Barthian thinking reverses the viewpoint from which Scripture argues its case. In Barth, we begin with a positive anthropology which comes from Christology – 'we participate in the human nature of Jesus'.[44] This, however, as Van Til points out, is not the order of Scripture, but a reverse of it: '[Barth] says that we receive our nature wholly from Jesus. Barth puts the matter this way because he wants to maintain that man's nature is what it is primarily because of the grace-relation that it sustains to God through Jesus.'[45] Van Til demonstrates that Barth, instead of starting with fallen man, as Scripture does, begins with Jesus of Nazareth, and is necessarily led into the speculation which abounds in his theology regarding the 'sin' of man, as a state in which there is no guilt, no wrath – an ontological impossibility.

Van Til delivers the following striking indictment of all of this: 'Barth's view of sin as something that is in advance destroyed by the grace of God requires the rejection both of the biblical view of sin and of the biblical view of grace. There is no transition from sin to grace in history in Barth's theology. And his views of both sin and grace are, it becomes increasingly clear, imbedded in and in turn permeate the whole of his theology.'[46]

Van Til's main emphasis in *Christianity and Barthianism* is to show that 'the theology of Barth is dialectical rather than biblical in character',[47] and it is in demonstration of this thesis that the remainder of the book is written. The setting forth of this thesis shows Van Til's extremely informed and acute grasp of his subject, and also what his biographer calls '[his] own fierce antagonism to the highly intellectualized but appealing unbelief that had become so deceptive to many'.[48] For Van Til regards Barthian thinking as apostate in character, springing out of the form-matter scheme of Greek philosophy, where the irrational was kept alive by the rational, and where a 'rational principle of continuity' and an 'irrational principle of discontinuity' are adopted as correlative. Barth, in Van Til's view, applies the same to theology and concludes that there can be no actual atonement because there is no transition from sin to grace in history. So Van Til: 'On this view, it is indeed possible for man to sin, but only in the sense that a child can disobey his parent. Man cannot sin in such a way as to require his being driven forth from the father's house.'[49] On this view also, evil is only a principle, as ultimate as good, and therefore the latter has no power inherent to destroy it.

Van Til's conclusion is that 'Barth does not, like Calvin, find God speaking directly to him in the facts of nature, history or Scripture.... To find the real man, we may therefore use Calvin's terminology but we must put it in the proper Christological framework.'[50] Faith, on the basis of Barth's Christology, is man's only choice. This is going far beyond Reformed thinking – this is 'the Christ of modern reconstruction...the Christ of the higher humanism'.[51] And, according to Van Til, the worst aspect of this is that it is paraded with the vocabulary of Reformed thought.

Conclusion

This chapter has been concerned with the question of whether or not Barth and the other Neo-orthodox thinkers we have been studying can legitimately be described as belonging to the Reformed tradition. Although it is not enough simply to compare and contrast traditions, it is quite clear that the divergence between the two streams of thought we have been studying is very wide indeed.

The Reformation theology begins with an acceptance of final, biblical authority. It theologises with constant reference to Scripture, and issues in the Gospel of a living and exalted Saviour. Neo-orthodoxy assumes the fallibility of scriptural dogma, and also the finality of experience. Its modus is the dialectic existentialism of the atheistic philosophers, and its outcome is that man is basically good, and certainly safe. Nothing could be more inimical to the spirit of the Gospel that declares man's total inability until saved by Jesus Christ.

NOTES

1. Kerr, H., 'Emil Brunner' in G.L. Hunt (ed) *Ten Makers of Modern Protestant Thought*, pp. 75-76.
2. Leith, J.H., *Introduction to the Reformed Tradition*, (1977), pp. 131-2.
3. Ibid., p. 21.
4. Ibid., p. 81.
5. Ibid., p. 100.
6. Whitney, *The New Heresy*, p. 182. Whitney is speaking here of the two contrasting views of Scripture in Karl Barth and the Reformed theology.
7. Ibid., p. 182.
8. Leith, op. cit., p. 97.
9. Whitney, op. cit., pp. 516-7.
10. Ibid., p. 183.
11. Ibid., p. 184. Whitney is here quoting Barth.
12. Webster on Karl Barth in the *New Dictionary of Theology*, p. 78.
13. Whitney, op. cit., p. 186.
14. Bloesch, D.S., *The Evangelical Renaissance*, (1974), p. 89.
15. Idem.
16. Whitney, op. cit., p. 186.
17. Leith, op. cit., p. 8.
18. Ibid., p. 18.
19. Ibid., p. 92.
20. Ibid., p. 93.
21. Whitney, op. cit., p. 187.
22. Whitney, *T.N.M.*, p. 155.
23. Leith, op. cit., p. 121.
24. Whitney, T.N.H., p. 143.
25. Leith, op. cit., p. 121.
26. Ibid., p. 128.
27. T.N.H., p. 490.
28. Leith, op. cit., p. 171.
29. White, W., *Van Til: Defender of the Faith*, Presbyterian and Reformed, 1979, p. 22.
30. *Ibid.*, p. 144.
31. Van Til, *Christianity and Barthianism*, (1962), p. vii.
32. Ibid., p. 2. Whitney also expresses the same admiration for Barth, but states at the same time that the important thing is one's view of Barth's

theological system, rather than his personal piety.

33. Ibid., p. 3.
34. Ibid., p. 4.
35. Ibid., p. 54.
36. Ibid., p. 57.
37. Ibid., p. 65.
38. Ibid., p. 66.
39. Wallis, N.W., Unpublished Th.D. thesis 'A Critique on Barth's Theology', p. 82.
40. Van Til, op. cit., p. 111. Part of the quotation is Berkouwer.
41. From Calvin on Psalm II, quoted in Miller, G., *Calvin's Wisdom*, Edinburgh: Banner of Truth, 1992, p. 346.
42. Van Til calls this 'the position of historic Christianity' (Ibid., p. 113).
43. Ibid., p. 157.
44. Ibid., p. 158.
45. Idem.
46. Ibid., p. 160.
47. Ibid., p. 203.
48. White, W., op. cit., p. 146.
49. Van Til, op. cit., p. 207.
50. Ibid., p. 442.
51. Ibid., p. 445.

Conclusion

Eta Linneman has written:

> 'Whoever maintains that the Bible can only be made understandable with the methods of critical historiography is putting a thoroughly atheistically conceived science in charge of the treasures of divine revelation. God's Word says to us that God controls the destinies of the nations; critical historiography refuses from the very start even to consider the possibility that God has worked in actual history.'[1]

The significance of Linneman's conclusion is that for many years she studied under Rudolf Bultmann, and rose to become Professor of New Testament at Marburg. An able exponent of the Bultmannian school, she taught the 'methods of critical historiography' to many students, and wrote highly acclaimed works.

These, she says, she eventually consigned to the rubbish-bin; and in her *Historical Criticism of the Bible*, urges those who have copies, to do the same.[2] The reason for such a radical rejection of her former position was the realisation that

> 'Both historical-critical theology and critical historiography have their basis in deception. Science is, accordingly, not the synonym for truth, but rather for rebellion against God which suppresses the truth in unrighteousness. The individual data which it unearths are marred and distorted, like a spoon's appearance is optically distorted in a glass of water.'[3]

This position is further clarified in Linneman's next book, *Is there a Synoptic Problem?* Here, Linneman's experience of Bultmannianism and her expertise in New Testament studies are employed to show how the Neo-orthodox method represents a distortion of truth. It is a method characterised by the fact that 'Basic philosophical principles, which have been established without reference to the Bible, must be harmonized with the actual biblical data.... Scientific biblical exegesis, for the most part, still follows the guidelines drawn up by the philosophers.'[4] This is the thesis presented by Dr. Whitney in these terms:

'Neo-orthodox thinkers have elaborated their view of Scripture without complete submission to Scripture. [They] have articulated a philosophical blueprint of their respective areas of interest and have super-imposed Scriptural insights upon their previously constructed, human philosophical creations.'[5]

Linneman applied these basic insights to the Synoptic question,[6] and showed how, in the interests of maintaining an atheistic position, University lecturers and students were theorizing unscientifically, and giving their theories the status of established fact. Linneman's conclusion is as follows:

'Either we follow the Lord Jesus in our theological work and cling loyally to his Word, or we pursue theology in the train of poets and philosophers who are declared enemies of our Lord Jesus.'[7]

The foregoing chapters have sought to demonstrate that the Reformed theology has consistently sought to maintain biblical emphases and biblical doctrines. Especially with regard to hamartology, it has sought to defend and maintain the high ground of biblical objectivity. But it has also been demonstrated that reactions to the Reformed position have veered in the direction of philosophy and subjectivism. So Dr. David Smith writes:

'Luther's unhappiness with conditions in the Roman Catholic church aroused dissatisfaction in others, not only with Catholicism but with the existing Reformation movements of the time. As a consequence, a variety of radical movements ensued. Some of these, reacting against the strong objective emphasis of Luther and Calvin, opted for a mystical approach to Christianity. Others, with similar reactions, moved toward a liberal rationalism.'[8]

Dr. Smith, summarising the reactions of Neo-orthodoxy, writes:

'Existentialism invested orthodox Christian terminology with new meaning. Its transformation of the doctrines of sin and salvation into psychological symbols removed it at a substantial distance from traditional theology. Like existentialism, neo-orthodoxy sought to renew orthodox Christian belief. It wanted to keep traditional doctrines while making the faith more relevant and believable for contemporary humans. The result was a considerably different emphasis on the doctrine of sin, more after the image of Søren Kierkegaard than that of orthodox Christianity.'[9]

There is a clear and radical divergence between orthodoxy and Neo-orthodoxy. While not all theologians of either stream agree wholly with each other, the most basic aspect of the cleavage is seen in the substitution of 'the infallibility of science for the infallibility of Scripture'.[10] The inevitable conclusion follows:

'where human experience displaces Divine declaration as the criterion for interpreting Scripture, Scripture is falsified, theology reduced to virtual anthropology, and the Christian faith transformed into either 'Christian Atheism' or Christian Agnosticism.'[11]

It is precisely this reductionist view of Scriptural truth that has been the legacy of Neo-orthodoxy. Despite the professed desire to return to Scripture and to the transcendence of God, Barthianism has paved the way for an unashamed universalism: in Barthian hermeneutics, 'if I would know what is right, I must acknowledge my status as a creature, as a sinful creature, as a sinful creature reconciled to God by God'.[12] One of the implications of this, as Biggar goes on to demonstrate, is that 'the Church is bound to regard the non-Christian as a virtual, if not actual, member of the community of hearing'.[13] This, more than anything else, demonstrates the subjectivism which Neo-orthodoxy inevitably leads to; the fact, as Linneman reminded us, that

'Because one has decided that the thought content of the Bible should actually be recognized independently, the unity of the Bible is dissolved and God's Word can no longer serve as its own interpreter. Consequently it is necessary to indulge in assumptions rather than to recognize facts, to connect hypotheses to other hypotheses until an entire house of cards is constructed using hypotheses. The decisive factor in the assessing and ordering of these hypotheses is the autonomous 'I', which judges God's Word according to its own discretion.'[14]

Whether the 'I' who interprets Scripture is in sympathy with its doctrines is beside the point; he or she may be the most rabid anti-theist in the world. But by crisis experience, by subjective criteria, by a 'non-rational, contemporary view of revelation',[15] Scripture is evacuated of its meaning and its objective character. As Whitney has it,

'The last thing the new theology appears to want to do is to try to see what the Scripture really teaches. It specialises rather in elaborate reappraisals, reinterpretations, reconstructions, reductions of the plain teaching of the Word of God. Theology has been cut off at the roots.'[16]

Linneman's conclusions regarding the place of evangelical theology will form a fitting conclusion to this study of the doctrine of sin:

> 'Claiming to be scientific means to regard the principles of science as foundational alongside God's Word. But these principles...turn out to be inimical to God when used in this way.... But giving up the claim to be scientific does not mean giving up competent intellectual work in theology.... Its passion is... the willingness humbly to serve the body of Christ, using the gifts of God wherever God should see fit.'[17]

Dr. D.L. Smith has said something similar:

> We need a revival of preaching against sin. The church seems to have lost its concern that those who persist in their sinful condition will go to hell and experience eternal loss. Many seem to follow the path of Karl Barth who believed that in Christ all human beings would avoid perdition. Such neglect goes against the tenor of the New Testament.[18]

Or, in the words of Dr. Whitney:

> 'Experience apart from Scripture is no safe guide to doctrine, for example, the Biblical doctrine of sin. This doctrine comes alone from Scripture; and only he who accepts Scripture as God's authoritative revelation and that of His self-identifying Son, will accept what the Bible says about himself as a sinner in God's sight.'[19]

Sin is not merely a psychological malfunction; it means that man has no personal relationship with God, but is under His wrath and curse. The modern Gospel that is rooted in Neo-orthodoxy does not allow this. It represents sin as malfunction, and salvation within man's reach. The Biblical, Reformation doctrine of salvation by Christ alone, and through faith alone – all of grace – can alone meet the condition of a fallen race.

'But God demonstrates His own love toward us, in that while we were yet sinners, Christ died for us' (Romans 5:8).

NOTES

1. Linneman, E., *Historical Criticism of the Bible*, Baker, 1990, p. 116.
2. Ibid., p. 20.
3. Ibid., p. 116.
4. Linneman, E., *Is there a Synoptic Problem?,* Baker, (1993), p. 20. cf. Dr. Wallis' assessment of Dr. Whitney's work *The New Infallibility:* Dr. Whitney, he argues, shows that 'the philosophical theories of Sartre and his followers have permeated the thinking of the Church, leading away from a Biblical theology to a theology of 'the ontological experience of the self and being' ' (*The Warhorse*, p.116.).
5. Whitney, H.J., *The New Heresy*, p. 5.
6. The subject of the literary dependence of the Gospels has been hotly debated in New Testament studies. One of Linneman's contentions is that 'The so-called Synoptic problem comprises about one-half of the ground on which the imposing edifice of New Testament science has been erected' (*Is there a Synoptic problem?*, p. 40).
7. Ibid., p. 42.
8. Smith, D.L., *With Willful Intent: A Theology of Sin*, (1994), p. 79.
9. Ibid., p. 113.
10. Whitney, H. *The New Infallibility*, p. 287.
11. Ibid., p. 303.
12. Biggar, N. in 'Hearing God's command and thinking about what's right: with and beyond Barth' in *Reckoning with Barth*, p. 105.
13. Ibid., p.110.
14. Linneman, *Historical Criticism and the Bible*, p. 121.
15. Whitney, *The New Heresy*, p. 508.
16. Ibid., pp. 507-8.
17. Linneman, op.cit., pp. 140-1.
18. Smith, op.cit., p. 410.
19. Whitney, op. cit., p. 519.

BIBLIOGRAPHY

Aalders, G.Ch., *Genesis*, Vol. 1, Bible Student's Commentary, (Tr. William Heynem), Zondervan, 1981

Alford, H., *The Greek Testament*, Vol I, Cambridge, 1874

Allen, E.L., *A Guide to the Thought of Emil Brunner*, Hodder and Stoughton (nd).

Allis, O.T., *The Unity of Isaiah*: A Study in Prophecy, Presbyterian and Reformed, 1977

Anderson, G.W., *The History and Religion of Israel*, Oxford University Press, 1965

A New Dictionary of Christian Theology, SCM Press, 1984

Atkinson, J., *Martin Luther and the Birth of Protestantism*, Marshall Morgan and Scott, 1982

Bainton, R., *Here I Stand*, Lion Publishing, 1983.

Barr, J., 'The Fundamentalist Understanding of Scripture', in *Conflicting ways of interpreting the Bible* (Kung/Moltmann, eds), Edinburgh, 1980

Barth, K., *Church Dogmatics*: Volume 4, The Doctrine of Reconciliation, Part I, T. & T. Clark, 1961

    —*Ibid*, Volume 4 Part II, 1958

    —*The Epistle to the Romans*, 6th ed., Oxford University Press, 1968

    —*Dogmatics in Outline*, SCM Press, 1949

    —*Evangelical Theology: An Introduction*, T. & T. Clark, 1979

Barthel, M. (tr. Mark Houson), *What the Bible Really Says*, Souvenir Press, 1982

Berkhof, L., *Systematic Theology*, Banner of Truth, 1959

Berkouwer, G.C., *The Triumph of Grace in the Theology of Karl Barth*, Eerdmans, 1956

    —*Studies in Dogmatics: SIN*, Eerdmans, 1971

Binnie, W., *The Psalms: Their History, Interpretation and Use*, 1870

Blanchard, J., *Truth for Life*, Walter Books, 1982

Bloesch, D.G., *The Evangelical Renaissance*, Hodder and Stoughton, 1974

Boettner, L. *The Reformed Doctrine of Predestination*, Eerdmans, 1932

Boice, J.M. *Foundations of the Christian Faith*, IVP, 1986

Bray, G., *Biblical Interpretation: past and present*, Apollos:IVP, 1996

Bright, J., *A History of Israel*, SCM Press, 1981

Bromiley, G.W., *Introduction to the Theology of Karl Barth*, Eerdmans, 1979

Brunner, E., *The Mediator*, Lutterworth Press, 1956

    —*Man in Revolt*: A Christian Anthropology, Lutterworth Press, 1939

    —*Our Faith*, SCM Press, 1949

    —*The Christian Doctrine of Creation and Redemption*, Dogmatics, Volume II, Lutterworth Press, 1952

Buis, H., *The Book of Revelation*, Presbyterian and Reformed, 1974

Bultmann, R., *Theology of the New Testament*, 2 vols, SCM Press, 1952 and 1955

    —*The Gospel of John*, Lutterworth Press, 1971

Busch, E., *Karl Barth: his Life from Letters and Autobiographical Texts*, SCM Press, 1976

Cadier, J., (tr. D. Johnson), *John Calvin: The Man God Mastered*, IVF, 1960

Cairns, D., 'The Theology of Emil Brunner', *Expository Times* 76.2, 1964

Calvin, J., *Genesis*, Edinburgh: Banner of Truth reprint, 1984

—*James*, reprinted Inverness, 1839

—*Sermons on Galatians*, Banner of Truth reprint, 1997

—*Commentary on Romans*, reprinted Edinburgh, 1850

Carson, D.A., 'Selected recent studies of the fourth gospel' in *Themelios* 14.2, Jan/Feb 1989

Clark, G.H., *Religion, Reason and Revelation*, The Craig Press, 1978

Craig, S.G., *Christianity Rightly So Called*, Tyndale Press, 1947

Cunningham, W., *The Reformers and the Theology of the Reformation*, Edinburgh, 1862

Donnelly, E., 'Paul: Kingdom Theologian', *Reformed Theological Journal*, Vol 2: November 1986

Dyrness, W., *Themes in Old Testament Theology*, Paternoster Press, 1979

Edwards, D.L., with John Stott, *Essentials: A liberal-evangelical dialogue*, Hodder and Stoughton, 1988

Eichrodt, W., *Theology of the Old Testament*, Vol. 2, English edition, SCM Press, 1967

Fairbairn, P., *The Interpretation of Prophecy*, 1964 Banner of Truth reprint of 1856 edition

Ferguson, S.B., Wright, D.F., and Packer J.I., (eds.) *New Dictionary of Theology*, IVP, 1988

Ford, D.F. (ed.), *The Modern Theologians: An introduction to Christian Theology in the Twentieth Century*, Blackwell, 1989, Volumes I and II

Gaffin, R.B., Jr. (ed.), *Redemptive History and Biblical Interpretation: The Shorter Writings of Geerhardus Vos*, Presbyterian and Reformed, 1980

Girdlestone, R.B., *Synonyms of the Old Testament: their bearing on Christian doctrine*, Eerdmans, 1978 reprint of 2nd edition of 1897

Grant, M.C., 'Sin and Human Responsibility in the Theology of Emil Brunner', unpublished Ph.D. thesis, University of Edinburgh, 1967

Guthrie, D., *New Testament Theology*, IVP, 1985

Harrison, R.K. *Introduction to the Old Testament*, Eerdmans, 1969

Hasel, G., *Old Testament Theology: Basic Issues in the Current Debate*, Eerdmans, 1982

Hebblethwaite, B., *The Christian Hope*, Eerdmans, 1986

Helm, P., 'History and Biblical Interpretation', *Banner of Truth*, 1973, p. 26

Hendriksen, W., *More than Conquerors*, Presbyterian and Reformed, 1974

Henry, C.F.H., *Frontiers in Modern Theology*, Moody Press, 1968

—*God, Revelation and Authority*, Vol IV, 1979

—(ed.) *Revelation and the Bible*, 1959

Heppe, H., *Reformed Dogmatics*, (tr. G.T. Thomson), 1950

Heron, A.I.C., *A Century of Protestant Theology*, Lutterworth Press, 1980

Hodge, A.A., *Evangelical Theology*, Nelson and Sons, 1890

Hooke, S.H., *Middle Eastern Mythology*, no date

Hooker, M.D., *Pauline Pieces*, no date

Horden, W., *New Directions in Theology Today, Volume 1: Introduction to Theology*, Lutterworth Press, 1968

Hughes, P.E., *Christianity and the Problem of Origins*, Presbyterian and Reformed, 1967

Hughes, P.E. (ed.), *Creative Minds in Contemporary Theology*, Eerdmans, 1966

James, E., *A Life of Bishop John A.T. Robinson*, Collins, 1987

Johnson, R. (ed.), *Rudolf Bultmann: Interpreting Faith for the Modern Era*, Collins, 1987

Kaiser, W.C., *Towards an Old Testament Theology*, USA, 1978

Kaiser, W.C., 'The Blessing of David: Humanity's Charter' in Skilton (ed), *The Law and the Prophets*, Presbyterian and Reformed, 1974

Kegley, C.W. (ed.), *The Theology of Emil Brunner*, Macmillan, 1962

Keller, W., *The Bible as History*, Hodder and Stoughton, 1977

Kittel, G., *Theological Dictionary of the New Testament*, Volume 1, Eerdmans, 1964

Klooster, F.H., *The Significance of Barth's Theology*, Baker Book House, 1961

Ladd, G.E., *Theology of the New Testament*, Lutterworth Press, 1987

Lane, A.N.S., 'Did Calvin believe in Free Will?', *Vox Evangelica*, XII, 1981

Linneman, E., *Historical Criticism of the Bible – Methodology or Ideology?*, tr. R.W. Yarbrough, Baker, 1990

——*Is there a Synoptic Problem?*, Baker, 1993

Lloyd-Jones, D.M., *Knowing the Times*, Banner of Truth, 1989

——Review of Emil Brunner Man in Revolt, in *Inter-Varsity*, 1940, pp29-30

Macdonald, H.D., *The Bible*, Hodder and Stoughton, 1979

Machen, J.G., *The Christian Faith in the Modern World*, Eerdmans, 1947

——*The Christian View of Man*, Eerdmans, 1947

——*The Origin of Paul's Religion*, Eerdmans, 1976

Mackay, J.L., 'Did the Prophets Prophesy better than they knew?' in *The Monthly Record of the Free Church of Scotland*, December, 1984

Macleod, D., 'Did Christ have a Fallen Human Nature?' in *The Monthly Record of the Free Church of Scotland*, March 1984

Macleod, D., *The Person of Christ*, IVP 1998

Marshall, I.H. (ed.), *New Testament Interpretation*, The Paternoster Press, 1979

Marty, M.E., and Peerman, D.G. (eds.), *A Handbook of Christian Theologians*, Lutterworth Press, 1984

McGrath, A.E., 'Justification: Barth, Trent and Kung', *Scottish Journal of Theology*, 34.6, 1981, pp517-30

——*Christian Theology: An Introduction*, 1994

Morris, L., *The Apostolic Preaching of the Cross*, Tyndale Press, 1955

Murray, J., *Principles of Conduct*, Tyndale Press, 1957

——*The Epistle of Paul to the Romans*, Marshall Morgan and Scott, 1960

——*Collected Writings*, Vol 2, Banner of Truth, 1977

New Bible Dictionary, IVP, 1986

Nicolson, W.B., *The Old Testament Church*, privately published, 1968.

Niesel, W., *The Theology of Calvin*, USA, 1980

O'Donovan, J.E., 'Man in the Image of God: The Disagreement between Barth and Brunner reconsidered', in *Scottish Journal of Theology*, 39.4, 1986, pp. 433-60

Packer, J., *Fundamentalism and the Word of God*, Tyndale Press, 1963

Pohier, J., *God – in Fragments*, SCM Press, 1985

Reardon, B.M.G., *Religious Thought in the Reformation*, Longman, 1986

Reymond, R.L., *Introductory Studies in Contemporary Theology*, Presbyterian and Reformed, 1968

Ridderbos, H.N., *Paul and Jesus*, USA, 1958

—*Studies in Scripture and Its Authority*, Eerdmans, 1978

—*Bultmann*, Presbyterian and Reformed, 1960

—'The Word became Flesh: Reflections on the Distinctive Characteristics of the Gospel of John', in *Through Christ's Word*, Presbyterian and Reformed, 1985

Robertson, O.P., *The Christ of the Covenants*, Presbyterian and Reformed, 1984

Sanderson, J.W., Review of Karl Barth: Church Dogmatics, Volume 4 in *Westminster Theological Journal*, 21.2, May 1959

Schaeffer, F., *Death in the City*, IVP, 1977

—*The Church Before the Watching World*, IVP, 1972

Schillebeeckx, E., *Jesus: An experiment in Christology*, London, 1983

Schrotenboer, P., *A New Apologetics: An Analysis and Appraisal of the Eristic Theology of Emil Brunner*, Holland, 1955

—'Review of Karl Barth: Church Dogmatics Volume 1 – The Doctrine of the Word of God' in *Westminster Theological Journal*, 19.2 (May 1957)

Smeaton, G., *The Doctrine of the Atonement*, Edinburgh, 1871

Smith, D.L., *With Wilful Intent: A Theology of Sin*, Victor Books, 1994

Sproul, R.C. (ed.), *Soli Deo Gloria: Essays in Reformed Theology*, Presbyterian and Reformed, 1976

Stonehouse, N. B., *The Witness of the Synoptic Gospels to Christ*, Presbyterian and Reformed,

—(ed.) *The Infallible Word*, Presbyterian and Reformed, 1946

Tenney, M., *New Testament Survey*, Eerdmans, 1982

The Bible Under Attack, Three papers read at the 1977 Conference of the British Evangelical Council, Evangelical Press, Evangelical Press, 1977

Theological Dictionary of the Old Testament, Vol. 1, Moody Press, 1981

Thompson, J., *Christ in Perspective in the Theology of Karl Barth*, St Andrew Press, 1978

Torrance, T.F., 'The Legacy of Karl Barth', *Scottish Journal of Theology*, 39.3, pp. 289-308

Trench, R.C., *Synonyms of the New Testament*, Eerdmans, 1976 reprint of 9th edition of 1880

Van Buren, P., *The Secular Meaning of the Gospel*, SCM Press, 1965

Van Til, C., Review of Karl Barth: Die Kirchliche Dogmatik 3:1, in *Westminster Theological Journal*, 22.1, November 1959

—*Christianity and Barthianism*, Presbyterian and Reformed, 1965

Van Til, C., *Has Karl Barth Become Orthodox?*, Presbyterian and Reformed, 1954
    —*The Later Heidegger and Theology*, Presbyterian and Reformed, 1964
Warfield, B.B., *Calvin and Augustine*, Presbyterian and Reformed, 1980
    —*Biblical and Theological Studies*, Presbyterian and Reformed, 1952
    —*The Person and Work of Christ*, Presbyterian and Reformed, 1950,
    reprinted 1980
    —*The Inspiration and Authority of the Bible*, Presbyterian and
    Reformed, 1948
    —*The Lord of Glory*, Hodder and Stoughton, 1907
    —*The Plan of Salvation*, Eerdmans, 1977
    —*Counterfeit Miracles*, Banner of Truth, reprinted 1976 (1st ed. 1918)
    —*Selected Shorter Writings*, Vol 1 (Meeter ed.), Presbyterian and
    Reformed, 1970
    —*Selected Shorter Writings*, Vol 2 (Meeter ed.), Presbyterian and
    Reformed, 1973
Wallis, N.W., *The Warhorse: The Life and Work of Harold J. Whitney*, Australia,
1986
    —*A Critique on the Theology of Karl Barth*, unpublished Th.D. thesis
    for the Central School of Religion, London, 1986
Webster, J., 'The Legacy of Barth and Bultmann', *Evangel*, 1.1 (January 1983),
pp. 8-11
Weiser, A., *Commentary on the Psalms*, SCM Press.
Wendel, F., *Calvin*, Collins, 1959
Whitcomb, J.C., and Morris, H.M., *The Genesis Flood*, Evangelical Press, 1969
White, W., *Defender of the Faith*, Thomas Nelson, 1979
Whitney, H.J., *The New 'Myth'-ology*, Presbyterian and Reformed, 1969
    —*The New Infallibility*, Presbyterian and Reformed, 1974
    —*The New Heresy*, Presbyterian and Reformed, 1974
    —*Evangelism the Heartbeat of the Church*, Mission Publications of
    Australia, 1987
Young, E.J., *Thy Word Is Truth*, Banner of Truth, 1972
Young, W., Review of Bultmann, Neibuhr and Tillich in *Westminster Theological
Journal* 19.2., May 1957

Glossary of Terms

Arminianism
A term describing a school of thought named after Jacobus Arminius (1560-1609). Its basic point was that God does not elect to life: he chooses those whom he foresees will choose him. In this way, Arminianism concedes the most important place in salvation to man's choice of God, rather than God's grace to man.

Augustianism
A term describing the thinking of Augustine (354-430), arguably the greatest of the Latin church fathers. Augustine's work both on theology and anthropology laid the foundation for later Protestant thought; while aspects of his work on the church were adopted by later Roman Catholicism.

Barthian
Adjective used to describe the thought of the Swiss theologian Karl Barth.

Calvinism
A term describing the stream of Reformed thought after John Calvin.

Demythologisation
A movement of thought associated with Rudolf Bultmann, which begins on the assumption that the Bible is written in terms of a world-view unrecognisable in this modern, scientific age. The 'myths' of the Bible therefore require to be re-read and re-interpreted to make the Bible meaningful to a modern audience.

Dialectic/Dialectical Theology
Dialectic refers to the search for truth through the resolution of apparent contradictions. It is a philosophical concept which has been carried over into theology; the modern school of theology examined in this book (especially Barth) would be classed as dialectic theologians, who seek to uncover truth on the interface between truths about God on the one hand, and truths about man on the other.

Evangelical
Relating to the Gospel (the Evangel); evangelical scholars emphasise the saving work of Christ on the cross as the heart of all truth.

Exegesis
The science of (literally) 'drawing out' of the Bible its meaning.

Existentialism
A philosophical school of thought which interprets all things in the light of our human existence.

Hamartology
The theological term for 'the doctrine of sin'.

Liberal theology
A general description for late nineteenth- and early twentieth-century theology which was concerned to interpret the Bible, and state the church's theology, in terms related to man's culture and civilisation. It is generally non-evangelical.

Neo-orthodoxy
A term which describes the theology of Barth and his successors; they claimed that their theology, though new ('neo-'), was rooted in the Reformation and its teachings ('orthodoxy').

Pelagianism
A term describing the thinking of Pelagius, whose work at the beginning of the 5th century insisted that human nature was essentially undamaged by the Fall. Augustine wrote much of his work in opposition to Pelagius' views.

Synoptic Gospels/Problem
The 'Synoptic' Gospels are Matthew, Mark and Luke, our three sources for the New Testament narrative of the life of Christ. The Synoptic 'problem' relates to the relationship and interdependence of these three sources.

PERSONS INDEX

SCRIPTURE INDEX

SUBJECT INDEX